Six Flags Over Texas

The First Fifty Years

A Pictorial History

Six Flags Over Texas

The First Fifty Years

A Pictorial History

by Davis G. McCown

For My Wife Lu, and my daughters Katie and Maegan.

Special Thanks to Marla Hohman and Six Flags Over Texas for providing photographs for inclusion in this book.

Table of Contents

FORWARD

An estimated one hundred and twenty million guests passed through the frontgate of *Six Flags Over Texas* before the end of its 50th season in 2010. During those fifty years, the park was constantly changing. Each season contributed to the creation of a new park built around a small group of time-honored favorite attractions.

This book is an effort to preserve the memory of the various attractions that provided hours of enjoyment and entertainment to those millions of guests. Effort has also been made to provide a wide range of photographs of the park and its attractions. Unfortunately, this work cannot be a comprehensive history of the park's first fifty years. It is not possible in a work of this size to include every individual, event, and change which are part of the park's heritage.

An attempt has been made to provide detailed information about the park's various attractions. Sometimes, however, these "details" change over the years. The number of units for an attraction may increase or decrease. Top speeds, "g" forces, hourly capacity, and even track length can change as rides are modified after installation. Generally, statistics provided for each attraction are for the time of installation.

In addition, many of the images were published in more than one form. An image identified as a postcard may have also been in a souvenir book, distributed as a public relations photograph, or published on a souvenir slide. Only one source, however, is provided for each image.

Additional information about the history of Six Flags Over Texas is available at the author's website, www.parktimes.com.

I hope you enjoy reminiscing over an exciting fifty years.

1.

BEFORE SIX FLAGS
1957 - 1961

Amusement parks have long been a source of entertainment around the United States. At their peak prior to the Great Depression, it is estimated that there were over 2,000 parks, with one in every major metropolitan area in the US. Frequently built on beaches and lakes, the parks provided a variety of entertainment. Typical activities included rides, midway games, shows, concert halls, swimming pools, and dance halls. These traditional amusement parks, however, often had reputations as seedy undesirable places. Frequently they were poorly constructed, staffed by unsavory transient workers, visited by rough guests, and located on unkempt grounds.

In addition to the traditional parks, a few small "attraction" parks existed around the country. Attraction parks were based on a single concept, such as cowboy towns, mother-goose lands, and Christmas villages. They generally consisted of themed exhibits, restaurants, stores, and possibly a show. They might also have a few themed rides, such as a stagecoach or snow-sleigh. In addition, some had small children's rides.

Disneyland. In 1955, Walt Disney opened *Disneyland* in Southern California, introducing the world to a completely new concept in amusement parks. In designing his park, Disney used a combination of movie sets, costumed workers, and themed rides to create a series of fantasy worlds within the park's borders. Disney then assured that the employees staffing these fantasy worlds were friendly respectful individuals whom he referred to as the park's "cast". His new park was clean, safe, and family friendly. This type of park became the model for the modern theme park.

At the time that Disney opened his new theme park in Southern California, Tommy Joe Vandergriff, the mayor of Arlington, Texas, was working on ways to boost his town's economic development. Located midway between the cities of Dallas to the east, and Fort Worth to the west, the town of 8,000 competed with both cities for industry and business.

Vandergriff was first elected mayor of Arlington in 1951 at the age of twenty-five. At that time, the small town was mainly known as the home of *Arlington State College*, now the *University of Texas at Arlington*. Vandergriff was working, however, to use the town's strategic location between the two cities to generate growth. He was off to an exceptional start. Under his leadership, the town was selected as the site of a major new General Motors assembly plant.

Vandergriff was not the only person then committed to the economic growth of Arlington. Angus Gilchrist Wynne, II, was President of the Great Southwest Corporation. This corporation was purchasing large quantities of land in Arlington and nearby Grand Prairie. In 1956, Wynne's Great Southwest Corp. purchased the Waggoner's 2,500 acre *Triple D Stock Ranch* located in Arlington near the site of the *Arlington Downs Race Track*. This was a separate ranch from the famous *Triple D Ranch* owned by the Waggoner's in Wilbarger and Baylor counties. In addition, the corporation purchased another 7,000 surrounding acres.

Angus Wynne, President of the Great Southwest Corporation and founder of Six Flags Over Texas. Six Flags' Gazette photograph, (Vol. 3, No. 1, pg. 2, 1963).

The corporation was buying the land for use in its planned Great Southwest Industrial District. This industrial district was designed to be the nation's largest planned industrial park, complete with railway service, warehouses, and a major freeway. The railway service was to be provided by the Great Southwest Railroad, a new railway created solely for the district.

While Wynne was planning his industrial district, Vandergriff visited the then new and unknown *Disneyland*. He was impressed with the park and saw the tremendous boost to the local economy that a theme park would bring. Wynne and his family also visited *Disneyland* and were just as impressed with the park as Vandergriff.

Having landed a major automobile assembly plant, Vandergriff was determined to bring an amusement park to Arlington. He went straight to the top, taking a request to Walt Disney himself. The young mayor proposed a second Disney park be built in Arlington, right in the middle of the Dallas-

Fort Worth metroplex. As part of the arrangement, Wynne agreed for Great Southwest Corp. to provide land for the project.

This was not the only request for a new *Disneyland* that Disney received. Officials of several cities saw the promise of a new theme park and brought location offers to him. Disney was open to reviewing these proposals. In fact, in 1960 Disney staff conducted a feasibility review of a proposed new park in St. Louis, Missouri. For whatever reason, however, the Arlington proposal did not appeal to him. He declined Vandergriff's offer for the Texas location.

Angus Wynne, however, was not deterred by Disney's response. Moreover, Wynne knew that it could take several years before his industrial district started generating enough income to repay his development costs. He was already exploring ways to generate immediate income during the time before the commercial property became profitable. An amusement park seemed the perfect solution. He figured that if Disney did not want to build a theme park in Texas, he would just build his own.

Looking west along Dallas-Fort Worth Turnpike (I-30) towards Fort Worth.
Site of future Six Flags is in the middle of the picture, to the South (left) of the
Turnpike and above Highway 360, which runs across the picture.
Texas Department of Highways picture taken approximately 1957.

Wynne's initial plans for an entertainment center were as grandiose as his plans for an industrial park. He would not build just a single Disney style theme park, but an entire entertainment district. In addition to an amusement park, it would include a family sports and games center, with activities such as bowling, shooting, fishing, golfing, and boating.

Wynne also knew that if the income from the entertainment projects fell off in the future, the land could easily be reclaimed and incorporated back into the expanding industrial warehouse district.

For his entertainment district, Wynne selected the most accessible location within Great Southwest's holdings. At the intersection of two of the area's key highways, the property was bordered on the north by the newly opened Dallas-Fort Worth Turnpike (now Interstate 30) and on the east by Interstate 360. At the time, property in the area was almost completely undeveloped. One lone exception was the *Arlington Downs Racetrack* located a few miles to the south.

Marco Engineering. Wynne and Vandergriff had resources and determination. They did not, however, have any experience in the design or operation of a theme park. For that, they turned to a third Texan central in the creation of *Six Flags Over Texas*, Cornelius Vanderbilt (C.V.) Wood Jr. Born in Oklahoma, and raised in Amarillo, Texas, Wood had what Vandergriff and Wynne lacked, experience in the creation of themed amusement parks.

Wood was a significant participant in the construction of *Disneyland*, working directly with Walt Disney on major issues involving the design and operation of the park. During *Disneyland's* first season, Wood served as Vice-President and General Manager of the new park. After the park was open, Wood left Disney to start his own themed entertainment design business, *Marco Engineering Company* of Los Angeles, California. The business was also referred to as *Marco Company* and as *Marco Engineering & Design*.

In order to start his new company, Wood hired many experienced designers and managers directly from Disney. In doing so, Wood created the first company outside the Disney organization with personnel experienced in the design, construction, and management of a modern themed amusement park. By the late 50's, Wood and *Marco* were involved in the design of three major theme parks around the nation. These were *Pleasure Island* near Boston, Massachusetts; *Magic Mountain* in Denver, Colorado; and *Freedomland USA* in New York City. (*Magic Mountain* was not connected to the later California amusement park of the same name.)

Marco Development team reviewing plans. Randall Duell is likely the individual sitting to the far left with glasses. CV Wood appears to be seated to the far right.
Six Flags' Gazette, (Vol. 1, No. 1, pg. 9, 1961).

Marco did not own these amusement parks. Rather, its personnel served as a staff of design and management consultants for each of the parks with which it was involved. Each of the parks were conceived and financed by other ventures that hired Marco for its expertise. This expertise was exactly what Vandergriff and Wynne needed to get their plans for a theme park off the ground. So, for professional assistance in designing the new amusement park, Wynne turned to fellow Texan Wood and his Marco Engineering.

Marco's first complete from scratch amusement park was *Magic Mountain*, built in Denver, Colorado. As Six Flags was themed on the history of Texas, *Magic Mountain* was themed on the history of Colorado. Development of the $3.5 million park started in 1957. The park managed to open in 1958, although it was only a partial opening as the park was not completely constructed. Once opened, the management dealt with constant financial difficulties. It closed at the end of the 1960 season, one year before *Six Flags* opened. Great Southwest Corp. purchased some of the defunct *Magic Mountain* props at auction for use at the new Arlington park.

In 1971, *Magic Mountain* reopened as *Heritage Square* shopping village, a local attraction with some new rides, as well as many of the original amusement park's buildings.

The second Marco designed park was *Pleasure Island*, a $4 million park built in Wakefield, Massachusetts. Work on the park started in late 1958. The park was known for its Moby Dick boat ride in which an animated whale rose up out of one of the park's ponds to threaten guests riding in whaling boats.

The third, and by far the largest, of the theme parks under development by Marco Engineering was *Freedomland USA*. Located in the Bronx of New York City, *Freedomland* was themed on the history and geography of the United States. Billed as the "*Disneyland* of the East Coast", it was laid out in the shape of the United States. With eighty-five acres allocated for the park proper, it was a large park; the park had more than twice as many acres as *Six Flags Over Texas* at its opening. While *Six Flags Over Texas* was themed on six different periods in Texas history, *Freedomland* was themed on seven different periods and regions of U.S. history.

Eventually Wood found himself in legal entanglements with Disney, some of which were due to his use of the *Disneyland* name in promoting *Freedomland USA*. In part as a result of these issues, Wood ended his participation in the theme park industry in the early 1960's. In 1968, he supervised bringing the *London Bridge*, brick by brick, from London, England, to Lake Havasu City, Arizona. In the early 1990's, he returned to the theme park business as President of Warner Brothers' Recreational Entertainment Division. There he designed *Warner Bros. Movie World* in Australia. He held this position when Warner Brothers first bought shares of Six Flags Corp. in 1990.

Randall Duell. The principal Marco designer working on the *Six Flags* project was Randall Duell. Before becoming an art director for Marco Engineering, Duell was an architect and Hollywood movie set designer. By the time he started work on *Six Flags Over Texas*, Duell was experienced in amusement park design, having worked on the design of both *Pleasure Island* and *Freedomland USA*.

As an amusement park designer, Duell relied on many techniques developed for creating fantasy movie sets to create fantasy amusement park environments. One such technique was the use of scaled down buildings. Buildings were designed with features on their front facades built to a slightly smaller scale than standard size. In some cases, the building appeared to have a second floor which was also scaled down. With all of the features in the same perspective, guests did not perceive these differences in size. This allowed structures to be built in a smaller space than otherwise required.

Concept art of the Confederate recruitment rally area.
Similar to movie storyboards, concept drawings were used in developing the park's attractions.
Such concept art was used on original souvenirs since photos were not yet available for printing.
All-Tom souvenir postcard P42683, published 1961.

Another technique was the use of curving pathways to create separation of the themed areas. With curving paths, attractions in adjacent sections are beyond the bend in the walkway. This removes attractions in one section from the view of guests standing in a different section. In the same manner, curving and dead-end streets are used on movie sets to hide structures and objects not intended to be viewed in a movie scene.

In order to help unify each section, a single pallet of coordinating colors was used to paint each of the buildings in a particular section. To distinguish the sections, the color pallet varied from section to section.

Duell also used what became known in the amusement park industry as the "Duell loop". The Duell loop was a single major looping pathway constructed through a park. Guests could follow this pathway in one direction and visit all of the park's attractions. Use of the loop also provided the curving path needed to separate the sections.

The use of the loop varied from the other major design pattern, Disney's "hub and spoke" design. In the hub and spoke design, a pathway from each of the major sections converges on a central section or area.

The loop is now considered inconsistent with the goals of some modern designers. They prefer random and disjointed paths with occasional dead-ends. Using less efficient pathways causes guests to repeat targeted areas and keeps guests in the park for longer periods of time. This increases the probability that they will purchase more food and gift items.

Although many of the amusement park designers and professionals which Marco hired were from Disney, Duell was not. In addition, he avoided visiting the Disney parks during his early park designing career. In this way, he hoped to avoid criticism that he was simply copying Disney's ideas.

Duell eventually took over the design of *Six Flags* for Marco and assumed responsibility for the design of additions to the park for several seasons. He established *R. Duell and Associates*, his own themed entertainment design company and participated in the design of most of the major amusement parks built in the 1960's and 1970's.

Initial Design.   Preliminary planning for the Arlington park began in 1957. Ideas for various rides and structures were developed and proposed layouts for the park were created. These designs were then represented in concept art drawings. Working with Wynne, it was decided that the park would consist of six themed areas. Each area would represent Texas as it existed under each of the six sovereignties which ruled over the land. These are: Spain (1519 to 1821); France (1685 to 1689); Mexico (1821-1836); the Republic of Texas (1836-1845); the United States (1845-1861); the Confederacy (1861-1865); and finally the United States again from 1865 to date.

Concept drawing depicting Happy Motoring Freeway. The concept drawing shows two tracks.
A second track was not added in the park, however, until the second season.
All-Tom postcard P42658, published 1961.

Duell later remarked that the Arlington site was the most beautiful property at which he designed a park. When he visited the proposed site, he decided to design the park around the property's exiting trees, landscaping, and terrain. Park publicity materials later boasted that only three trees were removed in order to construct the park. In addition, the building that became the *Old Red Schoolhouse* was already on the site.

Great Southwestland. In November 1957, Great Southwest released a preview of its proposed entertainment center. Described was a $34 million bifurcated entertainment center with a multifaceted sports and entertainment facility, as well as a separate amusement park. The entire complex was planned to be built on 203 acres of land located at the intersection of the Dallas-Fort Worth Turnpike (now I-30) and I-360.

The proposed sports facility was to be named the *"Great Southwest Sports Center"*. It was to be anchored by a 100,000 square foot sporting retail store at which visitors could practice their athletic skills and test new equipment. The site would include casting ponds, numerous types of shooting ranges, archery ranges, a boating lake, bowling lanes, and golf driving ranges. The sports center was to be open year round and would host guest appearances by popular sports figures.

The separate amusement park, which Marco Engineering was designing, was named *Great Southwestland*. According to information released by Great Southwest Corp., and published in the November 18, 1957, issue of *Billboard*, planned were "small towns, Indian encampments, canyons, cliff dwellers, stagecoach routes, saloons, oil fields, rides, and refreshment areas". Wood predicted the facility would host two million guests a year when fully operational.

Concept drawing of Spanish fort firing on French riverboat. An earlier version of this same sketch depicts a pirate flag on the riverboat, suggesting that the ride was considered as a pirate ride. All-Tom souvenir postcard P42684, published 1961

Principal investors in Great Southwest Corporation at the time were Angus Wynne; his uncle, Toddie Lee Wynne; Amon Carter, publisher of the Fort Worth Star-Telegram; William Zeckendorf and his New York real estate company, Webb & Knapp; the Development Corporation of America; and Rockefeller Center, Inc. Zeckendorf and Webb & Knapp, Inc. were also major investors in *Freedomland USA* and involved in efforts to refinance *Magic Mountain* in Denver.

In January of 1958, while in Dallas to conduct preliminary planning of *"Great Southwestland"*, Wood predicted that approximately twenty *Disneyland* style parks would open around the country in the next five years. This estimate proved to be extremely premature. It was closer to twenty years before twenty theme parks designed on the Disney model were constructed as predicted. What occurred in the next six years was that all but one of the major amusement park projects that Wood developed since *Disneyland* were closed or greatly scaled back. The sole exception was *Six Flags Over Texas*.

Concept picture of Texas section street. The last building to the far right resembles the building that became the bank building. All-Tom postcard P42682, published 1961.

In April 1958, more detailed plans for the new entertainment zone were announced. Still anticipated were both the amusement park *Great Southwestland* and the sports center, *Great Southwest Sports Center*.

The sports center plans remained as previously announced. Additional details, however, were provided for *Great Southwestland*. It was to be an amusement park designed on the previously developed theme of "Texas under Six Flags". As planned, the six historically themed sections would each represent Texas at a time that a different sovereign's flag flew over the land. Five would be based on Texas of the past, while the section representing the US flag would be based on a modern Texas. The sixty-acre park was predicted to be home to twenty rides.

The developers released a preliminary map for the planned Great Southwestland which was published in *Billboard Magazine* on April 7, 1958. Changes in the concepts for the park can be tracked through study of the various maps prepared prior to the final construction of the park. The preliminary park shown was much different from the one eventually built. The diagram, however, depicted the proposed amusement park at the same location, and in the same shape, in which it was eventually constructed.

The proposed park was bounded by the railroad, which followed the same track layout that was eventually built. There was one difference between the early concept map and the railroad as actually built. The track for the concept was depicted as passing on a bridge over the main entrance, rather than the actual passage under the entryway.

The Star Mall was also depicted very similar in its appearance to its original construction. Much of the proposed interior of the park, however, was changed significantly by the time the park was built three years later.

Near the amusement park, the *Great Southwest Sports Center* was depicted to the southeast of the amusement park, located on the property that is now home to the *Judge Roy Scream*. The first component of the sports facility to open was the *Great Southwest Bowling Lanes*, with 32 lanes. The bowling center, located directly west of the park, opened in July of 1958.

In January of 1959, Great Southwest Corp. announced that a 100-room hotel would also be built near the site of the planned amusement park.

In June of 1959, *Pleasure Island* opened in Massachusetts. The park only met one-half of it expected first year attendance goal of 750,000. By the end of the year, the company that built the park was in bankruptcy. Three different companies owned the park over the following years. After a series of weak seasons and financial difficulties, the final operator closed the park for good at the end of the 1969 season.

In May of 1959, Great Southwest Corp. announced an offer to sell to the public $18 million in additional stock. This was followed in January of 1960 with a Great Southwest announcement of the offer to sell $11.5 million of additional stock and debentures. Included in this offering was $3.7 million for the construction of the amusement park.

Great Southwest Corp. announced in February of 1960 that construction on the park would begin that year. The theme was still "Texas under Six Flags", although a specific name for the park was not mentioned. Cost of

Concept art of the Skull rock. The hanging figure was not part of the final Skull Island, although two similar hanging figures were part of the LaSalle's Riverboat ride.
All-Tom postcard P42674, published 1961.

construction was estimated at $7 million. Construction on the inn was also set to begin soon.

In April of 1960, Great Southwest Corp. announced that due to regulations regarding pending public offerings of securities, the company was under a news blackout so that no new additional updates could be released. Still being planned, however, was a 293-acre sports and entertainment center.

By June of 1960, park planners were drawing plans for a park that looked much more like the park that was finally constructed.

On June 19, 1960, a few months before actual construction of *Six Flags* began, *Freedomland USA* opened in New York. In many ways *Six Flags Over Texas* mirrored *Freedomland USA*. Both were designed by Marco Engineering, with many of the same individuals working on both parks. Each design was based on dividing the park into historical sections. One of the major investors in both parks was William Zeckendorf of New York and his investment firm, Webb and Knapp, Inc.

Versions of almost all of *Six Flags'* original attractions were already operating at *Freedomland USA*. These included a railroad; riverboat adventure ride; mule drawn carousel; sky-lift; stagecoaches; miniature motoring freeway; Indian village; dancing waters; and burro trail. In addition, the major additions that opened at Six Flags in 1962 were also already featured at *Freedomland USA*, including Indian war canoes, anti-gravity house, and an antique car ride.

Many of the ride units, such as the antique cars and stagecoaches, were supplied by the same companies and were virtually identical at each of the Marco parks. One such supplier at both parks was *Arrow Development. Arrow Development* was a California ride manufacturing company with experience developing theme park rides that began with *Disneyland*. Costumes and animations also came from common suppliers.

Another formal announcement regarding the park was made on August 23, 1960. Even though the final park plans were still under development, construction was scheduled to begin within two weeks. A construction budget was drafted, with final costs set at $10 million. The name "Great Southwestland" was reported to be the park's "tentative" name. It had already been decided that a one-price ticket would allow guests access to all attractions. A yearly capacity of two million visitors was estimated.

An updated design was provide in a map incorporated into a 1961 park "fact memorandum". The map depicted a park with the same basic shape as the final park, including the same layout for the railroad tracks. The star mall was shown as it was eventually built, although the park's main six flags were outside the Frontgate and not behind the star area.

The modern section was located in the same spot as it was ultimately built. It was shown, however, with a large outdoor mall area. The mall was a large plaza, with a dancing waters pond on the east side and a futuristic looking building on the west. Presumably, the futuristic building was an exhibits hall. A large structure similar to the San Jacinto Monument was shown next to the miniature freeway.

The section also contained the Astrolift station close to the location where it was eventually built. The design for the miniature freeway was larger and more elaborate than the one constructed.

As with the final park, the Mexican section was shown west of the Frontgate. A larger Indian village than the one eventually built was depicted in the northwestern part of the park. A stagecoach style ride was shown very close to where it was eventually built. An area apparently designed to replicate Palo Duro canyon extended from the area that became the Spanish section north into an area that is now used for the *Chaparral* ride. The replica canyon appears to have been the intended setting for a much more elaborate burro trail ride.

Concept art of Mexican Restaurant, originally operated by El Chico restaurants.
From postcard folder, P90601, published 1961.

A Boomtown area was depicted on the west side of the park, north of where the Texas train and *Astrolift* stations were eventually built.

LaSalle's River Adventure was depicted as loading from a replica of a large sailing vessel anchored in a lagoon. The ship was very similar to the pirate ship that was later constructed on *Skull Island*. It was reached by gangways connecting it to the shore. Riders loaded onto the riverboats by crossing another gangway connecting the ride's riverboats to the larger stationary ship. The river adventure itself was a larger ride, taking in the area that actually served as the river, as well as most of the area that actually became Boomtown.

The other side of the same sailing ship appears to be the loading point for the *Skull Island* rafts. Skull Island itself is shown with its trademark skull rock.

Construction.   Groundbreaking for the new park was held in August of 1960. Construction was to be complete in July of 1961, for an opening date in August of 1961. One hundred and five acres were set aside for the initial park, with thirty-five acres planned for the park itself. The other seventy acres were used for parking, storage, and other support needs. Luther D. Clark, Vice President of Construction for Great Southwest Corp., oversaw the construction of the park.

As construction began, the scope of the entertainment district was greatly scaled back. The *Great Southwest Sports Center* was no longer part of the proposed entertainment center. Only the bowling alley, and eventually the golf course, remained from the planned sports center. The amusement park, *Great Southwestland*, was now the major component of the development. As a result, the proposed costs dropped from $34 million to $10 million.

In December of 1960, Wynne took the press on a tour of the property under development. Only the concrete slabs for the building foundations were in place. At that time, the name "Great Southwestland" was no longer the name for the new amusement park. The new name was officially announced as "Texas under Six Flags". By April of 1961, however, the name for the amusement park was again changed. It was finalized as the much more appealing "Six Flags Over Texas".

The park was built in almost exactly one year. Four hundred craftsmen were employed to prepare the property, landscaping, and attractions. Heavy rains in February and March of 1961 slowed down construction and delayed the initial opening date, which was set to occur as soon as the park was constructed.

Concept art of Texas section. Note that the building to the left has two facades, each facing a different direction. From All-Tom souvenir postcard image book, published 1961.

In order to facilitate quick construction, diagrams of each of the key buildings were created at the design headquarters in California. A life size cardboard drawing of each building was then created and shipped in two boxcars to a woodmill in Texas. At the woodmill, carpenters used the life-sized drawings to cut the storefronts and other building parts from wood. The precut parts were then shipped to the park for rapid assembly.

In order to coordinate construction, each structure in the park was assigned a unique number based on its location. Construction workers used the numbers to locate and identify the building or area at which they were assigned to work.

In constructing the park, 250,000 yards of dirt were moved; 12,000 square feet of plaster was applied; two million square feet of paving was laid; and 100,000 feet of conduit and wiring were laid. In order to separate the fantasy world from reality, the park built 15,000 feet of fencing.

After the work was complete, the park held three million gallons of water in its man-made lakes and rivers, with another 50 million just outside the park in the larger reservoir.

In addition, in order to protect guests from the Texas heat, the park boasted three hundred tons of air conditioning and one hundred 53-inch hanging fans. Many of the air conditioning units and fans were located outside to cool down restaurant seating, attraction waiting areas, and pathways.

Carver Sound Equipment, Co. of Dallas installed the sound and music systems which piped music to the various areas of the park. Landscaping for the original park was designed by *Lambert Landscaping* of Dallas, Texas. The landscaping design firm won three awards for designs it implemented at *Six Flags Over Texas.*

The park's innovate lighting was designed and implemented at a cost of $300,000 by John Watson of *Watson Lighting* in Dallas. Watson later implemented lighting systems for *Busch Gardens* in Tampa Florida; *The Texas Pavilion* of the *1964 New York World's Fair; The San Antonio Riverwalk* project; and *Six Flags Over Georgia.*

The original costumes were designed by *Western Costume Company* of Hollywood, California. Western Costume is one of the oldest businesses in Hollywood and has furnished movie industry costumes since 1912. It furnished uniforms and costumes for other of Marco Engineering's theme parks, including *Freedomland USA.*

Animations for the park were constructed by *Special Effects*, a company owned by Winfield H. Hubbard of Morrison, Colorado. Hubbard also did animations for *Freedomland USA* and *Magic Mountain, Colorado.* Like many of the individuals then involved in amusement park design and construction, Hubbard began his career in the movie industry. He was previously MGM's chief special effects designer.

Also contributing to animation design and creation were LTV and Peter Wolf, both from Dallas.

Masonry work was performed by *Prewitt & McFaul* of Dallas, Texas. *William H LaDew, Inc.* of Dallas, Texas, provided fire suppression equipment. Plumbing installation was provided by *Beard Plumbing Company* of Dallas, Texas. Electrical work was completed by *Burton Brothers Electric Company* of Fort Worth, Texas.

To help develop the area, a major baseball park was also planned nearby.

In May of 1961, after a mere eight months of construction, the park was reported to be 75% percent complete. Officials with Great Southwest Corp. estimated that the park would be finished in ninety days. On June 4, 1961, with the park approximately 80% complete, Wynne announced opening day: Sunday, August 6, 1961. By the time August arrived, the grand opening date was moved forward one day to Saturday, August 5, 1961. The total cost of construction was $10 million dollars.

Six Flags Frontgate and Ticket Plaza.
Dancing Waters behind Star Mall. Entrance to Mexico on left.
Astrolift in background.
Souvenir slide, 1962.

Six Flags' public relations aerial photograph, pre-opening 1961.
Construction is ongoing at the time of this picture.
The ride labeled as the "Missile Chaser" is what was later
named the "Sidewinder" roller coaster.
The "Missilechaser" ride is not shown on the photo.
The "Mission" is the Conquistador Burro Ride.

2.

THE ORIGINAL PARK

1961

In keeping with the original historical concept, the final park design divided the park into six sections. Each section was based on life in Texas at the time when one of the state's six sovereigns ruled over the land. The sections were not laid out in historical order. Starting at the Frontgate and moving clockwise, the Mexican section was the first section, not the Spanish section. Likewise, the French section sat between the Confederacy and the Modern USA, rather than next to Spain.

Originally, park literature referred to each of the park's six sections as a "trail to adventure". Guests would travel each "trail" as they explored the park.

To help define each section, many of the rides were design to replicate an actual experience from the era depicted. The steam train departed from a turn of the century station house in the "old west" Texas section; the raft ride and stagecoach were in the Confederate section; and the futuristic *Astrolift* ride was based in the Modern USA section. The riverboats in the French section simulated a trip by French explorers scouting areas of Texas. Each attraction brought to life unique experiences corresponding with the section's period in Texas history.

Wynne knew that the rides, while important, were just part of the formula. He felt that a successful park must also provide professional quality shows to entertain the guests in the park. For the new park, he planned two types of shows. One type was traditional theater style productions. In addition to these, he planned numerous "street" shows for the crowds. These included gunfighters, period characters, clowns, and marching bands.

The street shows in particular added to each section's atmosphere, with period costumed characters and street performers located in the various sections they represented. In the Confederacy, civil war reenactment soldiers not only marched in formation and drilled with their weapons, but also caught and executed Union spies. In the Texas section, cowboys robbed the bank and were arrested by lawmen. A Mariachi band performed live music as they

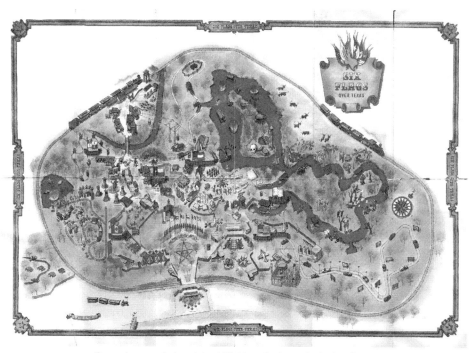

Souvenir map of the original 1961 park, from Author's collection.

strolled through the Mexican section. Many of the reenactment characters were available between their performances to educate guests regarding the lifestyle of the characters that they portrayed.

In addition to unique rides and entertaining shows, Wynne wanted a beautiful park. He used extensive landscaping and entertaining theming to ensure that the park was both interesting and visually attractive throughout.

The theming was carried out in the souvenir stores. The stores in each section sold merchandise characteristic of the section. The Mexican store was full of colorful sombreros, baskets, pottery, and other items typical of a Mexican market. The *Indian Trading Post* sold cowboy and Indian toys, as well as western style souvenirs.

As with the shops, the food was also selected to fit the atmosphere of the section in which it was sold. An *El Chico* Mexican diner was the major restaurant of the Mexican section; *Naler's Fried Chicken Plantation* dominated the Confederate section; and hamburgers and hotdogs were sold in the USA section. *Naler's* and the *El Chico* were considered as the original park's two major restaurants.

Other activities and exhibits were located in each section to provide additional atmosphere. An animated prisoner snored away in the jailhouse in the Texas section. The Confederate section was home to a recruitment center with tents framed by large recruitment banners hanging above.

Integral to the theming was the music piped into each historical section. The music for each section was carefully selected to match the mood and atmosphere of the area. Playing softly in the background, the musical selections provided subliminal atmosphere for the guests as the moved from place to place within the park.

All of Wynne's efforts to create an exciting and interesting park were tied together by his three overall principals for the park. The first was that the park should provide "unique and wholesome entertainment". To keep the attractions unique, new ones should be added each season.

Second, the park should be kept immaculately clean. To meet this goal, Wynne assured that every employee in the park was responsible for keeping the park clean. Every employee, including supervisors and management staff, were taught to pick up any trash they saw anytime they walked through the park. Wynne lead by example and enjoyed being seen by his staff picking up and throwing away discarded cigarette butts and soft drink cups.

Finally, Wynne avoided hiring the "carny" type of transient works frequently associated with amusement parks and fairs. Instead, he hired responsible and clean-cut college students to run the park. As time passed, enthusiastic high school students were also hired to staff the park. These students were not only trained in their jobs, but they were trained to always politely interact with the guests. Each employee received a training manual regarding the park and its policies. One section emphasized using phrases such as "yes sir" and "thank you". Employees were also taught the importance of always smiling.

Opening Day.   The grand opening for *Six Flags Over Texas* was held on Saturday, August 5, 1961. The opening ceremonies began at 9:00 am and the park officially opened to the public at 10:00 am.

The official opening ceremonies were held inside the Frontgate, in front of the park's six flagpoles. Tom Vandergriff, mayor of Arlington and a driving force behind the park's creation in Arlington, was present. He was accompanied by Mayors John Justin of Fort Worth; Earl Cabell of Dallas; Gene Goren of Grand Prairie; and Lynn Brown of Irving.

Angus Wynne, Jr., developer of Six Flags, and President of the Great Southwest Corporation, spoke regarding his vision that became Six Flags. Very accurately, he promised that, "Six Flags was not complete and will never be complete. We shall continue to build what we consider an institution".

After the speeches were concluded, the Six Flags Marching Band played the official *Six Flags March* as each of the six flags were hoisted up their respective flag poles. A Marine honor guard raised the US flag, while Six Flags security officers raised the others. When the flags reached the top, the *Dancing Waters* were turned on in front of the flags. With the end of the ceremonies, Six Flags was officially opened to the public.

The original plan was for all of the first day tickets to be sold in advance. The Junior Leagues of Dallas and Fort Worth were asked to sell the tickets. Their ticket sales ended on Friday. They sold 15,000 tickets, although these tickets could be used on days other than the grand opening. Due to the demand at the gate, however, tickets were sold at the park on opening day as well. For the opening day, 8,734 guests visited the park.

Unlike the openings at several of the major parks, including *Disneyland*, Wynne was proud to announce that there were "no problems" during the opening day. He stated later that he was advised by "the people from Marco Development that it was 'one of the smoothest park openings' that they had been involved with."

The following day the park received favorable reviews in all of the local papers. Elston Brooks, noted columnist for the *Fort Worth Star-Telegram*, in particular wrote about his pleasant impressions of the park.

Although August 5 was the official opening day, it was not the first day that guests had entered the park. A week long "soft opening", which allowed the park staff to test its systems and make last minute adjustments to the rides and attractions, preceded the official opening. The very first visitors to these "dress rehearsals" were 20,000 employees of Ling-Temco-Vought (LTV). Not only was LTV one of the area's largest employers, but the company helped supply some of the animations used in the park. They were followed during the week by guests from other area employers. Friday, the day before the official *Grand Opening*, was "press" day, with invitations to visit the park extended to media representatives and other selected individuals.

Frontgate area with iconic Six Flags, Dancing Waters, and Marching Band. Souvenir slide, circa 1961.

Frontgate.

The Frontgate area represents all of the sections, but is not officially a part of any. For the opening season, the center of the Frontgate area consisted of the *Star Plaza*, a large floral arrangement in the shape of the Texas Lone Star. A guest path circled the star lawn.

Framing the garden directly across from the entry gate was the *Dancing Waters*, a seventy-five foot long water show. The water show used water cannons to shoot water into the air at various heights and angles. The water was choreographed to music, hence the name "dancing waters". The show was particularly impressive at night when bright spotlights, also synchronized to the music, changed the color of the streams as they shot into the air.

The water fountains are still present at their original location. They now spray only in a generic cycle and no longer constitute a water show.

Behind the *Dancing Waters* stood the symbol of the park, the six flags themselves, flying forty-feet high from poles at the back of the entryway.

In keeping with Randall Duell's approach to amusement park design, the main path through the park was originally laid out basically as a Duell loop. There was one side path in the Texas section that branched off the loop. This path crossed a bridge to an additional Texas area which contained the railroad and *Astrolift* stations.

The Frontgate area was designed to split arriving guests in two opposite directions, thus spreading them throughout the park. Guests could go east, into the Modern section, and then on to the French and Confederate sections. Others could travel west, going first into Mexico, then into Spain and Texas.

USA – The Modern Section.

Prior to joining the United States of America, Texas was an independent nation, the Republic of Texas. Although the Republic won its independence from Mexico, it was still threatened by the more powerful nation to the

Modern USA section from 1961 souvenir map. Part of the French section is visible at the top of the segment. The rocket structure decorating the Missilechaser was not built.

south. Seeking protection from Mexico, the Republic of Texas became the 38th State in 1845.

The USA section represents Texas since it joined the United States. It is also known as the "modern" section, since the section represents the Texas of the day, while the other sections all represent some period from Texas' more distant historical past. It is "modern" Texas, with a hint of Texas of the future added for excitement. This is the Texas of sports cars, jet planes, and astronauts.

Exhibit Halls. Immediately to the left, upon entering the USA section from the Frontgate, were the park's exhibit halls. Such exhibits, usually sponsored by large corporations, were a common sight at state and world fairs. Typically, they consisted of an educational display that promoted the sponsor's corporate goals and products. The exhibits generated additional income for the park, as the corporations paid a fee for use of the exhibit space.

In addition to the exhibits, several major corporations sponsored rides and attractions in the park. CV Wood was a strong proponent of the use of corporate sponsors to generate additional income for the parks he developed. He relied on them at both *Six Flags* and *Freedomland*.

The initial park also relied heavily on leasees, independent businesses that pay a fee to operate their restaurant or shop inside the park. Since the leasees typically covered their own expenses for supplies and inventory, they lowered start-up costs for the park management. In addition, their business expertise insured smoother operations. Some of the first year leasees included the *El Chico Mexican Restaurant*; the *Indian Village*; *Naler's Chicken Plantation*; *Mrs. Goff's Ice Cream Shop*; and the *Leonard's* store.

The first booth nearest the Frontgate was the *Eastman Kodak* display. Here guests could rent cameras and obtain film and supplies. Guests without their own cameras could also purchase professionally shot images of the park on photographs, movies, and slides. Also available was advice on taking pictures in the park. Kodak later sponsored signs marking recommended picture taking spots around the park.

Next to the Kodak building was the exhibits hall. For the opening season, exhibits on display were: *The Story of Color* sponsored by Jones-Blair paints; *The Story of Industry* by the park's parent company, the Great Southwest Corporation; *The Story of Power ~ Power for Progress* by Texas Electric Service Company; and the *Electric Kitchens – Yesterday, Today and Tomorrow* by Westinghouse.

The Westinghouse exhibit ended after the 1962 season. In 1964, Braniff Airways added an exhibit. In 1965, Great Southwest ended its exhibit. In 1966, American Airlines replaced the Braniff Airways exhibit. Both the American Airlines and Jones Blair exhibits ended in 1967, leaving Texas Electric as the sole exhibit. The Texas Electric exhibit lasted until 1972.

The building that was the home to the exhibits is now the *Looney Tunes Souvenir Shop*, located in the northern portion of Looney Tunes' USA.

Animal Kingdom.   Directly south of the exhibits building was the *Animal Kingdom* petting zoo. The zoo, initially sponsored by *Southwestern Life Insurance Company*, was a place where guests could visit and touch friendly animals, such as donkeys, cows, and goats. Also on display were more exotic animals, such as a burro, llamas, deer, and monkeys. One resident was a giant tortoise. The animals on display were changed from time to time. For a nominal fee, guests could purchase fish to feed seals swimming in a pool.

The highlight attraction of the *Animal Kingdom* was "Sis Flagg", the baby Asian elephant. Baby elephants grow so fast that Sis had to be replaced every season or two with a smaller, younger, elephant. The original Sis was purchased from Thailand for $2,000. Sis's companion was a white burro named Tulip.

The zoo was a significant attraction in the park until the early 70s. It was then gradually downsized until nothing remained of it. It was completely removed in 1982 to make room for *Pac-Man Land*. *Looney Tunes USA* now occupies the area that originally held the zoo.

Southwest Life sponsored the Zoo until 1968. For the 1970 season, Ralston Purina pet food became the sponsor.

Missilechaser.   Behind the exhibit halls, and across the walk from the Zoo, was the *Missilechaser*. The *Missilechaser* was a standard scrambler style ride, commonly seen at traveling carnivals and county fairs. Although it was a standard carnival ride, it was at the time a state-of-the-art carnival ride. The ride, as well as its name, emphasized the modern aspects of the section.

Southwest Life Insurance Petting Zoo (1961-1982) in the USA section.
Initial plans for the petting zoo to be based on a "stranded circus" were dropped.
All-Tom postcard number P43935, 1961.

The ride was removed from the park at the end of the 1977 season. The area where it was located was later used for the *Sensational Sense Machine* attraction. This area is no longer open to the public. The ride was the first of three scrambler rides installed in the park.

Sidewinder.   To the east of the petting zoo was the *Sidewinder* roller coaster. "Sidewinder" is a name used to describe an unsavory cowboy. The term for the deceitful cowboy originated with the detested *Sidewinder* rattlesnake. In keeping with the modern aspects of the section, the ride was certainly named for the "Sidewinder" air-to-air missile, which uses an infrared system to locate targets. The missile, however, also takes its name from the rattlesnake, which also uses an infrared mechanism to help it locate its prey. Both names, *Missilechaser* and *Sidewinder*, defined the space age concept of the Modern USA section.

The *Sidewinder* has the distinction of being the first in a long line of roller coasters at *Six Flags*. It was the only roller coaster in the park during the first four years of operations. The ride was manufactured by the Herschell Company.

The ride was a "Wild Mouse" or "Mad Mouse" style metal roller coaster. The ride units were not attached in a train, but rather ran as individual cars, each of which held two riders. As with most coasters, the cars are pulled up a lift hill. Instead of traveling down a steep initial drop, however, they descended a winding track with sharp side-to-side turns. The front wheels of the cars were set back towards the middle of the ride. As a result, as the car approached a curve, the front end stuck out over the edge of the track before the front wheels started turning. This design created the illusion that the cars were constantly about to run off the track.

On display in front of the *Sidewinder* was a retired Grumman F9F-6 Cougar Navy jet fighter. A character dressed in a space age pressure suit answered questions about the aircraft and the possibility of space travel. The plane, on loan from the nearby Naval Air Station, added to the atmosphere of the "modern" Texas.

These two rides, the *Missilechaser* and the *Sidewinder,* have the distinction of being the only "off the shelf" carnival rides in the original park. Not being specifically designed for the park, the *Sidewinder* and the *Missilechaser* are also the only rides not featured in any early postcards or guidebooks. They are only mentioned in passing in early park public relations materials. The 1962 employee handbook does not describe the *Sidewinder* as a "roller coaster", but rather refers to it as a "fast moving rail ride".

The ride only operated as the *Sidewinder* for the seventy days of the short 1961 season. For 1962, it was relocated to the Mexican section and renamed the *La Cucaracha*.

Happy Motoring.   Immediately next to the *Sidewinder* was the *Humble Happy Motoring Freeway*. The attraction, sponsored by the Humble Oil Company, consisted of small go-cart sized vehicles with sports car bodies. The phrase "Happy Motoring" was a Humble logo. Humble was the predecessor

*Happy Motoring Cars (1961-1986) with
Sidewinder roller coaster (1961–1964) in the background.
1965 All-Tom souvenir book, picture 1961.*

of Exxon. Humble Oil was also a Great Southwest Corp. industrial park
client.

The ride was designed and built by Arrow Development Company of
Mountain View, California. It utilized the same car design as a similar attraction installed at *Freedomland USA*. There were twenty-three cars on the freeway
when the ride opened in 1961. The cars had 7½ horsepower single-cycle rear
engines with which the vehicles could race along at 40 mph. The engines,
however, were adjusted so that the maximum speed at which the guests could
travel topped out at 6 mph. The gas pedal on the driver's side actually controlled the speed of the car, while the steering wheel controlled the direction
of the car's travel. Each car cost the park $1,700.00.

The cars traveled around a half-mile long track, passing billboards
and waving by-passers. To keep the vehicles on the freeway, the roadway
contained a metal guide-strip located directly in the middle of the track. The
guide-strip, designed by Arrow Development, prevented the cars from leaving
the roadway while at the same time allowing the driver the feel of steering the
cars to the left and right. This was an innovation over *Freedomland USA*, which
instead ran the cars in a depressed roadway.

The ride was favored by the younger crowd because it allowed them
to actually "drive" the car, controlling both the speed, and within limits, the
position of the car on the roadway.

Due to the popularity of the ride, a second *Happy Motoring Freeway* was
added in 1962 to the south of the first track. The queue house used by the

Original Happy Motoring Cars.
Gasoline engines were in the rear.
Six Flags' public relations photo, ca. 1970.

Sidewinder roller coaster became the queue house for the second automobile ride.

In 1973, the body style of the cars was changed in order to keep the appearance of the cars up to date with actual car styles and designs.

Astrolift.   The USA section was also home to one of the two *Astrolift* terminals. Rising to a height of fifty-five feet, the Swiss made cable car ride carried up to four adults in gondolas across the park on a 2,100-foot long steel cable. As the steel cable consisted of a loop, the actual distance between the stations was roughly half the length of the cable. The USA station was the drive station, housing the motor that turned the cable. It was also home to the side tracks used to store most of the ride units when they were not in use.

The second terminal was in the Texas section. This station was the tension station. It housed a counterweight suspended in a vertical shaft under the cable-wheel housed in the station. The counterweight was used to keep the cable at the same tension, no matter how much weight it was holding. The station had a sidetrack much smaller than the one at the modern station. This track was used to hold a maintenance unit and a few of the unused gondolas.

Four towers supported the cable. One was located in the Modern section; one just outside the amphitheater in the Confederacy; and two were grouped together in the Texas section. When the *Southern Palace Theater* was built, the amphitheater tower was replaced by a tower on the roof of the theater.

On all but the most crowded days, riders could ride "one-way" to the other station, or "round-trip" back to the section at which they started. In this manner, the ride served as a means for people to cross the park quickly and comfortably. On crowded days, trips could be limited to "one way" only.

The ride was built by Von Roll of Berne, Switzerland. Von Roll was the primary builder worldwide of cable car rides of this type. Modeled after a ski lift, the ride cost $300,000 to construct. It was erected by F.B. McIntire Equipment Company of Fort Worth.

The ride was a model 101 Sky Ride. Von Roll built over one hundred "101" Sky Rides at amusement parks and locations around the world. Sky rides of this nature were constructed in almost all new themes parks built during the 60's and 70's. The last was installed in 1977, at *Marriott Great America*, in Chicago, Illinois, now *Six Flags Great America*. The rides have now been removed from most parks.

Six Flags Gazette photo of Modern USA Astrolift station (1961-1980).
Queue house is to the left and storage tracks are on the right. (Vol 1, No. 4, pg. 5, 1961).

The Modern section was also the location of one of the park's dining areas. The eating area was a large patio restaurant that sold traditional hamburgers and hot dogs. Originally, it was simply referred to as "refreshment stand" on park maps. It was named the *Pit Stop* in 1973. It was also enlarged and remodeled several times, beginning with an enlargement in 1966. The larger *All American Cafe* now exists in basically the same location as the original refreshment stand.

The section also contained a *Pom Pom* hat store located at the end of the exhibit hall. The store sold a wide variety of hats. Guests could have their name sewn onto the front of many of the hat varieties. The hats were a very popular souvenir. Garnet N. Walker and Company sold the hats in the park. The shop was renamed *USA Hat Shop* in 1977.

Live entertainment in the section included the *Six Flags Marching Band,* which periodically marched through the section. A clown on high stilts named "Shorty" was also a popular figure with the crowd.

The French Section.

During the 1600's, Spain, England, and France were racing to stake claims on the "new world". While Spain had several communities in Texas, France had established colonies mainly in Canada and Louisiana. France's claim to Texas consisted of a single colony, which is now referred to as Fort Saint Louis. The outpost was established near Matagorda Bay by the expedition's leader, René Robert Cavelier, Sieur de La Salle.

LaSalle's original outpost was rather small, consisting of a two-story headquarters blockhouse, six or so surrounding structures and eight cannon. The settlement, however, was not ever intended as a permanent community. Located near the mouth of the Lavaca River, it was simply intended as a base of operations while La Salle explored the Lavaca and the surrounding area looking for his original destination, the Mississippi River.

La Salle originally sought the Mississippi River because he felt that control of the mouth of the Mississippi would lead to control of the southern half of the continent. Finding the Mississippi became even more critical, however, as his group became stranded in Texas. He knew that the waterway connected the French outposts in Louisiana with those in Canada. If he could locate the massive river, he could follow it north into familiar French territories.

In the end, the colony stood from 1685 to 1689 and was a complete disaster. Unfortunately for LaSalle and his followers, he never found the Mississippi, which was 400 miles to the east. Instead, La Salle ended up dead at the hands of his own people. Those remaining in the colony that did not die were captured by Indians. The Spanish later discovered the former site of the colony after it was completely destroyed. La Salle's efforts, however, did concern the Spanish enough that they increased their presence in Texas.

The entire French section at *Six Flags* was designed to recreate historic Fort Saint Louis. The fort contained a small play area with a two-story block-house, a catwalk, and cannon. Guests could climb on the catwalk and enter the blockhouse. A garden growing corn recreated the gardens used by the explorers.

Pierre's Treasures was a small gift store built in a log building which matched the rest of the fort. This particular building was an effort to recreate a building similar in style and appearance to an actual family dwelling built by the French settlers at historical Fort St. Louis. It was filled with the usual assortment of souvenirs, postcards, and maps of the park. As it was a "treasure" store, it specialized in rocks and gems, both loose and mounted in jewelry.

In 1969, the name was changed to *Jacques' Treasures*. Jacques and Pierre were the names of the two river scout characters in *La Salle's River Adventure*.

Pierre's Treasures, gift store in French Section.
In keeping with the treasure theme, the store specialized in rocks, minerals, and jewelry.
All-Tom postcard P57504, published 1963.

After 1981, the building was no longer used as a souvenir shop. The front was removed and the location was used for various other activities, such as a t-shirt customization shop, an artist drawing area, and an encyclopedia sales stand.

La Salle's River Adventure.   Across from the small store was the centerpiece of the French section, *La Salle's River Adventure*. The ride was designed to commemorate La Salle's expedition to Texas in search of the Mississippi. Guests traveled the replica Lavaca River in twenty-five foot "riverboats" manufactured by the Willis Boat Company of Dallas, Texas.

LaSalle's Riverboat Ride as depicted on 1962 souvenir map.
Amphitheater is shown in upper left corner.

The ride consisted of a series of animated scenes, each part of the fictionalized account of La Salle's adventures in Texas. The entire ride was narrated by the boat's "captain" standing at the front of the boat. The "captain" recited a spiel that explained each scene that the boat traveled passed.

As the boat left the dock, the captain educated the guests as to the history on which the ride was based. The passengers were told how La Salle explored the Lavaca River in search of a route to the Mississippi. As the route had not yet been located, the captain explained, on their trip they would be searching further. In order to assist their efforts, the captain sent ahead two river scouts to guide them on the journey. Until they are located, the Captain warns the crew, "anything can happen".

The first scene on the attraction was the outpost of the river scouts. The captain was expecting to pick them up at their camp. Originally, the outpost was abandoned, leaving the crew of the riverboat to wonder what happened to the scouts. In later years, a more dramatic scene depicted an outpost that had been attacked and was in ruins. In view was the body of a riverboat pilot with an Indian arrow in his back, as well as the bodies of dead Indian warriors. The captain notes that the river scouts are not present and exclaims that he hopes that they can be found as they continue with their journey.

Around the first turn, a lone wolf was spotted howling to the sky. This scene was later enlarged to include a family of wolves sitting in front of a cave protecting the bones left from their last meal.

The next scene was one of the highlights of the ride, a Spanish fort sitting at a bend in the river. Prominent were three menacing cannon protruding through a stockade wall. The fort was a threat, the captain explained, since the French and Spanish were at war over the "little territory known as *Texas*".

As the boat approached the stockade, a Spanish Conquistador rose up from behind the wall. In the flash of an eye, he swung his sword down. As his sword went down, a tremendous "boom" was heard and one of the fort's three cannons exploded with fire. Immediately a large pillar of water shot up next to the right side of the boat. The first shot missed; there was another boom, another cannon spit fire, and another column of water shot into the air on the other side of the boat. The cannons continue to fire as the captain put the engine into "full speed ahead". The shooting stopped as the boat traveled out of the line of fire of the cannon.

Upon passing the fort, the Captain called everyone's attention to a scene on the other side of the river. Two Frenchmen, who the Captain confirmed were the two missing river scouts, Jacques and Pierre, were seen hanging by their necks from a tree. In the early 80's this rather gruesome scene was replaced with a more family friendly French trading post.

Spanish fort firing on French riverboat.
Souvenir slide, circa 1961.

Next, the crew came upon a lone French scout, François, sitting watch high in a tree. The captain asks François if it was "safe to go on?" François signals back that it is not.

Despite the warning, the unknown danger ahead does not seem unreasonable when compared to turning around and risking another run by the Spanish fort, so the boat continued on. As the captain cautiously piloted the boat down the river, explosions were heard again. While not as loud as the cannons, they were disconcerting just the same. Moments later the boat traveled into the middle of a battle between Native Americans on one side of the river and French explorers on the other. Caught in the crossfire, the captain ordered everyone to take cover.

Portion of Indian village scene from LaSalle's River Adventure.
Photo by Author, 1975.

As the boat passed the crossfire, it left the domain of the French explorers and entered the land of the Indians. As the journey continued, all of the remaining scenes related to either Native Americans or the wildlife living along the riverbank. The boat passed by such things as alligators, flamingos, and bears. A cougar on a tree limb threatened to jump into the boat. An Indian war canoe appeared from nowhere, its warriors threatening the boat with bows and arrows at the ready. One of the larger scenes was of a peaceful Indian village, with children playing, women preparing a meal, and a medicine man dancing around a fire.

Originally, the ride displayed fifteen live alligators, as well as live flamingos. These proved too troublesome, however, and soon the flamingos were removed and the alligators replaced with fiberglass counterparts. The alligators refusal to stay in their assigned areas was noted as one of the few problems on the park's opening day.

The loading dock of LaSalle's River Adventure (1961–1982),
with Astrolift (1961-1980) at top right and Sky Crane (1963–1968) in the background.
Tourist photo from author's collection, circa 1965.

Toward the end of the ride, the boat passed a den of beavers working on their dam. The largest was gnawing on a rather tall tree. As the boat passed by, the tree suddenly started to fall, heading directly for the side of the boat. The tree splashed into the water, merely inches from the side of the boat.

After the beaver tree, the river split in two directions. The captain would stop the boat to consider the options, finally deciding to take the branch to the left. As the boat turned the bend, however, it appeared that the captain made a terrible mistake. Directly in front of the boat stood a waterfall. Behind the waterfall was a solid rock wall. The captain again stopped the boat. Here, however, the river was too narrow to turn around. As the crew listened to the captain explaining that this could be the end of the trip, the waterfall started to change. The water, which had been flowing down in front of the rock wall, slowly diverted its path and began traveling down the sides of the rocks. The rock wall, which stood behind the flow of the water, slowly split into two and opened, revealing an ominous cave.

Slowly, the boat crept forward into the dark cave. Just as it cleared the rock doors, they closed behind the boat, sealing off any exit. At the same time, the guest could hear the water again begin to fall in front of the rock entrance.

Though dark, the cave was not empty. There, just out of reach, were treasures and bounty, including a treasure chest full of gold and jewelry. The cave was also filled with skeletons and skulls. The items in the cave were fluorescent and illuminated with blacklights, creating an ominous atmosphere. A skeleton guarding the treasure chest jumped out from the wall as the boat traveled passed. The captain speculated that the souls lost in the cave were probably doomed for trying to vandalize the treasures and warned everyone not to touch anything.

After the boat entered the cave, it became clear that yet another rock wall prevented any exit. As the boat approached the next wall, however, it also began to slowly open in front of the boat. As the boat came out of the dark cave, the captain pointed out the golden fleur-de-lis of France, the flag of France, flying high from Fort Saint Louis. The boat turned a corner, bringing it back into view of the dock. Another crew had survived the perils of the Lavaca River. The captain speculated that the crew was released alive from the cave as a reward for not taking any of the gold or treasures.

The river scenes changed some over the years, mostly with the addition of new scenes and the addition of details to older ones. One addition was a peaceful scene of an Indian burial scaffold. A bear fighting a pack of timber wolves was added in 1966. A whirlpool, with some poor soul being pulled down to a watery grave, was installed just before the beaver tree. Guests could only see his hand sticking up, holding onto a small stick, which twirled around as he tried to fight the forces of the water.

In 1970, a large scene with a Spanish monk supervising four friendly Tejas Indians in the construction of the Mission San Francisco De Los Tejas was added just after the encampment ruins and before the Spanish Fort. That same season, animated Indian warriors were added on both sides of the river just in front of the cave's entrance.

While the animations created an impressive ride, the spiel of the captain created the show like component of the ride. The humor and enthusiasm of the captain on each tour of the river made the ride one of the favorites in the park.

The ride's riverboats were originally powered by gasoline engines. The gas engines were later converted to electric engines powered by large rechargeable batteries. While the captain controlled the speed of the boat, the direction of travel was controlled by a channel under the boat.

The track system was designed and patented by Arrow Development as a means to control the travel of a boat ride on a river or pond. The system used tires mounted sideways on axles descending from the bottom of the front and the back of the boat. These tires rested sideways inside a small channel at the bottom of the river. The boat traveled with the channel. This system provided smooth control over the direction of the boat.

The outside walls of Fort St. Louis still define the French section of the park. The Riverboat ride, however, was removed during 1982 to make way for the *Roaring Rapids* ride.

The Confederacy.

Between 1861 and 1865, Texas, along with 12 other southern states, was a member of the *Confederate States of America*. This time period is recreated in the park's Confederate section, located roughly in the middle of the park. The section, which is now often referred to as the "Old South" section, was designed to recreate the feel of visiting a typical southern civil war era town.

The Confederate section originally connected to the French section through the west gate of Fort Saint Louis and to the Texas section at two different locations. Additional paths into the area have been added and removed over the years.

Amphitheater.   The Confederate section was home to the park's largest show production, simply referred to as the "Amphitheater". The 1,200-seat amphitheater was the first attraction in the Confederate section upon entering from the French section.

The Broadway style shows were produced by Six Flags' own staff members. They featured singing, dancing, comedy, and special talents, such as ventriloquism. The first show in the amphitheater was a variety show. Beginning in 1962, the *Campus Revue* was produced at the amphitheater. Each season's *Campus Revue* was a completely new show.

The Lil' Dixie Carousel (Flying Jenny)(1961–1974) is shown at bottom.
The Astrolift (1961–1980) is heading across the Confederacy towards the USA section.
The Amphitheater (1961-1967) is in the middle of the left side. Souvenir slide, circa 1962.

Confederate firing squad executes Union spy in front of Recruitment Center.
Souvenir slide circa 1961.

Rather than professional performers, the talent for each show consisted of college students. Beginning with the first season, the park conducted extensive auditions for performers at college campuses all over the state. Wynne himself frequently participated in the selection process. The early amphitheater shows, as well as the later Southern Palace shows, were frequently reviewed in the entertainment sections of the local newspapers.

The amphitheater hosted shows until the end of the 1967 season. In 1968, it was replaced at the same location by the indoor *Southern Palace Theater.* The same types of shows were produced in the Southern Palace.

Across the walkway from the Amphitheater was a small juice stand.

Lil' Dixie Carousel.   Located directly in front of the *Amphitheater* was the *Lil' Dixie Carousel.* The *Lil' Dixie* was a small carousel with bench seating. The ride was powered by a mule named Joe. Joe walked in a circle, pulling the ride seats around as he went. The ride was renamed the *Flying Jenny* in 1963 to avoid confusion with the traditional carousel added in the Boomtown section. "Jenny" is a term for a female donkey or mule.

After the 1967 season, the ride was moved west to a spot near the entrance to the *Cave* ride. The move was needed to make room for the conversion of the *Amphitheater* into the *Southern Palace.*

Above: Preconstruction concept drawing of Naler's Chicken Plantation.
All-Tom postcard P42667, published 1961.
Below: The same building thirty-five years later, rethemed as Gator McGee's restaurants.
It was later JB's Smokehouse Barbecue. Photograph by Author, 2006.

Naler's Chicken Plantation. The largest restaurant in the section, and one of the largest in the park, was *Naler's Chicken Plantation House.* Resembling a southern plantation house, the specialty of the establishment was the southern fried chicken basket. Seating was available on a large patio outside the restaurant. In order to keep the diners comfortable, outdoor fans blew air down from the trees above. The patio featured a scenic view of the *Skull Island* waterway and rafts.

Confederate Reenactment Players. Located to the south of the *Amphitheater* stood another of the park's historical recreations: *The Confederate Soldier's Headquarters and Recruitment Station.* This area was a recreation of a small confederate encampment. It included a group of large military tents, protected by cannon. The area was framed by colorful civil war recruitment banners mounted on scaffolding above the tents. A bandstand stood in front of the area.

At the recruitment station, park guests could "enlist" in the Confederate army by signing on the dotted line. The boys could sign up as "soldiers" and the girls could sign up as "nurses". In addition, guests could interact with the reenactment players, who displayed their knowledge of life during civil war times.

The reenactment players were outfitted in the distinctive gray uniform associated with the Confederate States of America. They marched through the streets of the Confederate section and performed precision drills with their rifles. From time to time during the day, a union spy would be reported in the crowd. The confederate soldiers would then search the area, discover the spy, and execute him by firing squad.

Stagecoach (1961–1967) traveling through a creek.
Guests rode both in, and on top of, the coach.
Six Flags' public relations photograph, circa 1961.

Butterfield Overland Stagecoach. Behind *Nalers* stood the *Butterfield Overland Stagecoach* station. The attraction offered guests the experience of a ride on an authentic stagecoach. The coaches were manufactured by the Gignac Company of Chicago, Illinois, and were identical to those built by Gignac for *Freedomland USA* and *Pleasure Island.*

The ride was based on the historical *Butterfield Overland Stagecoach* which provided mail and passenger service from the Mississippi river, through the heart of Texas, and on to California. The line ran from 1857 to 1861. Butterfield was later taken over by Wells Fargo.

Setting was available both inside the coach and outside on the top of the coach. The loading dock consisted of a two-story tower used to load and unload guests onto the ride. The tower's top level was used to provide access to the top level of the stagecoaches. In 1962, a second tower was added, so that loading and unloading could take place at the same time. Both two and four horse teams were used with the ride's three coaches. Each coach carried up to twenty guests on a half-mile course.

The coaches traveled through the backwoods of the park, where the guests viewed various scenes, including live buffalo. At one point, the coaches crossed a small creek. Beginning with the 1964 season, the coaches also passed through a small "ghost town", home to the "Ghost Town Saloon". At the saloon, a skeleton bartender stood serving drinks to his four skeleton customers. When the stagecoach ride was removed, the saloon and its inhabitants were moved near the mine train at a location viewable by passengers on the *Six Flags Railroad.*

The loading area and route where changed several times over the life of the ride. In 1963, the queue house and loading area were moved north in order to make room for the new arcade building. In 1964, the loading area was

Skull Island as depicted in 1961 souvenir map. To the far left is part of the Texas section, including the Astrolift station and Watermelon Garden.

Skull slide in Skull Rock (1961-1978) on Skull Island (1961-1982).
All-Tom postcard number P43955, 1961.

again moved, and the route was shortened, to make room for the *Speelunker's Cave* ride. The attraction was removed at the end of the 1967 season.

Skull Island.   Another major attraction in the Confederate section was Skull Island. Originally to be named, "Outlaw Island", the name became "Skull Island" in homage to the island's most noted feature, the large "Skull Rock". The island was a large play area that was almost a themed section of its own. Skull Island depicted a fictitious Texas coast island used by the pirate Jean Lafitte to hide his treasures. Lafitte was a French pirate that operated in the Gulf of Mexico in the early 1800's.

Originally, the island was reached by motorized rafts that were boarded on a dock next to the *Amphitheater*. The rafts were reminiscent of 18th century river barges and referred to in some early park materials as "cotton barges" and "river barges". The rafts were powered by gasoline motors and driven by the ride operators. The raft traveled down the man-made river towards *Naler's* restaurant, turned north and moved away from the Confederate section. They then turned back to the east and docked on the far side of the island, out of view of the remainder of the Confederate section. They returned along the same route.

The island was full of paths, trees, and greenery. The centerpiece of *Skull Island* was *Skull Rock*, the landmark for which the island was named. The huge artificial rock was formed in the shape of a skull. The skull housed a thirty-foot slide that ran out the ear hole on the left side of the skull, turned, and traveled to the front of the rock.

A short-lived idea for *Skull Island* was guest fishing from the shore. The 1961 souvenir map indicates two fishing areas, with a fishing and bait shop nearby.

Skull Island Rafts (1961 - 1976) took guests to and from
Skull Island and the dock in the Confederate Section.
Souvenir Slide, circa 1964.

Tree Slide. **T**aller than the skull slide was the tree slide, which stood nearly forty-feet high. The slide was accessible through a circular staircase that wound upward next to the tree. The circular slide itself was contained inside of the tree trunk shaped structure. Burlap sacks were provided to each guest to sit on as they spiraled down through the dark to the ground.

The original tree slide was acquired from the University of Texas. There it was a fire escape slide in a dormitory in which Angus Wynne, Sr. resided. Having fond memories of sliding down the slide for entertainment purposes, Wynne Sr. suggested use of the slide at the park.

Skull Island was expanded over the first few years of the park's operation, adding more slides, suspension bridges, barrel bridges, and other activities.

With the addition of the *Tower* in 1969, portions of the *Skull Island* were removed. The island started a slow decline, with various attractions being removed over the following seasons. What remained of the attraction was completely removed in 1982 in order to make room for the *Roaring Rapids Raft Ride*.

Confederate Section Shopping. Several specialty stores offering more than just traditional souvenirs were located in the Confederate section. The streets of the replica southern town offered a diversity of shopping and exhibits. One was a newspaper building, with an antique printing press, sponsored by *The Fort Worth Star-Telegram* and the *Dallas Times Herald* and operated by the *Daily News Texan*. Guests could purchase items such as wanted posters, newspaper frontpages, or show bills. After purchase, the guest could have a name printed predominately on the item.

One leasee shop was *Leonards*, sponsored by the local *Leonards Department Store*. In 1963, the *Emporium* replaced *Leonards*. Next to *Leonards*, *Miss Abigail's Gift Shop* provided traditional souvenirs.

Both new and used books were sold at the *Highland Historical Press* bookstore. The store specialized in history books and historical maps, with

Above: Concept art of store in the Confederate section.
The building originally housed the book store and flag shop.
From All-Tom postcard folder P90601, 1961.
Below: The actual building forty-five years later after being converted to a restaurant.
Photograph by Author, 2005.

some rare items on display in the store. After the first season the bookstore became the *Artist Colony*.

In keeping with the park's theme, the *Flag Shop* sold popular flags, including the flags of each section and pirate flags for *Skull Island*. The *Flag Shop* and bookstore were located together in the last building in the Confederate section, next to the white columns.

At the other end of the street, across from the carousel, stood a souvenir stand named "Yankee Notions". Items sold at the stand included typical souvenirs, such as maps, guidebooks, postcards, as well as other useful items such as sunglasses and camera film. In the mid-70s, the stand was converted into a portrait studio.

For refreshment, ice cream was available at *Mrs. Goff's Ice Cream* shop, also known as *Mrs. Goff's Frozen Sweets*. Ice cream has been sold at this location, near the entrance into the Texas section, throughout the history of the park. The store has had many names, including *Smith's Ice Cream Parlor* beginning in 1964; the *Old South Ice Cream Parlor* in 1967; the *Ice Cream Palace* in 1970; and *Borden's Ice Cream Palace* for 1986. In 1987, it became the *Ice Cream Palace*. By 1998 it was *Smith Street Ice Cream Parlor*. In 2005, it became *Ben and Jerry's Ice Cream*.

In addition to the performances by the Confederate reenactment actors, live street shows included periodic performances by a Dixieland band.

A set of large white columns, two on each side of the pathway, mark the border between the Texas section and the Confederate section. The columns were salvaged from an actual plantation house. The Confederate section is to the north of the columns, the Texas section to the south. The guest pathway also turns approximately 90 degrees between each section, in a manner designed to help visually separate the sections.

The Sovereign Nation of Texas.

After the revolution from Mexico, the independent Republic of Texas was formed. The new nation covered much more than what we now consider Texas. In addition to the land that is the state of Texas, the nation also claimed land into part of what is now New Mexico, with claims as far north and west into what is now Wyoming. The Republic of Texas existed from 1836 to 1845. In 1845, still threatened by Mexico, Texas became the twenty-eighth state in the United States.

When the park opened in 1961, Western culture was extremely popular. The top three shows on television, *Gunsmoke*, *Bonanza*, and *Wagon Train* were all westerns. It is not surprising then that the "Old-West Texas" section became one of the largest sections in the park. The section recreated the days when Texas was home to cowboys, gunfighters, and outlaws.

Having a Texas section at the park may seem a little redundant, since all of the sections represented Texas at some point in time. In keeping with the master theme, however, the Texas section represented Texas at the time that it was a sovereign nation. The "Texas" section was, therefore, themed on the Texas of the old west. Technically, the section represented a time period from 1836 to 1845.

The section brought to life a western town, straight out of a cowboy movie. All of the typical buildings were present, including a saloon, bank, courthouse, jail, schoolhouse, post office, train depot, and hotel.

The original Texas section was one long street, known as "Texas Street". The street extended from the *Old Red Schoolhouse* near the middle of the park to the Texas depot on the west end of the park. The street curves slightly to the north as it travels to the west.

If you start nearest the center of the park, the first building in the section is the *Little Red Schoolhouse*, officially known as the *Johnson Creek Schoolhouse*. Reportedly, this building was the only structure in the park before construction began. This is also the first building in the section that guests observe as they enter the section from the Confederate section to the north.

Texas section as depicted in 1961 souvenir map.

The schoolhouse is the home to administrative offices and served as the park's original "lost children" waiting area. Complete with a bell tower, the building façade is virtually unchanged after more than fifty years in the park. The lost children area, however, was moved to a caboose in the Modern section in 1963.

Next to the antebellum pillars marking the entrance into the Confederacy was the *Artistic Tonsorial Saloon* (Barbershop), and the *Doggie Hotel*. ("*Doggie*" is a term for an orphan calf in a herd of cattle.) The lobby to the *Doggie Hotel* was furnished as a period hotel lobby and was open to the public. The lobby was the home of a talking parrot. The parrot could tell jokes and appear to banter with the guest on any topic of interest. In fact, an employee spoke for the parrot using a hidden microphone, hidden speaker, and a one-way mirror. This set up created the illusion that the bird was talking with the guests. The attraction was similar to a *Freedomland USA* attraction at which guests conversed with a talking gas pump.

The *Doggie Hotel* and the *Tonsorial Saloon* were actually the same building. Using a Hollywood set design technique, the façade for the hotel faced to the south and the façade for the barbershop faced to the west, creating the appearance that there were two different buildings.

45

The Johnson Creek Schoolhouse.
Photograph by Author, 2005.

Next to the hotel and barbershop stood the *Sheriff's Office and Jailhouse*. At the jail, guests could peer through a barred window and see an animated prisoner snoring loudly as he slept on a cot. In 1978, the corner on which the *Jail, Hotel,* and *Tonsorial Saloon* were located was rebuilt and they were replaced by the *Buckeye Gallery* electronic shooting gallery.

The Crazy Horse Saloon.　　On the south side of the street, across from the hotel and *Sheriff's Office*, sat the *Crazy Horse Saloon. The Crazy Horse* is a show saloon, complete with a small stage for singing and dancing, a piano, and several tables for the guests.

In keeping with the park's historical emphasis, the entire back bar of the saloon is an antique bar from an 1890 vintage saloon. Carpenters crafted a new front bar to conform to the antique back bar. Antique tables and chairs were acquired from a saloon in Little Rock, Arkansas. In keeping with the park's family friendly atmosphere, various park promotional materials make it very clear that "although it is a *saloon,* only soft-drinks are sold there". The show was sponsored by both Dr. Pepper and Coke-a-Cola.

The theater was expanded in 1964 to a capacity of 250. It is still rather small when compared to the 1,200-seat amphitheater. Rather than have a specific show, the performers originally staged various numbers throughout the day. Typically, four or five performers in saloon costumes sang period songs, danced on the stage, and mingled with the guests.

The *Crazy Horse* was the park's first indoor theater. It continued as the park's only indoor show until 1968 when the larger *Southern Palace Theater* and the theater in Good Times Square were opened. Still operating at its original location, the *Crazy Horse Saloon* is the longest running theater in the park.

Being the early park's only indoor theater, the *Crazy Horse* also served as an employee auditorium for orientation sessions, training, and meetings.

Crazy Horse Saloon performers at the original entrance.
All-Tom postcard P43945, published 1961.

During the first season, the *Camark Pottery* store shared the building with the *Crazy Horse Saloon*, occupying the eastern half of the building. *Camark Pottery* was an Arkansas pottery company and a Great Southwest Industrial warehouse client. During the first season, their park store sold various items of pottery. During the second season, the pottery shop was replaced with *Mrs. Wood's Pastry Shop*. The space became a coffee shop in 1963. In 1964, the *Crazy Horse* was expanded to take in the entire building.

Next to the *Crazy Horse*, the guest-way branched around the corner and entered the Mexican section. The *Indian Village* sat across from the theater on the path leading into the Mexican section.

Across the pathway was the *Texas Bank & Trust Company*, sponsored by a local bank of the same name. The building was purchased in Tom Bean, Texas, and moved to its location in the park. The building was designated as a bank until 1965.

Next to the bank was *Armour's Meat Market*, sponsored by Armour and Company. The *Meat Market* was a small café with some outdoor seating. Although Armour's sponsorship was dropped before the 1967 season, the *Meat Market* remained at the location until 1974. Armour and Company was also a Great Southwest Industrial Park tenant.

Gunfighters. *Judge Roy Bean's Courthouse and Law Office* sat across Texas Street from the bank and meat market, next to the Sheriff's office. Roy Bean was a historical Texas figure. In the 1880's he was Justice of the Peace in Val Verde County, Texas, and was known as the "Law West of the Pecos". He was reported to have held court in his saloon, the "Jersey Lilly". (Due to a later subdivision of Val Verde County, the actual location of Bean's saloon court is now in Pecos County.)

In 1963, a recreation of the Jersey Lilly was added in the Texas section. Six Flags again memorialized Roy Bean when the park's first wooden roller coaster was named the "Judge Roy Scream", with the tagline "Awe west of the Pecos".

The area in front of the courthouse was a frequent location for the gunfighters' street show. Periodically during the day, outlaws would rob the bank across the street. Quickly, the sheriff and his deputies jumped to their feet to apprehend the hombres. On the street, the inevitable quick draw gunfight would entertain the guests and put an end to the lawlessness. Between shows, Judge Roy Bean often sat playing checkers and talking with the crowds on the porch of the courthouse.

Six Flags postcard depicting gunfighters in front of the Texas Courthouse. Judge Roy Bean is standing on the steps holding a rope. Note park photographer in stripped dress left of mid-center. She sold Polaroid pictures to guests. All-Tom postcard P43952, published 1961.

The gunfighters also performed at other locations throughout the Texas section. One routine involved the outlaws riding along and "robbing" the train, followed by Western justice in the form of a shoot-out with the sheriff at the train station.

Neither the park's designers, nor the guests, seemed to be bothered by the fact that Judge Roy Bean did not preside in Texas until the 1870's, well after the time that Texas was no longer an independent nation.

Next door to the courthouse was the *Prairie General Merchandise* souvenir store, which contained the *Potter's Wheel* pottery shop. The store also had a front façade indicating it was a blacksmith shop.

Across the street from the general merchandise store was a single building housing both the *Post Office* and *Waples Platter Grocery Store*. Ice tea, coffee, and pastries were sold at the "grocery store". The sponsor, Waples Platter, was a Texas based grocery store supply company. The Waples sponsorship lasted until 1967. At the *Post Office*, guests could purchase stamps and post cards. They could also mail items from this location. In 1974, both the *Post Office* and the *General Store* became the *Hanging Tree Gift Store*.

The *Sheriff's Office*, *Jail*, and *Courthouse* were actually only facades attached to administrative buildings that were not open to the public. Using this technique, administrative buildings were "hidden" within the park.

At this point in the street, there was an interruption in the Texas section. Tucked into the southwest corner of the bend in the street, next to the grocery store and post office, was the Spanish section.

Directly across from the Spanish section was a second pathway connecting to the Confederate section. Along this pathway, next to the general merchandise and pottery store was the *Sorghum Mill*, a reproduction mill where early methods of making syrup were demonstrated. Traveling the path past the *Sorghum Mill* brought guests to the *Butterfield Stagecoach* ride in the Confederate section

The Texas section is divided into two distinct areas by the creek running through the park. A small bridge spans the creek and connects the two portions.

On the east side of the Texas Bridge, next to the burro ride entrance was one of the park's Pom Pom hat shops. As with the hat store in the Modern section, this shop sold all types of souvenir hats. In 1964, the *Pom Pom Hat Shop* was moved across the pathway.

To the right, upon crossing the bridge and entering the second portion of the Texas section, was *Jean's Western Wear Store*. *Jean's* was another leasee specialty shop with boots, saddles, western clothes, and accessories. The shop became the *Western Shop* in 1966. It remained a western shop until 1974.

Dogie Hotel, located in the Texas Section, near the entrance to the Confederacy.
The Tonsorial (Barber Shop) facade is built into the right side of the building.
Postcard P42664, published 1961.

Astrolift cars viewed from Texas Lift. (1961–1980).
Photo by Author, 1976.

Next to the *Western Wear* was the *Western Trading Post* gift store. The *Western Trading Post* was renamed to *Annie's General Store* in 1973; *Annie's Country Christmas* in 1984; and *Annie's Notions and Dry Goods* in 1985. It became a woodcrafts store in 1987.

The first building on the left as you crossed the bridge, sitting across from the *Western Wear*, was *Mrs. Bowie's Candy Shop*. While remaining a candy store, the shop was renamed several times. It became the *Kandy Kitchen* in 1964. With the installation of the *Texas Giant* in 1990, it became *Giant Sweets*. It was renamed again in 1991 to the *Texas Candy Kitchen*.

Next to the candy shop was the Depot Cafe, a medium sized outdoor eating area. The cafe served hamburgers, hot dogs, and soft drinks. It was renamed to the Iron Horse Café in 1973.

Next to the *Depot Cafe* was the Texas station of the *Six Flags Railroad*. The history and operation of the railroad is discussed in Chapter 3, "The Six Flags Railroad".

Astrolift.   Across from the railroad station was the Texas station of the *Astrolift* ride. The *Texas Astrolift* terminal was the last building on the east side of the pathway. The path curves more at this point, so that while the *Western Wear* next to the terminal was facing somewhat towards the south, the terminal itself faced more to the west.

The *Astrolift* provided a panoramic view of the park. It provided the only aerial view of the park until the Sky Crane was installed in 1963. Riders could view most of the Confederate section; France; and parts of the Modern USA section, before descending into the USA section.

The *Boot Scootin'* ride, and the souvenir stand at the exit to the *Texas Giant*, now occupy the space where the *Texas Astrolift* was located. Inside the queue house was a large sign crediting the Von Roll Company of Berne, Switzerland with the design and installation of the *Astrolift* ride.

For the first season, the *Watermelon Garden* was located at the end of the pathway between the *Astrolift* station and the train station. There guests could purchase ice-cold watermelons by the slice. For the second season, the *Chaparral* car ride was placed at the site of the watermelon garden.

The Indian Village. Although Native Americans did not have a flag to be recognized in the park's theme, an area representing their contribution to the State was appropriate. The *Indian Trading Post and Village* sat on the border between the Mexican and Texas sections. Various park materials referred to the village as being in the Texas section, the Mexican section, and even the Spanish section, which was directly behind it. In particular, materials released before the park was complete indicated that the *Indian Village* would be part of the Spanish section.

The front of the *Indian Village* was the *Trading Post*. The *Trading Post* was a large souvenir shop selling Western and Indian related items, including fine jewelry. This was one of the original park's largest souvenir stores.

In addition to the items for sale, the trading post contained displays of many authentic Native American relics. The relics were owned by Skeet Richardson, who leased the space for the store from Six Flags.

Indian Village dancers (1961–1967) displaying Hoop Dance hoops.
Souvenir slide, circa 1963.

Behind the trading post was the actual Indian village. A set of four teepees were reconstructed in the corners of a small square performance area. In this area, Native Americas performed authentic dances during the day. Typically, two Native Americans performed a traditional dance, while a third performer marked the time on an Indian tom-tom. One such dance was the Hoop dance, performed with wooden hoops resembling a hula-hoop. Many of the performers were from the Kiowa tribe of Oklahoma.

The *Indian Trading Post* building still sits at is original location. The *Indian Village*, with its native dancers, however, was removed following the 1967 season.

The Spanish Section.

The Spanish were the first Europeans to reach Texas. They started colonizing the area that is now Texas as part of a broader claim to parts of what is now the western United States, Mexico, Central America, and much of South America. The Spanish claims to Texas started with Alonso Álvarez de Pineda in 1519 and lasted until the Mexican Revolution of 1821.

The Spanish section recreated the ruins of the 1690 Spanish mission *San Francisco de los Tejas*, the first mission built by the Spanish in Texas. To replicate the Spanish style, the buildings in the section are rock, unlike most of the wooden buildings in the Texas section.

Conquistador Burro Ride. The site of the mission was also the location for the only attraction in the original Spanish section, the *Conquistador Burro Ride*. Here Six Flags honored the Spanish contribution to the history of Texas by recreating the adventures of Conquistador Francisco Vasquez de

Conquistadors, (1961–1962) such as this one, lead a train of burros.
Six Flags' public relations photograph, circa 1961.

Coronado. In 1539, Coronado led an exploration looking for gold and riches. In 1541, he searched the Texas panhandle for the legendary seven cities of gold. Although he located some Native American cities, he never found the gold and riches that he sought. It is his expedition into Palo Duro Canyon that was represented by the ride.

The ride was a scaled down version of an earlier one proposed in pre-opening materials. This earlier version was larger and had scenery designed to look like a replica of Palo Duro canyon.

The burro ride was a live animal ride. While each guest rode on a small burro, the host, dressed as a Spanish Conquistador, road on a larger mule. The Conquistador led the burros as if the guests were traveling through *Palo Duro Canyon*. The riders went in search of the fabled seven cities of gold. The ride followed a winding trail through the trees and brush before returning to the mission from which it started. The path was located in the area of the park now occupied by the park's first *Log Flume Ride*.

The burro ride was the shortest-lived ride in the park and was the first of the original attractions to be removed. Weight restrictions of 150 pounds per rider, as well as limited ride capacity, seriously hampered the ride's viability. The burro ride was removed at the end of the 1962 season, after only two seasons in the park, to make room for the log flume ride. The flume closely follows the same path through the trees as that used with the burros.

The Mexican Section.

The colonists in Mexico revolted from Spanish control in 1821 and the independent nation of Mexico was formed. The new nation included what is now Texas. The colorful Mexican section displayed life in Texas during the Mexican reign.

Canopied Garden Covered Walkway from Mexican section to Frontgate.
All-Tom postcard P43943, published circa 1961.

Mexican section from 1963 souvenir map. Indian Village is middle top.
The La Cucaracha roller coaster is to the right.

The Mexican section recreated a generic Mexican village, with colorful sights, a bazaar, market, entertainment, and Mexican food. The entrance into the section from the Frontgate was through the *Canopied Garden Walkway*. Brightly colored triangular shaped canopies covered the walkway and gardens from the Frontgate to the Mexican section. Lighting on the canopies created a colorful special effect at night.

The section also connected to the *Indian Village*, located between the Mexican section and the Texas section.

The bazaar and marketplace, *Casa De Regals*, was the section's major store. It had a traditional Mexican market flavor and the items sold there replicated the items sold at a traditional Mexican market place. Among the many colorful items sold were sombrero hats, ponchos, and Mexican pottery. As with other shops in the park, there were also postcards, large park maps, and other traditional souvenirs. The store was located at the end of the *Canopied Walkway* and still serves as a Mexican themed souvenir shop.

Live entertainment in the section was provided during the day by a Mariachi band performing traditional Mariachi music throughout the section.

Across the path from the market was an *El Chico* Mexican food restaurant, one of the major eating establishments in the park. With both indoor and outdoor seating for 250, the restaurant provided traditional Mexican food items. *El Chico* was a leasee and operated several local Mexican food restaurants outside the park. *El Chico* operated the restaurant until 1972 when *Six Flags* took it over and it became simply the *Mexican Restaurant*.

More modern fast foods were provided at the *La Tarraza (The Terrace) Snack Stand* across from the *Goat Carts*. The stand was renamed the "La Cantina" snack shop in 1973.

Ferrocarril Fiesta Train.   The main attraction of the Mexican section was the *Ferrocarril Fiesta Train*, which translates to the "party train". Like the larger *Six Flags Railroad*, the *Fiesta* trains ran on a narrow gauge track. Both of the two engines were diesel powered. One engine was named the "El Cho Cho" and the other the "El Cha Cha". The modern diesel engines were hidden behind an ornamental frame which gave the engines the appearance of a quaint trolley.

The two engines each pulled nine little square cars. The cars could seat four adults, for a total capacity of 36 riders on a train. All were painted in bright pastel colors. For a roof, each of the cars had a giant colorfully painted sombrero, inevitably leading to the ride being called the "hat train" and the "sombrero train". In addition, in keeping with the sombrero theme, many of the characters viewed on the ride also wore a sombrero.

The ride was an outdoor "pretzel" style ride; that is a ride whose track curves in and out several times, like a giant pretzel. This technique allows different isolated scenes to be observed by riders, without distractions from the previous or upcoming scenes.

The trains pulled away from the small station to loudly playing Mexican music. Around the first bend riders viewed an animated band of Mexican musicians, with large sombreros, constantly playing their pleasant tunes. The train turned another bend and riders spotted a troop of dancing tamales, some as tall as people. The tamales constantly turned as they danced to another gleeful song. Dancing with the tamales were other characters, such as onions.

Fiesta Train (aka the Hat Train) (1961–1967), in the Mexican section.
All-Tom postcard P43967, 1961.

Inside Mexican section Market, Casa De Regalos, or "House of Gifts".
All-Tom postcard P51025, 1962.

Around the next bend was a more comical scene, a group of oversized travelers, sitting on much too small burros, rocking back and forth, as they headed off to some unknown destination. The next bend revealed a sleepy little village, where characters in large sombreros took a siesta in the afternoon sun.

A major scene was the *Gardens of Xochimilcho*, with its picturesque scenery. The scene recreated the famous floating Aztec gardens of Mexico City. In the gardens, a small pond contained a fountain and small boat. On board the boat, a boy serenaded his lovely partner. Another mariachi band performed in the gardens.

The final scene was a bull-fighting arena, the *Plaza De Los Toros*. Here a matador challenged a large black bull, while a crowd cheered him on. As the bull moved through its paces, it appeared for a moment as if it were charging the train, leaving the riders with a bit of a fright.

The train then pulled back into the station to end the ride.

The ride's animations were built by Peter Wolf of Dallas.

The ride was significantly reconstructed in 1968, with redesign work by Sid and Marty Krofft. These modifications are detailed in the 1968 section of this book. The ride was removed at the end of the 1978 season. The ride's queue house was used by the *El Sombrero* beginning in 1980. The queue house is now used by the Mexican teacup ride. In 1986, the *Avalanche Bobsled* ride was installed in an area that overlapped some of the area used by the train ride.

Children riding the Las Cabras goat cart ride. (1961–1963)
Six Flags' public relations photograph circa 1961.

Goat Cart Ride.　　Across from the *Fiesta Train* was the other ride in the section, the *Las Cabras,* or "cart ride". The goat carts were small wooden carts in which two or three young children sat. The cart was pulled around a dirt path by a goat. The ride path was bordered by a small wooden fence to keep the goats from wondering off track. An attendant walked along with the cart to keep the goat moving.

The goat carts were short lived and were removed from the park at the end of the 1963 season. It was the second original ride removed from the park.

Helicopter Rides.　　In addition to the attractions in the park, there was an additional ride on the outside. Pilot Tommy Blankenship flew guests in a Bell Ranger helicopter around the park for an aerial view of all of the attractions. The five-minute ride was an extra $3.00 per person. After the ride, the pilot signed the front of ticket, certifying that the holder traveled in the helicopter and creating an instant souvenir of the journey.

Tickets.　　For the first season, ticket prices were $2.75 for adults and $2.25 for children under 12 years of age. Initially, unused tickets purchased during any season were valid during any subsequent seasons.

One of the innovations of Six Flags was the one price ticket. Rather than sell individual tickets for each visit to an attraction, guests in the park could visit each attraction as many times as desired. Planned since the inception of the park, this policy was unique for a major amusement park at that time. Most of the major amusement parks built after Six Flags, however, imitated this policy. In contrast, *Disneyland* did not abandon its letter-coded system of individual ride tickets until June of 1982.

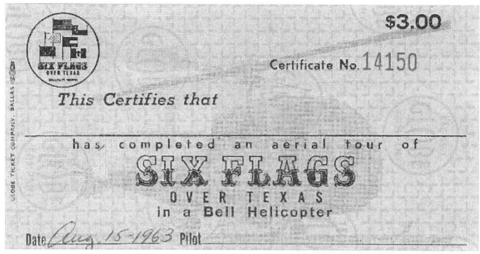

Helicopter Ticket documenting the guests ride on the Six Flags Helicopter.
From Author's Collection.

In the early years, non-ride tickets were also sold for individuals desiring to visit the park without riding on any attractions. These were $2.00 for adults and $1.70 for children. Visitors with ride-tickets were stamped on the hand with an ultraviolet (blacklight) ink stamp. At each ride entrance a large ultraviolet light was used to check guests' hands for the rider stamp. The lights and stamps were the same as those used at the frontgate for read-mittance after leaving the park. Guests with non-ride tickets could, however, purchase individual ride tickets at a ticket booth across from the *Little Red Schoolhouse* located in the Texas Section.

Parking for the first season was 50¢; soft drinks were 10¢; and a ham-burger cost 35¢. Park hours were 10:00 am to midnight, seven days a week. Initially, a season was planned to last from Easter to Thanksgiving of each year, with weekend only operations while schools were in session. The park estimated that two million individuals would visit the park during each regular season.

With over 600 employees, total parkwide ride capacity was estimated at 14,000 to 15,000 riders an hour, and park capacity at 30,000 guests. For the first season, 564,000 guests visited the park. When the park opened, the parking lot held 3,700 cars. The park utilized parking lot trams to carry the guests between their cars and the park entrance.

The first season was a short season. Including the five-day soft opening, the park was open just seventy-days between August 1, 1961 and November 26, 1961. This was, however, long enough to prove the concept of the park and build a reputation as a quality attraction.

3.

Six Flags Railroad

One single ride remains from Six Flags' inaugural season, the *Six Flags Railroad*. The ride is noted for its two steam engines, each of which has its own interesting history. The park's two trains travel at up to ten mph on a one and one-half mile run around the park.

Rolling Stock.   Engine Number 1 of the *Six Flags Railroad* is known as the "Green Train" due to its green paint scheme. It is powered by a 12-ton engine manufactured in 1901 as engine number 1280 by the Dickson Works of the American Locomotive Company (ALCO). The engine's build year is sometimes given as 1902. The year 1901 is, however, the year on the train's faceplate and sources indicate that the engine was built in October of 1901. The year 1902 may be the year that the engine was actually delivered to its original owner. It became operational in the park on July 13, 1961.

Engine Number 2 is known as the "Red Train" for its red color scheme. It is both the older and smaller of the two engines. It is powered by a 10-ton engine manufactured in August of 1897 as engine number 1754 of the Porter Company. Remodeling of the engine was not complete for Six Flags' first season. The engine became operational at the park on July 5, 1962, nearly a year after the first train.

The trains run on narrow gauge track, with thirty-six inches between the two rails. This is a shorter distance between the rails than the standard track on which most American commercial railroads run. The smaller gauge, however, allows for better maneuverability on tight tracks. Such narrower track was common with smaller railroads that did not require interoperability with main line railroads. In particular, narrow gauge trains were common at sugar plantations and logging operations sites.

Both engines were originally built for the Enterprise Plantation, a sugar cane plantation in Patoutville, Louisiana. The plantation was owned by the Patout family. The railroad was used to haul sugar cane from the fields to the mills. The two engines were part of a fleet of eight engines and 220 four-ton cars eventually owned by the plantation railroad.

The Red Train was originally a 0-4-0 engine named the "Lydia". Lydia was the Enterprise's first engine and tender. The Green Train was originally a 0-4-4T named the "Mary Ann". This was the Enterprise's second engine and tender.

Both engines were leased to *Six Flags Over Texas* by the Patout Family when the park opened in 1961. The trains were obtained through a lease agreement, as the will of Hippolyte Patout specified that the engines were not to be sold.

Engine Number One, the General Sam Houston, aka "The Green Train".
Photograph by Author, 1998.

The engines had not been run since the plantation replaced the railroad with a fleet of trucks in 1945. As a result, when the park received them in 1961 they required extensive overhauling and remodeling. The engines were refurbished by Smike L. Watson and Leroy Shirley at an estimated cost of $50,000 each. The railroad track and bed was built by W.H Nichols & Co. of Dallas, which also built the Great Southwest Railroad.

Several structural modifications were made to each engine. Although still steam engines, they no longer burn wood, but instead run on diesel fuel. The tenders were also converted accordingly. So that the engines would appear more like the ones seen by the public in western movies and shows, a lantern and cattle guard were added to the front end of the each train.

Additional guide wheels were added to the front of each engine under the cattle guards, converting both trains to 2-4-2 engines. In addition, the front smoke stack on the Green train was modified. On the Red train, the cabin for the engineer and fireman was moved back on the engine and additional windows were added.

The Green train was renamed by Six Flags from the "Mary Ann" to the "General Sam Houston". Sam Houston was the first President of the Republic of Texas. Typically pulling four passenger cars, this train is the larger of the two trains and generally the primary train of the railroad. Over the years, it typically has operated on slower days when only one of the two trains was needed.

The Red train was renamed from the "Lydia" to the "Maribeu B. Lamar". Lamar was the second President of the Republic of Texas. Over the years, this train has generally run as an extra train on crowded days.

Due to the long bench seats on the passenger cars, the number of guests per car can vary. It is generally estimated that each passenger car can hold up to 100 passengers. The green train typically is configured with four passenger cars, for a total of 400 riders. The Red Train is generally run with three passenger cars for 300 guests. The passenger cars were built for the park using parts from old boxcar frames.

Photographs of both the original "Lydia" and the "Mary Ann", as they appeared prior to their reconstruction, hang in the lobby of the Texas station. Most guests would fail to recognize the engines due to their extensive modifications by the park.

The home to the trains is an engine house built in the southwest corner of the park, outside of the Spanish and Mexican sections. The engine house is visible by guests as they ride the trains.

The Charlie Patton, known as the "Red Train".
Photograph by Author, 1985.

Engineers.   Authentic steam engines require experienced engineers to operate them properly. In order to staff its railroad, Six Flags had to search for qualified railroad engineers. Three engineers, George Ankele, Elbert Gaddis, and Charles (Charlie) Jefferson Patton, were hired by the park. All three were retired Texas & Pacific Railroad engineers with years of experience operating steam engines. All three were over seventy years of age at the time that the park opened.

Ankele was an engineer for the Texas and Pacific Railroad from 1918 to 1960. Gaddis began his carrier with the Texas and Pacific in 1909.

Above: Preconstruction concept art of Texas station,
All-Tom postcard P42754, Published 1961.
Below, Texas Station nearly fifty years later.
Photograph by Author, 2010.

Charlie Patton was the first of the engineers to operate one of the engines on the park's track. Patton was the perfect person for the job, having started shoveling coal on the railroad in 1907 at the age of nineteen. Born in 1888, he was just a few years older than the park's two engines. He retired from the T&P in 1960. At the time he started with Six Flags, he had been in railroading for fifty-three years, with forty years experience as a passenger train engineer. Most of this career was spent running a train between Fort Worth and Texarkana. He retired from the Texas and Pacific at the age of seventy-two and began working for Six Flags six months later.

Patton continued to operate the trains until he retired from the park in 1982 at the age of ninety-four. During the twenty-one years he worked at the park, Patton trained most of the engineers and firemen who subsequently ran the engines. Most of these individuals had no prior experience with steam engine operations. The engineer passed away in June of 1990 at the age of 102.

The Red train has since been renamed the "Charles Jefferson Patton", in honor of the park's long term engineer. Patton preferred running this engine to the larger Green Train.

Spiel and cenes.　The ride was originally enhanced by the "spiel of the conductor", in which a conductor standing at the back of the train pointed out sights for the riders, highlighting interesting facts about the park and providing some entertainment. The spiel changed over the years as new attractions were added and others were removed.

The spiel was abandoned for several seasons beginning in the 1990s. A live spiel is now occasionally heard. When the spiel is not given live, a recorded spiel is played over the speakers as the trains travel around the track.

"Ghost Town Saloon" scene viewed from the Railroad. This scene is based on a scene originally located at the Stagecoach ride. Photograph by Author, 2010.

Good Time Square Railroad Depot.
Photograph by Author, 1985.

For the first two seasons, the trains operated only out of the Six Flags railroad station in the Texas section. The station was officially named the "Great Southwest Station". Trains left the Texas station heading north. They made a non-stop round-trip run around the park, which was completely enclosed by the tracks. Along the way, riders could see many of the park's rides and attractions. Additional sights were added to the undeveloped areas of the park. In the area that later became the Boomtown area of the park, the train riders viewed live roaming buffalo and longhorn cattle.

On occasion the train would be "robbed" by the gunfighters. Of course, such robberies always ended badly for the desperadoes when the sheriff and his deputies arrived on the scene.

Boomtown, along with the new Boomtown station, was added in 1963. With the addition of the second station, the trains began stopping on the east side of the park so riders could embark and disembark. The Boomtown station was an actual MK&T train station moved from Lake Dallas, Texas. It was created from a railroad boxcar.

Ride times can vary, depending on the speed at which the engineer runs the route. Typically, however, a round-trip ride lasts twelve to fourteen minutes.

When the stagecoach ride closed, the ghost town saloon scene was moved to become part of the train's landscape. Likewise, in 1968 when the *Fiesta Train* was rebuilt, the train's landscape became the home of several of the original *Fiesta Train's* animations, including the "dancing tamales" and burro riders. This section of the landscape became known as "Mexican Junction", although the trains never actually stop there.

The ride stayed basically the same until Six Flags added Good Times Square in 1973. At that time, the original Boomtown station house was replaced by the Good Times Square station. The new Good Times Square section sat outside of the railroad tracks, so the new station house was also built on the outside of the track. The passenger cars were modified accordingly so that they could be entered from either side.

Tamales dancing at the "Mexican Junction" of the Six Flags Railroad.
Formerly from the Fiesta Train, the tamales have been in the park for over fifty years.
Photograph by Maegan McCown, 2014.

The Indian Village scene near the railroad engine house.
Photograph by Author, 1998.

At the same time that the Good Times Square station was added, the trains were "turned" for the first time. After turning, they ran in the opposite direction, leaving the Texas station heading south, towards the flume. The trains were "turned" again for the 1989 season, so that they depart Texas heading north, as they did from 1961 to 1973.

At the end of the 1996 season, the Good Time Square station was removed to make way for the *Mr. Freeze* ride. At that time, a new Boomtown station was built near the location of the original Boomtown station.

The Texas station has now been renamed from "Great Southwest Station" to the "Johnson Creek Station".

An official Texas historical plaque, placed in 1966, hangs on the outside of Texas Station. It documents the history of narrow gauge railroads in Texas.

Railroad water tower scene near Modern USA section.
Photo by Author, 2012.

4.

WYNNE DEVELOPMENT YEARS CONTINUE
1962 – 1970

1962

Even before finishing its first, highly successful season, Six Flags' management was working on expanding and improving the park. The first season guidebook predicted, "[a] continuing policy of adding new and fresh attractions will assure constant growth and further planned development of this remarkable wonderland". True to the promise, beginning with the second season, at least one new major attraction was added ever year up to 1970.

In fact, 1962 saw the addition of five acres of land and three major new attractions and the expansion of two other attractions. A total of $700,000 was spent on additions and improvements. Expansion included nearly doubling the amount of air-conditioning, bringing the total capacity to 600 tons.

Prices for all types of tickets, as well as parking, stayed at the first year rates. Non-ride tickets, referred to as "General Admission" tickets, were $2.00 for adults and $1.70 for children under 12. Parking remained at 50¢.

The park opened for its first full season on Friday, April 20, 1962. Governor Price Daniels and four area mayors were the featured guests. The season was scheduled for 105 days, nearly double the length of the initial season.

Chaparral Cars.   The *Chaparral* automobiles were added in an area north of the *Astrolift* and train station in the Texas section. This area of the park was previously undeveloped, except for a small portion that was originally occupied by the *Watermelon Garden*. The *Watermelon Garden* was moved a short distance south, next to the *Depot Café*. At that time, it was renamed the *Watermelon Patch*.

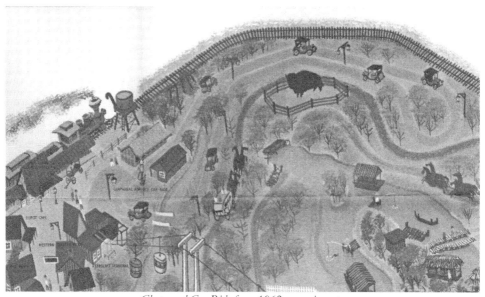

Chaparral Car Ride from 1962 souvenir map.
Stagecoach and Skull Island are to the right.
Texas section is to lower left.

The ride consists of vintage automobiles running on a "guide-rail" track. Except for the design of the car bodies, the attraction was identical to the *Happy Motoring Freeway* ride. As with the *Happy Motoring* cars, the guests control the acceleration and steering of each of the gas-powered vehicles, while the metal guide in the middle of the road prevents the cars from leaving the roadway.

Unlike the *Happy Motor* cars, which were a tight fit for two, the larger *Chaparral* cars seat four adults comfortably, with two in the front seat and two in the back.

The 3/10ths of a mile *Chaparral* roadway runs north, parallel to the railroad track. It then turns and returns to the ride station, crossing Johnson Creek by a bridge near the end of the ride. The cars governors are set to allow the seven horsepower engines to run at a maximum 8 miles per hour for a three minute and forty-five second ride.

The *Chaparral* cars are three-fourth scale replicas of a 1911 Cadillac. Although modeled on the Cadillac, they were named for the Chaparral automobile. The Chaparral was one of three models of cars produced by the Cleburne Motor Car Manufacturing Company of Cleburne, Texas, in 1911 and 1912. The automobile model was in turn named for the Texas Roadrunner, known as the Chaparral. The ride is known as "Chaps" to employees.

For the ride's opening, the park acquired fourteen vehicles. Another six cars were added in 1963. Originally, the cars had tops. The tops, however, are not now being used with the vehicles.

When the ride opened, the employees wore period costumes consisting of knee length "driving coats" with a driving cap.

Above: Chaparral Automobile with original hoods, circa 1964
The second oldest operating ride in the park, opening in 1962.
Photograph by: Robert Lee Hohman, 1966, courtesy of Marla Hohman.

Below: Chaparral automobile without hoods.
Queue house inthe background.
Photograph by Author, 2007.

As with the *Happy Motoring* cars, the *Chaparral* cars were built by the Arrow Development company. Identical versions of the cars were operated as the "Jennys" at *Pleasure Island* and the "Horseless Carriage" at *Freedomland USA*. The ride was also popular at other theme parks that opened later.

The ride is the now the second oldest continuously operating ride in the park, behind only the *Six Flags Railroad*.

Casa Magnetica. Also opening with the second season was *Casa Magnetica*, translated as "the Magnetic House". *Casa* was a walk-through attraction located in the Spanish section next to the burro ride. The front of the attraction and queue-house were built incorporating part of the structure that served as the recreation of the mission *San Francisco de los Tejas*.

Both the house floor, as well as the pathways through the house, were built at a twenty-six degree angle. While this made walking through the attraction somewhat difficult, it creates an optical illusion regarding the horizon. As a result of this illusion, items that are actually flowing or rolling downhill appeared to be "defying gravity" and moving uphill. The illusion was used for several special effects in the house.

After wondering through a small garden, guests entered the first, and smaller, of the house's two rooms. There a guide dressed in period costume told the story

with no small amount of pleasure

ANGUS G. WYNNE, JR.
President, Great Southwest Corporation

cordially invites

YOU AND YOUR FAMILY

to the

SPECIAL PRESS PREMIERE

of the

2ND SEASON

of

SIX FLAGS
OVER TEXAS

to be held at the Park

Thursday, April 19, 1962

2 p.m. to 10 p.m.

Arrive Hungry and Attired for Fun

(There'll be thrilling explorations into New Territories with all the hot dogs and hamburgers you can eat — and all the soft drinks you can down!!!!!)

LOCATION: *Great Southwest Industrial District.*

Dallas-Fort Worth Turnpike, Exit at Hwy. 360 or take Hwy. 360 off Hwy. 80 at Arlington or take Hwy. 360 from Hwy. 183 at Carter Field.

Front of the invitation to the Press Preview for the 2nd season. Invited reporters and guests visited the new attractions and saw a skit in which a fleeing outlaw, driving one of the new Chaparral cars, was apprehended by a security officer pursing him in a Happy Motoring vehicle.
From author's collection.

of the history of the house and its designer. The name for the designer varied over the years. Official spiels and publicity materials have used the names: Don Pedro, Don Pablo, Don Salvador, and Don Juan.

According to the legend, "Don" was an inventor and a hermit who did not like visitors. Several of the house's features were specifically designed to deter visitors. While telling Don's story, the guide demonstrated various tricks based on the anti-gravity illusion, including a chain that appeared to be hanging at an unnatural angle and a broom that sat at a similar angle.

After viewing the sights of the first room, the guests moved into the larger second room. There guest witnessed more impressive illusions, with "fruit" balls rolling uphill through a series of shelves and then uphill across a dinner table.

Room one of Casa Magnetica "the Crooked House". The table was Don's early garbage disposal. Items rolled up the table and out the window. Photograph by Author, 2004.

Given the fact that the same group of visitors viewed the exhibit in both the first and second rooms, it remains to be determined why one room was designed significantly smaller than the other.

After the tour, guests left through the patio, which was home to the wishing well. There guests could hear their voices echo indefinitely in the "bottomless" well.

Casa Magnetica has remained in the park since it opened in 1962. In 1979, the attraction was completely rethemed as *The Lost Temple of the Chisos*. The theme change lasted only for one season. In 1997, the attraction was closed, not to reopen until 2004. It then remained open until the end of the 2007 season, when it closed again. It reopened for the 2011 season in connection with the 50th anniversary.

Similar attractions were built at other amusement parks and tourist attractions. They are frequently known generically as "anti-gravity houses". A 1961 "Fact Memorandum", issued by Great Southwest before the park was completed, refers to the attraction as the *"Magnetic Mine"*. The memorandum anticipated that it would be open for the first season. Other early materials use the name of *"Casa Loco"*, or the "Crazy House". Although this was not the name finally selected, this was the name used for the attraction at *Freedomland,*

In the second room of Casa, guests watched wooden "fruit" roll out the side of the cabinet, "up" the wall shelves and onto the table. Photo by Author, 1985.

USA, and later at *Six Flags Over Georgia*. A similar attraction was named the *Slanty Shanty* at *Pleasure Island*.

Caddo Indians Canoes. The third completely new attraction was the *Caddo Indian Canoes*. The Caddo are an Indian tribe native to Texas. Much in the style of the park's original rides, this ride recreated a ride on an Indian war canoe. The four long canoes each held up to twenty guests on ten benches of two adults each. They were steadied and steered by an employee at the back of the canoe dressed in a Native American costume. Occasionally, another sat at front of the canoe as well. In addition to actually steering the canoe, the employee would often entertain the guests with instructions on how to paddle, as well as jokes and antidotes about the park and sights along the ride.

The canoes traveled around a small pond named "Caddo Lake". In the middle of the water was a small island, named "Caddo Island", also sometimes referred to as "Indian Island". The island contained a small Indian village, complete with teepees. The canoes traveled completely around the small island and then returned to the dock.

Much to the surprise of many of the guests, who frequently believed that the ride worked with some type of hidden motor or track, the canoes had no method of propulsion other than guest paddling. In addition, the canoes were not on any type of track or guide rail. In fact, the Indians often tried to pass other canoes during the trip around the island and encouraged their guests to race other canoes back to the dock.

The original loading dock for the ride was behind the *Amphitheater* and accessible at the end of a path located between the *Amphitheater* and the *Skull Island* waterway. This dock was used for the 1962 and 1963 seasons. In

1964, the queue house and loading dock were moved to Boomtown. In 1970, additional props were added at the Indian village on *Indian Island*.

The canoes were removed from the park at the end of the 1983 season to make room for the *Great Air Racer*, which was built on *Caddo Island*.

Caddo War Canoes leaving the original dock.
All-Tom postcard P51069, 1962.

Campus Revue.   Angus Wynne and the other park developers were firmly committed that quality shows were as important to the park's success as were the rides. As part of the effort to produce high quality entertainment, the *Six Flags Campus Revues* began in the park's amphitheater in 1962. The first revue was a 55-minute performance by 26 college students.

The revues were produced by David Blackburn, Stanley McIlvaine, and Charles Meeker. Meeker also wrote the shows. Each revue was set at "Gilchrist University". The name "Gilchrist" was taken from Angus Wynne's middle name. Some of the productions were also set at "Bedford Hall" at Gilchrist University. Bedford Hall was named for Wynne's brother, Bedford Wynne.

Eugene Patrick, a member of the orchestra, wrote and arranged much of the music. Patrick went on to become an amusement park and entertainment center designer and consultant, a profession he held for thirty years. He eventually became Vice-President of Marriott's Great America Parks. After retiring from the entertainment industry, he returned to Arlington and served on the city council for 8 years.

Happy Motoring Track II.   While not an entirely new ride to the park, the second season also saw the addition of a second track for the *Happy Motoring Freeway*. The second track was located to the south of the original track and used the queue house previously used for the *Sidewinder* roller coaster. This increased the number of cars on both of the tracks to thirty-eight.

Six Flags operated the two *Happy Motoring* tracks until the end of the 1979 season. At that time, the original track was removed. The track added in 1962 continued to operate as the lone track until 1986, when it also was removed.

In order to make room for this second track, the *Sidewinder* was moved to the Mexican section. There it was renamed the "La Cucaracha", Spanish for the "Cockroach". The name also refers to the festive Spanish folk song.

In addition to expanding *Happy Motoring Freeway*, *Skull Island* was also expanded. A second area, named "Pirate Island" was added behind *Skull Island*, between the original *Skull Island* and the railroad tracks. *Pirate Island* was separated from *Skull Island* by a small creek. It was accessed from *Skull Island* by way of a barrel bridge.

On *Pirate Island* guests could explore a cave and a pirate ship docked in a small artificial lagoon. In order to explore *Pirate Island*, guests had to cross the deck of the pirate ship and "walk the plank" onto the island. The cave contained various paths and was the home of the "Mad Organist".

Added to the Confederate section was the park's third major eating facility, *Miss Amanda's Pancake House*. The new restaurant was built in front of the Confederate recruiting area and across from the *Amphitheater*. The restaurant was renamed *Shady Oak Cafeteria* in 1963. The name was changed to *Bluebonnet Manor Cafeteria* in 1973; *Dixie Belle's Hickory House* in 1977; and *Dixie Belle's Barbecue Specialties* in 1980. The addition of the new restaurant significantly reduced the size of the Confederate enlistment rally area.

In the Mexican section, a small souvenir shop was added between the *El Chico* and the covered canopied walkway. In 1973, it was named *Los Amigos Souvenirs*, or "Friends' Souvenirs".

The park saw consistent attendance increases during the 1962 season. Expectations were for daily attendance between 4,000 and 30,000 guests. On July 21, 1962, the park set an attendance record of 16,635. This was exceeded the very next week, when on Saturday, July 28, the park broke the 20,000 mark with 20,181 guests in a single day. The higher 21,000 mark was exceeded twice before the season ended. This mark was passed on Saturday, August 25, with 21,317 visitors and again on Sunday, September 2, 1962, with 21,917 guests.

The park was seen by 1,272,489 visitors during the park's 115 day second season. Although the park did not meet its anticipated visitor goal of 1,500,000 guests, overall the season was still considered a success. In July of 1962, fourteen-year-old Patty Cipriano became the one-millionth visitor to the park.

Not all changes where additions. With each season, the management developed a better idea of which attractions were successful and which were less popular. At the end of the 1962 season, the *Conquistador Burro* ride was removed to allow space for the log flume ride. The burro ride lasted only two seasons and was the first ride to be removed from the park.

Inn of Six Flags.   *The Inn of Six Flags* opened in May of 1962, across the turnpike (now I-30) from Six Flags. The Inn provided a convenient

The live animal Conquistador Burro Ride was present only for the 1961 and 1962 seasons.
It was removed before the 1963 season to make room for the log flume ride.
All-Tom postcard P43947, 1961.

hotel for the park's guests. Built at a cost of $1.1 million, guest accommodations included 100 rooms decorated in themes based on Texas history. The hotel provided two guest pools, meeting rooms, and banquet halls. The hotel also boosted an Acapulco suite with three rooms, living area, kitchen, and private pool. All rooms included a TV, HiFi music, and an ice-maker.

A sixty-seven seat double deck red touring bus was also acquired for the 1962 season. The bus was a vintage 1925 bus originally used by the *5th Ave Bus Lines* of New York City. The bus traveled at a top speed of 44 mph and got a mere 3.5 miles per gallon. The bus made round-trips between the Inn and the park's entrance, allowing inn guests convenient access to the park.

1963

By the time that the park was ready for its third season, Six Flags had hosted over 1.8 million visitors. Opening date for the third season was April 20, 1963. Arlington Mayor Vandergriff and Angus Wynne, II, were on hand to open the park. Ticket prices increased to $3.50 for an adult and to $2.50 for children under 12. "General Admission" non-ride tickets increased to $2.75 for adults and $2.00 for children under 12.

Riding on the first two successful seasons, Six Flags again expanded significantly in 1963. For the third season, the park added its first entirely new section, as well as three new rides. In addition, the park expanded existing attractions. The park now proclaimed that it had 115 acres, ten more than at opening. In addition, 50 tons of air conditioning was added, bringing the total to 650 tons. Total ride capacity was estimated at 20,000 riders per hour, up from 15,000 the season before.

Boomtown. The new section was named "*Boomtown USA*". In keeping with the park's overall system of themes, Boomtown technically fell under the US flag. Now two different park sections represented the USA flag, the Modern USA section and the new Boomtown USA section. The Boomtown section was likely part of the original plans, as a similar area was depicted in pre-opening concept maps of the parks.

The six-acre Boomtown section replicated a typical turn of the century Texas oil town. Such towns were known as "boomtowns" due to the rapid manner in which they sprang into existence whenever oil was located nearby.

As with the other sections, Boomtown offered a mixture of rides, stores, food concessions, and entertainment.

Billed as a "million dollar expansion", the section contained several era buildings. For atmosphere, "Hobo Jungle", a scene replicating a hobo village, complete with shacks and characters, sat next to the new train station.

Boomtown section from 1963 map.

In anticipation of the new section, an authentic oil derrick was installed in the park the season before. The 68-foot tall oil derrick was a reconstruction of Crowley Number 1, which was drilled north of Breckenridge, Texas. The tools and rigging from the then forty-year-old derrick were moved from the actual well site. Much of the wooden parts of the structure, however, had to be rebuilt. The derrick, now over ninety years old, is still in the Boomtown section, although it has been moved twice to accommodate other attractions.

Also on display was an early oil tool equipment supply store exhibit sponsored by Mid-Continent Oil Well Supply Company. The Mid-Continent display became the *Boomtown Arcade* in 1971.

For souvenirs, there was a pom-pom hat store, similar to the ones in the Texas and Modern sections. The shop was later named *Boomtown Hats*. A souvenir shop was located next to the *Sky Hook* queue house.

A small medicine wagon located in the middle of the section provided entertainment in the form of a puppet show.

For food, the *Hash House* sat across from the Hobo Jungle. The *Hash House* became *Dry Hole Charlies* in 1972.

The section was built in a previously undeveloped area. During the first two seasons it was home to a few longhorns and buffalo that were visible from the train ride. The new area was accessible by a pathway extended from the Modern section. After visiting the section, guests could leave the area following the same path back into the Modern section.

In addition to the footpath, guests could reach the new section by way of the *Six Flags Railroad*. With the addition of a second station at Boomtown, the railroad now stopped on two sides of the park. This supplemented the *Astrolift* as a convenient means for guests to travel around the park.

Sky Crane Ride.   The main attraction of the new Boomtown was the 190-foot tall *Sky Crane* ride. This unique ride was adapted from a cargo crane. The ride units consisted of two metal teardrop shaped baskets, each of which held 14 to 18 guests sitting on a bench which circled the inside of the basket. Each enclosed basket was attached to a cable at the end of one of the structure's "Y" shaped girder arms.

After guests boarded a basket, it was lifted into the air by the cable. As one basket rose up the height of the structure, the other slowly went downward. At the same time, the arms rotated 180 degrees. The descending basket reached the ground when the other was a total of 155 feet in the air. At that time, the one on the ground was loaded and unloaded. Once loaded, the other basket rose. As it rose into the air, the arms again rotated and the other

Runaway Mine Train (1966) in front of Sky Crane ride (1963–1968).
Six Flags' public relations photo, circa 1967.

basket descended back to the dock to be unloaded. While the ground basket was unloaded and reloaded, guests in the other basket enjoyed a panoramic view of the park and surrounding communities. Riders could see both downtown Fort Worth and Dallas, each 15 miles away.

While not strictly Boomtown related, the ride had an industrial look and feel that fit into the concept of the industrial age section. It provided a unique aerial view of the park unmatched by any ride in the park. Standing nearly four times as high as the *Astrolift*, it was also the only attraction easily seen from outside the park. As such, it provided a visual identity for the park until 1968 when it was removed.

The ride had quite a history of its own, having first thrilled visitors to the *Brussels' World's Fair* of 1958. From there it came to Texas in 1963, where it served for six seasons. After being removed from *Six Flags Over Texas* in 1968, the ride was dismantled and moved to the newly built sister park, *Six Flags Over Georgia*, where it stood as that park's major focal point from 1969 until 1977. Finally, it was sold to *Magic Springs* amusement park in Arkansas, where it operated for several years. During a major remodeling of that park in 1995, it was dismantled and sold for scrap metal.

A similar version of the ride was installed at the *1964 New York World's Fair* and later moved to *Pirate's World* in Florida. At 120 feet, this ride was shorter than the *Sky Crane*. It did, however, have four arms with baskets, rather than two.

Carousel.   In addition to the *Sky Crane*, the new section contained another ride new to the park, the *Six Flags Carousel*. Like the *Sky Crane*, the then twenty-six year old carousel had already operated at another location.

The ride was manufactured by the Dentzel Carousel Company of Philadelphia in 1925 or 1926. Gustav Dentzel founded the carousel company,

Riders enjoying view in one of the two Sky Crane Baskets (1963–1968).
Photograph by Robert Lee Hohman, 1966; courtesy of Marla Hohman.

producing his first carousel in 1867. His company was the first American man-ufacturing company to build carousels on a regular full time basis. Dentzel's carousel horses and menagerie animals were each individually crafted from wood by skilled wood carvers. In 1928, the Dentzel Company was sold to another major ride producer of the day, the Philadelphia Toboggan Company.

The *Six Flags Carousel* has been said to be the last Dentzel carousel produced. Given the production dates, this is possible. The company was not, however, sold to the Philadelphia Toboggan Company for two to three more years after manufacturing this particular carousel. The ride is one of twen-ty-eight original surviving Dentzel carousels.

Six Flags Carousel in original location in Boomtown. The ride was later renamed the "Silver Star Carousel" and moved to the Frontgate. Photograph by Author, 1985.

The sixty-six horse carousel has four rows of horses: fifty jumpers and sixteen "standers". The standers do not move up and down as the ride turns. In addition to the horses, there are two double bench chariots. The ride contains only horses; it does not have any menagerie animals. The horses are not the original animals built with the ride. The horses are from different time periods. Some of the horses are actually older than the ride itself. Three of the standers were crafted in 1900.

Neither the brass ring machine, nor the band organ, still operate. The organ has been removed. The ride rotates at 3 mph.

The ride was originally operated at *Rockaway Playland* amusement park. The carousel was one of several operated at Rockaway Beach on Long Island in Queens, New York. *Rockaway Playland*, then known as *L.A. Thompson Amusement Park*, acquired the ride new from the manufacturer in 1925. Six Flags purchased the carousel in 1962 from *Rockaway* for approximately $25,000. *Rockaway Playland* closed in 1985. The park's founder, LaMarcus A.

Silver Star Carousel after refurbishment and move to Frontgate.
Photograph by Author, 1998.

Thompson is credited with popularizing the modern roller coaster and holds the first U.S. patent for a roller coaster.

When Boomtown opened, the ride was located north of the Boomtown train station, at the current location of the *Texas Gunslinger* swing ride. It was originally simply referred to as the "Merry-go-Round" ride. The ride was removed from Boomtown after the 1985 season for restoration. [See the 1988 subchapter for additional information regarding the renovations.]

Only three rides have operated in the park longer than the *Carousel*: the *Six Flags Railroad*, *Chaparral* cars, and the *Flume*. The *Carousel* opened the same season as the *Flume* ride, but has operated in the park for fewer years, due to the three years that it was out of service for remodeling.

During the early 1970's, when the ride was in Boomtown, the railroad spiel stated that the ride was identical to one at the Smithsonian Institute. There have been two different carousels operating on the mall of the Smithsonian. Both carousels were built by Allan Herschell Co. and were not identical to the park's ride. The spiel referred to another carousel purchased prior to the bicentennial by the Smithsonian. This was a Dentzel carousel similar to the Six Flags' ride.

The Smithsonian did not restore or display this ride and it was held in storage until 2005. It was subsequently restored and moved to the *Please Touch Museum*, in Philadelphia, Pennsylvania, where it is now operational. While similar in design to the Six Flags' ride, it has only 52 animals in three rows. This ride also originally operated in the Rockaway area of Queens, although not at the same *Playland* amusement park.

The carousel at the State Fairgrounds in Dallas is also a Dentzel, manufactured around 1914. The Carousel that was at Astroworld was an even older Dentzel, manufactured in 1907. The carousel that most closely matches the Six Flags' ride is at *Kennywood Amusement Park* in Pittsburgh, Pennsylvania. It was also manufactured in 1926 and has the same basic configuration as the Six Flags model.

Log Flume Ride.   Not content with adding an entire section, 1963 also saw the addition of one of the park's most famous and innovative rides, the *Log Flume* ride. The Six Flags Flume ride was a first of its kind ride, engineered and designed for *Six Flags Over Texas* by the Arrow Development Company.

The ride is officially named *El Aserradero*, which translates to "the sawmill". This name is taken from the mill building, complete with a lumber saw, through which the logs pass as they travel over the ride's first lift. The ride is much more commonly known as the "flume ride" or just the "log ride".

The ride was inspired in part by the western log flumes used to move lumber down the sides of mountain. Such flumes were made famous by a story written by H.J. Ramsdell, a newspaper reporter. In 1875, Ramsdell chronicled a ride he took down such a flume with millionaires James Flood and Jim Fair. Flood and Fair owned a flume used to move lumber fifteen miles down a mountain from the top of the High Sierras to Carson Valley, Nevada. Ramsdell's story told of a thirty-minute adventure that he, Flood, and Fair had in a small watercraft traveling at an average of 30 mph down the flume.

The flume ride was placed at the site of the burro ride, which was closed at the end of the 1962 season. In fact, the flume layout closely follows the path through the trees used by the burro path. In addition, the ride uses the same queue house and entryway that was used for the burro ride.

Sawmill, from which the Flume ride takes its official name of "El Aserradero".
Photograph by Author, 1985.

The eight-foot fiberglass units in which the guests ride are designed to resemble hollowed out logs. They travel through the 1,200-foot long flume at 10 feet per second. The highlight of the ride is a 44-foot drop set at a 45-degree angle. This final fall creates a major "splash" to end the ride. The ride lasts three minutes and thirty seconds.

Reportedly, Six Flags' management was unhappy with the amount of water originally thrown onto the guests. They did not want the guests actually getting wet. As a result, Arrow's engineers adjusted the ride so that less water was thrown back onto the guest. After the adjustments, the ride's popularity dropped off. Accordingly, Six Flag's management had Arrow reconfigure the ride so that the splash went back into the logs. Even so, the actual water thrown onto the guests is minimal when compared to current water rides, such as the *Splashdown Falls* and the *Roaring Rapids*.

The ride uses two pumps and a 500,000-gallon reservoir to supply the ride with 36,000 gallons of water per minute.

The park invested $300,000 dollars in the new ride, of which $52,000 was for research and engineering. The investment paid off, as the ride was an immediate success. A second log flume opened later in 1963 at *Cedar Point* in Sandusky, Ohio; another opened the following year as part of the rides at the *1964 New York World's Fair.* The ride became a basic addition to nearly every new amusement park built. In 1968, a second flume was added at Six Flags to keep up with the demand for the ride. It is estimated that by 1979, fifty of the rides where built by Arrow Development at various locations.

In addition to adding a whole section and three rides, other changes were made around the park.

Flume log heading down the main drop.
Photograph by Author, 2008.

The highlight of the Flume ride is the splashdown at the bottom of the last lift.
Photograph by Author, 1976.

Lost Parents.　In the Modern section, a retired caboose was converted into the *Lost Parents* station. Children whose parents become lost during
their visit could wait in the caboose until they were located. Overseen by an
attendant, the youngsters could explore the inside of the authentic caboose
or spend their time with books and toys. The caboose was located near the
railroad tracks between the Frontgate and the petting zoo. Due to its prox-
imity to the zoo, small animals were occasionally brought in to entertain the
children.

In order to accommodate the Boomtown section, the route of the
original *Humble Motoring* track was shortened, making it closer in length to the
newer second track.

Skull Island.　On *Skull Island*, a multistory activity center was added
between the main island and Pirate Island. The activity area included a second
story bridge that led from a treehouse on *Skull Island* to the top of two slides
on the Pirate Island side. The treehouse was accessible by stairs. The treehouse
was designed after an ocean-side cabana from the Texas coast.

Arcade.　An old fashion arcade, with working antique games and
attractions, was added on the edge of the Confederate section. The arcade
was fashioned after a turn of the century penny arcade. Unlike the state of
the art arcades that would follow in later years, this arcade was filled with
antique machines that had been restored to working condition. Around twenty
machines were located and restored for the arcade at a cost of $20,000. Some
of the machines were from the 1900's.

The antique machines included a mutoscope, in which viewers
watched 'movies' created by rapidly flipping individual photographs; a
mechanical soccer game from 1915; a baseball game from the 1900s; and a

Skull Island from 1963 souvenir map. New for the year was the activity center to the left of the pirate boat. "Pirate Island" is the area with the cave and pirate ship. "Caddo", or "Indian Island", is the one with the three teepees. Indian island was later connected to Pirate Island by two bridges. The Canoe dock is between the skull and the teepees.

jukebox containing its own instruments which actually played music. There was also the classic strength testing machine, fortune teller, and a metal imprinter with which guest could imprint words on a small aluminum blank.

Jersey Lilly.   In the Texas section, a reproduction of Judge Roy Bean's saloon, the *Jersey Lilly*, was built in the area of the *Sorghum Mill*. The mill was moved a little north to accommodate the new building, which was used as a barbecue restaurant.

Beginning in 1963, park maps indicate that the building next door to the Courthouse, which was known as *Prairie General Merchandise*, became the "tobacco shop". Cigarettes and tobacco supplies were available at the store. A *Blacksmith Shop* was also indicated for the location, although this name was mostly for atmosphere. The building remained the *Tobacco Shop* and *Blacksmith Shop* until the 1979 season.

Gilchrist Glitters.   In the Confederate section, the 1963 *Gilchrist Glitters* was the second campus revue performed in the 1,250-seat amphitheater. The show was again produced and directed by Charles Meeker Jr., David T. Blackburn, and Stanley McIlvaine. It ran three times an evening. The live show featured twenty-six cast members and a seventeen musician live orchestra directed by cast member Gene Patrick. Over 800 performers auditioned for spots in the cast.

Peter Wolf Associates designed the special effects and sets for the show.

In the Confederate section, the park's third major eating facility, *Miss Amanda's Pancake House*, was renamed as *Shady Oak Cafeteria*. It was a general cafeteria with indoor and outdoor seating.

84

Reproduction of the historical "Jersey Lilly Saloon", named for the opera singer Lillie Langtry.
Judge Roy Bean owned the Jersey Lilly and also used it as his courtroom.
Photograph by Author, 2005.

The pom-pom hat store in the Texas section was moved to the other side of the street next to the Texas bridge in order to make room for a new entrance to the *Flume* ride.

In the Modern section, the *Power for Progress in the Opportunity Frontier of Texas* was added to the Texas Electric exhibit.

At the end of the 1963 season, the goat cart ride, with its very limited ride capacity, was removed.

By the time of the second anniversary date, Six Flags had hosted 2.5 million guests. The two millionth visitor walked through the gates on June 3, 1963. Daily attendance averaged 12,000, up from 5,900 for the first season, with 1,436,000 total visitors during the 130 day third season. Attendance was very close to the anticipated level of 1,500,000. On May 4, 1963, a new daily attendance record of 22,617 was set. This was nearly a thousand guests over the previous daily record.

The park was closed for the last weekend in November of 1963, in honor of President Kennedy, following his assassination in Dallas on November 22.

In July of 1963, The Six Flags Regional Shopping Center was announced. The $14 million complex was planned for Highway 80 and 360. Construction was set to begin in 1964 and be completed in 1966.

In June of 1963, Legend City opened in Phoenix, Arizona. It was the first modern theme park to open since Six Flags. The park was the first non-Disney theme park not designed by Marco Engineering. The park was themed on Arizona history and was similar to the other theme parks built to date. Attractions included a riverboat ride, antique cars, modern cars, a railroad, canoes, gunfighters, Indian dancers, burro ride, anti-gravity house, astrolift, a dark ride, and theaters. While not built by Marco, Randall Duel was hired to complete the design of the park after the original designer resigned.

1964

A light rain greeted visitors to the park's opening on April 18, 1964. The season was noted for both a major new dark ride and further expansion to *Skull Island*. Ticket prices for all types of ticket stayed at the same rates as for 1963. Parking remained at 50¢.

The Speelunker's Cave. For the fourth season, Six Flags added its first dark ride, the *Speelunkers' Cave*, also known as the *Cave Ride*.

The ride was designed in collaboration between Angus Wynne and Randall Duell and Associates. Walter McKeegan, an art director for several popular TV shows, including "I Love Lucy", "Green Acres", and the "Beverly Hillbillies" is credited with the design of the unique creatures. Gene Patrick selected the unique music and sounds effects and helped design the props and scenes.

Built at a cost of $300,000, the ride took eight months to construct. The design of the ride borrowed heavily from the design of the log flume ride. Like the log ride, the cave ride used fiberglass crafts floating in a flume style waterway. The 600-foot cave flume, however, lacks any major drop. The lift is five feet high. Arrow Development designed and built the ride portions of the attraction.

In keeping with the historical theme of the park, the original tubs were designed to resemble bull boats. Bull boats were small boats constructed by the Plains Indians using buffalo hides stretched over a wooden frame. Like bull boats, the original boats on the ride were round, allowing up to six guests to sit in a circle inside of the tub. The round boats would also spin slightly with the water flow, changing the riders' view of the various scenes.

Over the years, the design of the tubs changed from the original round tubs to oval tubs with a single bench seat running from the front to the back of the tub. The tubs were later changed for a second time and now riders sit side by side on two bench style seats that cross the width of the oval tubs.

Two pumps each lift 900 gallons a minute to the top of the ride's small lift to move the water in the flume at a flow rate of $3\frac{1}{2}$ feet per second. The ride takes approximately four minutes to complete.

The ride's waterway ran through a 13,300 square foot building designed to recreate the inside of a Texas cave. Totally unique to Six Flags, this cave was populated with Speelunkers, small creatures that stood three feet high. The spelling of the name of the characters was also unique. While a "spelunker" is an individual that explores caves, Six Flags distinguished these creatures by spelling their name with two "e"s, coining the name "speelunkers". The name is also spelled as "spee-lunkers" in some park materials. The park may have coined the hyphenated "spee-lunkers" form so that guest would realize that the word was not inadvertently misspelled.

The most memorable characteristics of the Speelunkers were their large banana shaped heads, oversized ears and large eyes. Their banana shaped heads were said to have been inspired by the stalactites and stalagmites that develop in the caves of Texas. Originally, twenty-eight of the characters populated the ride as a part of a total of fifty-two animations and props.

In order to increase the ominous nature of the cave, objects in the cave were painted with incandescent paint and illuminated with strategically placed blacklights. The lights were designed to illuminate a particular scene only from the spot at which it was viewed during the ride. The remaining areas were either dark or illuminated with soft mood lights. The incandescent colors, juxtaposed with the surrounding dark, gave the entire ride a mystical surreal feel.

Closely integrated with the visual effects was carefully selected music that blended seamlessly from one scene to the next. Each piece was designed to reflect the mood of the scene.

There was no particular story line to the ride. As the riders floated through the cave, they visited the world of the speelunkers and viewed the playful creatures in various settings. In order to keep the ride fresh, various scenes in the ride were modified or replaced over the seasons.

The ominous music riders heard as they entered the ride was the first few moments of *Gigues* from Debussy's *Images pour orchestra*. For years, the first scene consisted of the Speelunker King and his servant, greeting the riders

Entrance to Speelunkers' Cave. Shown are oval tubs with front to back seating.
Photograph by Author, 1985.

at the entrance to the cave. These were followed by the "chiseller", a lone speelunker constantly chiseling a stone tablet with a hammer and large spike. Perhaps he recorded the names of all who entered the cave. The sound track included a distinct and eerie hammering sound to accompany the striking of his hammer.

Next, the tubs floated passed a Speelunker sitting at a large pipe organ. As he performed on the keyboard, another character pushed and pulled on a bar that appeared to pump the organ.

Across from the organist were three Speelunkers riding giant turtles as they raced each other in an endless circle. This was later replaced with a larger scene of several young speelunkers in a classroom. Included were speelunkers playing on a seesaw; a teacher; a "dunce" student; a boy flying a paper airplane; a boy pulling a girl's hair; and a student with a slingshot. Just past the school scene, a truant office caught another student speelunker fishing when he too should be in class.

Speelunker Harp Choir seated on giant mushrooms.
Photograph by Author, 1985.

At this point, the flume made a "u" turn. Here riders discovered that the speelunkers were not the only creatures in the cave. Following the classroom scene, a giant spider threatened riders from the dark.

A little further, two speelunkers stood on opposite sides of the waterway, tossing a bolder back and forth. The tubs went directly under the threatening bolder as it crossed in the air above.

As the tub passed the menacing bolder, riders were threatened by both flying and hanging bats that inhabited the next section of the cave. The river

Prisoner Speelunker in the brig.
Photograph by Author, 1985.

again made a "u" turn. In the corner to the right, the tubs passed a large idol head visible across the river from the bats. As the tubs started back in the other direction, two more non-speelunker creatures came into view.

The next scene featured a speelunker lobster-driver using a whip to keep three giant lobsters in line, while holding onto each with a leash. The musical piece *Tabu* played in the background. The distinct sound of the lobsters' pinchers opening and closing was timed with the rhythm of the music.

A scene added later appeared to be a speelunker nightclub. While one speelunker rode a bucking armadillo, another savored a drink, and a third flew a kite. Directly across the river, other speelunkers played music and danced. At one time, the music played was *Yakety Sax*.

At this point, the ride made a ninety-degree turn as the tubs floated onto the small lift for the ride. The lift was located roughly halfway through the ride. As the tubs came down the small drop following the lift, the scenes changed so that it no longer seemed as if the river were inside a cave. Instead, the scenes portrayed a coastal bay area. With the change in view, the ride's scenes became less playful and much more ominous. The ride's music reflected this change in atmosphere.

After traveling over the lift, the tubs floated past a group of speelunkers in a round tub, similar to, but smaller than, the one in which the guests rode. The tub appeared out of control and the speelunkers appeared to be in distress. The next speelunker viewed was in a tub that was sinking. Not only was his tub going down, but he was using a sword to fight off a shark lurking up out of the water, ready to devour him. In a similar scene, a speelunker was sword fighting with a swordfish. These views were followed by a pirate speelunker guarding a treasure chest. The treasure chest contained different treasures over the seasons, including replicas of small gas cans during the gasoline shortage of the 1970s.

Next, an orchestra of four speelunkers each sat on something resembling giant mushrooms while they performed on harps. A fifth directed them with a baton. The music accompanying the harp choir was from Rossini's *William Tell Opera*, although it was not the section made famous as the Lone Ranger theme music.

Riders then viewed a doomed sailing ship that seemed to be wrecked in the bay. A seven-ton hull was used to create the ship. A lightening storm was visible across from the ship. As the tub passed through the storm, loud thunder was accompanied by the sight of lightning bolts on the horizon. Portions of Stravinsky's *The Firebird* were heard near the storm scene.

After turning the corner, the boats seemed to be inside the ship they had just traveled passed. The riders viewed the ship's brig, where a Speelunker sat sawing through the bars of his cell with a small saw. Other sailors sat at a table playing cards, while yet another played the *Sailor's Hornpipe* on his accordion. Passed the boat scene, the tub sailed through a series of columns. The columns rocked back and forth as if ready to fall onto the small boat at any time.

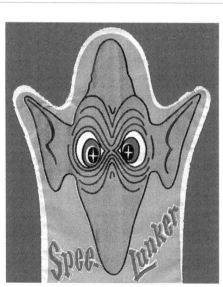

Plastic Speelunker Puppet with Six Flags ad on the back. These were given away as promotional items.
From Author's collection.

The river turned ninety degrees and the tubs entered into a barrel like tunnel within the cave. The tunnel rotated around the flume as the tubs floated through it. The barrel's rotation around the tubs gave riders a disorienting feeling that made it seem as though the entire flume was rotating and would soon turn completely over. At the end of the barrel were dancing mops.

The finale was one of the largest scenes. It included a group of speelunkers each dressed in outfits based on one of Texas' six flags. The waterway and room holding the finale were added after the ride opened.

One of the favorite features of the cave is the forty-tons of air conditioning used to cool the building, making the ride a wonderful escape from the Texas heat. A long-term feature of the ride was a blast of cooled air shot at the riders just before they arrived at the unloading dock. This blast was followed by a blast of water shot at the unsuspecting guests.

The cave ride is the fifth oldest operating ride in the park. The Speelunkers inhabited the cave for twenty-eight years, until the end of the 1991 season. Before the 1992 season, they were removed to make room for *Looney Tunes* characters. At that time, the name of the ride changed to "Yosemite Sam's Gold River Adventure". [See the 1992 subchapter for more details regarding *Gold River*.]

Finale of Speelunker's Cave ride.
Photograph by Author, 1985.

In order to accommodate the entrance to the cave ride, the run for the stagecoach was shortened and the loading dock was moved back.

Across from the *Ice Cream Parlor* in the Confederate section, the *Artist Colony* and *Flag Shop* were converted into a restaurant named *The Steak House*.

In the amphitheater, the third Campus Revue, *The Singing Flags*, was performed by a cast of twenty-seven, accompanied by a fifteen piece live orchestra. One of the cast members was sixteen-year old Betty Lynn Buckley. Buckley went on to become a star of TV and Broadway.

As it had been every year, *Skull Island* was once again expanded. A cluster of three swamp tree slides, like the single one already on *Skull Island*, was added to the small island east of *Pirate Island*. Know as *Indian Island*, this was the island circled by the route of the *Caddo Indian War Canoes*. (*Indian Island* was later referred to as "Caddo" Island.)

The new slides were accessible by a bridge from *Pirate Island*, as well as a 28-foot high rope suspension bridge that started on *Pirate Island* and went across the water to the top entrance of the forty-foot tree slides on *Indian Island*.

With the addition of these new activities, *Skull Island* was the largest size it would ever reach.

To accommodate the *Skull Island* expansion, the canoe dock was moved from its original location behind the amphitheater to a location in Boomtown, near the *Skyhook*. The Caddo canoes still made the same circle around *Caddo Island*; they just started and ended from a different point on the lake. In addition, they now traveled under the series of new bridges connecting the two islands.

In the Mexican section, a *Mexican Bazaar* was added at the site of the removed goat cart ride. Included were a *Leather Store*, *Flower Market*, and a *Portrait Artist* studio. The bazaar carried authentic native curios and related souvenirs.

In Boomtown, puppets *Punch and Judy* entertained the crowds from a small wagon. *Punch and Judy* is a traditional British puppet show dating to the 1600's. The show was performed by John Hardman. Hardman later performed in the park as *Argyle the Snake*. He also worked for Sid and Marty Krofft.

The building between the *Mid-Continent Supply House* and the souvenir shop became the *AAPI* (American Association of Professional Landmen) *Land Office*. The building, later renamed the *Luther Clark Land Office*, became the home of the *Travel Exhibit* in 1970.

Caddo War Canoes (1962-1983) traveling under Skull Island bridges.
One of the new tree slides is shown as the end of the suspension bride to the right.
Six Flags' public relations photograph, circa 1964.

Pink Things.   In 1995, Six Flags registered the trademark for *Pink Things*, the ice cream treats that became an icon of the park. The registration cited 1964 as the date of the first use of the phrase as a trademark. The funnel shaped ice cream was sold on a plastic handle. Attached to the handle, and surrounded by the ice cream, was a small plastic cut out character. Part of the fun of the treat was eating through the ice cream to discover the character buried inside.

Although flat, the characters were cut out of the plastic, with details engraved on both sides. The original characters varied widely and included such things as cowboys, Indians, soldiers, animals, and circus performers.

Six Flags Pink Thing Sticks. Left are older and include dog, pirate, elephant, large cat and donkey. On right are newer ones with Sylvester the Cat (left) and the Tasmanian Devil (right) imposed on them. From author's collection.

The various buried characters were changed to Looney Tunes characters after the rights to the characters were licensed from Warner. They were represented by a relief on a half-oval shaped background instead of being cutouts.

The ice cream treats were sold from small ice cream stands. During their hay-day in the early and mid-70s, *Pink Thing* stands were located all around the park. In 2011, the original cherry flavor of the treat was changed to something more in the nature of cotton candy. The hidden characters were changed to stick whistles.

In April of 1964, additions to the Inn of Six Flags tripled its current capacity from 100 rooms to 308 rooms. Additional meeting rooms and other support facilities were also added.

In Mexico, the park's only roller coaster, the *El Cucaracha* was removed at the end of the 1964 season. With the removal of the *El Cucaracha*, there was no roller coaster in the park until the end of the 1966 season when the *Runaway Mine Train* was ready for performance testing. At that time, the ride was occasionally opened for guests to experience.

A landmark was reached for Six Flags in 1964 when it became the most visited tourist attraction in Texas, pushing ahead of the Alamo, which had been in the number one position. Six Flags had 1,622,432 visitors for the year, exceeding its anticipated yearly goal of 1,600,000. A new daily attendance record was set on June 2, 1964, the day the *Speelunker Cave* opened, with 27,850 guests.

1964 New York World's Fair.   In November of 1962, Angus Wynne signed contracts to manage the *Texas Pavilion* of the *1964 New York World's Fair*. His involvement was at the specific request of then Vice President Lyndon Johnson and Texas Governor Price Daniels. In doing so, Wynne personally financed the *Texas Pavilion* and personally guaranteed the money loaned to build the exhibit. The fair was set to formally open in April of 1964.

On February 27, 1964, the opening ceremonies were held for the *Texas Pavilion*. The pavilion consisted of an indoor theater with seating for 2,400, twice the size of the *Southern Palace*. The 90-minute show produced at the theater was *To Broadway with Love*. The pavilion also contained the *Frontier Palace*, an old west style restaurant, capable of serving 50,000 guests a day. There were also several Texas exhibits in the pavilion, including *Life on the Range* and *Art in Texas*. An exhibit on the exploration of outer space exhibited items on loan from NASA. The six flags of Texas flew in front of the theater.

Although not part of the *Texas Pavilion*, the fair had other attractions similar to those at Six Flags. These included a log flume ride; a sky crane ride with four arms instead of two; and a dancing waters attraction. Sid and Marty Krofft, puppeteers who would later play a major role in developments at Six Flags, presented a puppet show, similar to the one to be installed in the Arlington park. The pavilion was designed by Six Flags designer Randall Duell and his firm.

In sharp contrast to the success of the Texas amusement park, the *Texas Pavilion* lost millions of dollars. Although an elaborate production, a Broadway type show in the home of Broadway shows was not very attractive either to New Yorkers or tourists.

Pour attendance, however, was not due just to the show's competition with Broadway. The entire fair never meet its overall attendance expectations. Over its two-season run, attendance was twenty million less than the seventy million projected. In addition, the *Texas Pavilion* was assigned to the *Lake Amusement Area*, a section of the fair that hosted rides. To reach this separate area, visitors had to walk a long footbridge over the Long Island Expressway.

Besides being separated from the fairgrounds, most of *The Lake Amusement Area* attractions, including the *Texas Pavilion* show, required a fee to enjoy. These paid exhibits competed with free exhibits, such as Disney's *It's a Small World* ride, on the main fair grounds. In addition to competing with these free exhibits, the attractions in the area had to compete for visitors' limited cash with other paid attractions, as well as with the concession stands and restaurants.

As a result of these and other factors, the entire *Lake Amusement Area* was poorly attended, with several of the area's pavilions scaling back or shutting down prematurely. In order to cover losses generated by the *Texas Pavilion*, Wynne began selling his shares in the Great Southwest Corp. He sold a substantial portion of his interest in the company to the Pennsylvania Company, a wholly-owned subsidiary company of the Pennsylvania Railroad. The sale of these shares, as well as subsequent sales to the Pennsylvania Company, later became pivotal to the ownership and control of Six Flags.

In contrast to the extreme success of Six Flags, *Freedomland USA* was not fairing so well. It saw less than profitable crowds. Poor reviews followed. Unable to compete with the *1964 New York World's Fair*, in September of 1964 the park filed bankruptcy a mere four years after its opening. The largest amusement park in the country was torn down in 1965.

1965

For 1965, a $600,000 expansion of the park saw the addition of one new ride and one new theater. The park opened on April 16, 1965. As part of the opening, Angus Wynne, Jr., cut a string holding 600 balloons. The balloons carried coupons for free admission to the park for whoever found them. For those not lucky enough to find a free pass, ticket prices remained the same as for 1964.

El Sombrero Ride. The *El Sombrero* (the Hat) ride was introduced at the former site of the *La Cucaracha* roller coaster. The ride, manufactured by the Chance ride company, is a standard *Trabant* ride. "Trabant" is German for satellite, since the ride is typically configured to resemble a flying saucer. Instead, the park's *Sombrero* ride is designed to resemble a 1,000-gallon sombrero. Chance began offering the ride in 1963 and installed over 250.

El Sombrero Ride, introduced into the park in 1965. Originally painted blue, it is now yellow. Photograph by Author, 2011.

The ride is commonly known as the "Hat" ride by guests. It spins at twenty-two rpm. It was the second off the shelf carnival style "flat ride"added to the park. The ride stayed in its original location until the 1986 season. It was then moved a little west, to a location which was part of the former site of the *Fiesta Train*. It was again moved for the 2006 season to a spot next to the Mexican restaurant, where it sits almost directly across the pathway from its original location.

The ride is the sixth oldest operating ride in the park. It has been replaced on more than one occasion over the years with a newer model.

Outdoor Arena. The fifth season also saw the addition of a 2,500 seat outdoor arena. In early park materials, it was also referred to as the "County Fair Area". The first arena show was a circus, so the area was also named the "Six Flags Circus". Fourteen acts performed in the arena's three-rings, three times daily. The show included typical circus acts, with clowns, animals, and acrobats. The circus lasted one season only. It was replaced by a *Wild West Show* in 1966.

The theater was later named the *Texas Pavilion*, although it was also referred to as the *Texas Arena*. The arena was located to the west of the Texas section, across the railroad tracks from the *Texas Railroad Station*. The arena, therefore, has the distinction of being the first Six Flags attraction located outside the perimeter of the railroad tracks that circle the park.

The arena was accessible by a walkway that went over the railroad tracks to the south of the flume ride and by a passageway under the railroad tracks between the flume ride and the watermelon patch. The overpass is now gone, while the underpass now leads to the Titan.

Guests join Apache Indian Dancers in the entertainment for the finale of the Western Show at the Texas Arena. Photograph by Robert Lee Hohman, 1966; courtesy of Marla Hohman.

The arena offered the opportunity for a variety of special shows and productions to be offered at the park. The arena was closed at the end of the 1974 season, replaced by the *Music Mill Theater*, which opened earlier that same season.

In addition to the new ride and arena, design changes were made in the landscaping at the Frontgate. The star shaped flowerbed at the star plaza of the Frontgate was removed and the plaza redesigned, complemented by new hanging baskets.

Another addition for the season was the landmark Courthouse facade, with its four-side clock tower, built behind the Frontgate. Designed to resemble the Parker County Courthouse, the clock facade was constructed on the top of a building containing an ice-house and is not a guest attraction.

The Clock Tower was added behind the Frontgate in 1965 on top of the park's ice-house. The ice-house is capable of producing 4,500,000 pounds of ice per season. Photograph by Author, 1985.

The season also saw the addition of several historic displays around the park. Western photographs by Erwin Smith were displayed in the *Cattleman's Exhibit*, located in the bank building in the Texas section. A branding iron collection from famous Texas ranches was also displayed in the Texas section. The collection included over 100 irons.

J. Bean's Shootin' Irons, the Texas shooting gallery, was added by the arcade in the Texas section between the Confederate and Texas sections. The shooting gallery was a traditional carnival style shooting gallery. Guests shot small bb like projectiles at tin ducks and other objects that traveled across the back of the gallery in various rows and patterns. The gallery was coin operated and originally cost 25¢ for 15 shoots.

The *Texas Shooting Gallery* stayed in the park until the end of the 1982 season when it was converted into the *Texas Games* arcade. After the arcade was closed, the building was at times used as a display area and more frequently used as a souvenir shop. The original building which housed the shooting gallery was dismantled in 2006 to make room for the *Rodeo* bull ride.

In the Modern section, the *Animal Kingdom* (petting Zoo) added a walk through aviary with a hundred exotic birds.

The *Amphitheater Campus Revue* for the season was *Thank You Mr. President*, subtitled *A New Play with Old Music*. The story line involved the visit by the President of the United States to the fictional Gilchrist University.

J. Bean's Shootin' Irons (1965-1982).
Six Flags BB-gun style shooting gallery in Texas Section.
Photograph by Author, 1998.

The trio of Charles R. Meeker Jr., David Blackburn and Stanley McIlvaine were again responsible for producing the show. This season's production featured twenty-five performers selected from 1,200 college students that auditioned in the spring. Gene Patrick again provided the musical orchestrations.

The *Camus Revue* was presented in the summer months, while a variety show was produced during weekend operations. Management estimates were that 300,000 guests attended the *Campus Revue* shows a year.

In an effort not to offend visitors from the North, the Confederate reenactment characters took up the practice of shooting a Confederate deserter instead of a Yankee spy.

Also in the Confederate section, the Steak House was renamed to *Colonel's Café*. This became *Colonel's Café and Bar B-Q* in 1974. Beginning in 1978, it was designated on park map's simply as "Chicken Fried Steak", although in 1981 it was referred to as "Colonel's Chicken Fried Steak."

A candy store was added in the exhibit hall area of the Modern section.

Since the *El Cucaracha* was removed at the end of the 1964 season, 1965 was the first year, and only full season, that Six Flags operated without any type of roller coaster in the park.

On May 14, 1965, five-year-old Yon Robinson became the five millionth visitor to the park. Total visits to the park set another seasonal record with 1,713,000 guests, 446,000 more than the yearly attendance at the Alamo. The target number of guests for the season was 1,750,000.

At the end of the season, *Skull Island* started a downsizing that would continue over several seasons. The walk through cave and the pirate boat were removed from Pirate Island; the area in which the small cave was located was no longer accessible to guests; and the pirate boat was replaced by a simple pathway.

In addition, 1965 was the last season for the helicopter rides around the park.

Reminiscent of the original plan for a large sport entertainment center, the eighteen hole *Great Southwest Golf Course* was completed in 1965. It was located north of the *Inn of Six Flags*. The par 71 course was designed by Ralph Plummer, with Byron Nelson, and cost $500,000 to construct. The course also featured a nine hole lighted course.

1966

The 1966 season marked the park's fifth anniversary. The landmark season opened on Friday, April 15, 1966, with perfect weather. The season brought the construction of the park's first major thrill ride, a custom designed roller coaster. For the fourth straight season, tickets prices remained at $3.50 for adults and $2.50 for children under twelve.

Six Flags' official first guest, Teresa Poole, celebrating the park's fifth anniversary.
She is holding a photograph of herself waiting to enter the gate on opening day.
Six Flags' public relations photograph, August 5, 1966.

By the start of the 1966 season, Great Southwest had invested over $15 million dollars in the park with original construction, as well as improvements and additions to the park.

Runaway Mine Train.   The park's first coaster, the *El Cucaracha*, was simply a carnival ride obtained by Six Flags and assembled in the park. The park's next coaster, the *Runaway Mine Train*, was designed specifically for *Six Flags Over Texas* by the Arrow Development Company. The roller coaster cost the park one million dollars, one-tenth of the park's total construction cost five years earlier. The ride's development costs were $250,000.

Although the new *Mine Train* was displayed on the 1966 souvenir maps, the ride was under construction during most of the season. In July, the ride unofficially became operational for soft testing. During that time, it was occasionally open for guests to ride. Riders were allowed to ride, even before all of the display elements, such as the rock crusher at the second lift, were finished. The ride was not officially finished until the winter of 1966.

As with Arrow Development's flume ride added in 1963, the *Runaway Mine Train* was the first of its kind when built, but became nearly a required element of all successful amusement parks to follow.

Located in Boomtown, very close to the site of the *Sky Hook Ride*, one of the elements that made the Runaway Mine Train unique at the time was the use of tubular steel tracks and nylon coated wheels. Although there were other metal roller coasters at the time, they ran on a flat track.

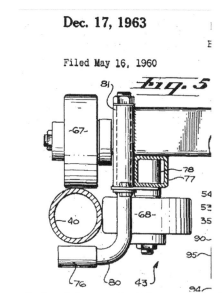

Portion of figure number 5, from patent number 3,114,332, filed May 16, 1960, by Karl Bacon and Edgar Morgan of Arrow Development for a bobsled style tubular roller coaster. This portion of the diagram shows the newly designed roller coaster wheel system. The tubular track is item "40". The top wheels (67) are now referred to as the "running wheels" and the side wheels (68) are the "guide wheels". Below the track (76) are the "up-stop wheels", which the patent states can also be rollers. Right image shows tubular roller coaster wheels on Titan.

The tubular steel tack opened the door to extensive creativity in roller coaster design. The track allows the trains to run with traditional wheels on each unit. The tubular design, however, also allows wheels to attach both below and on the sides of the track. These side and bottom wheels keep the trains on the track and running smoothly in loops and highly banked turns. This innovation led the way for loops, corkscrews, and other exciting elements that were not possible with the traditional flat track metal coaster. In fact, this innovation paved the way for all of the high thrill roller coasters of today.

The use of tubular steel track was originally developed by Arrow for *Disneyland*'s highly successfully *Matterhorn Bobsled* ride. Disney, however, only ran the *Matterhorn* with single ride units until 1978. The *Mine Train* went the next step in development and added several cars linked together to form a roller coaster train. This is the basis for most modern steel roller coasters today.

The ride was the first major thrill ride in the park. It was also heavily themed for the Boomtown section where it was constructed. The ride was inspired by the small mine trains used to carry equipment and personnel into underground mines and to haul rock, dirt, coal, and other materials out. The queue house is designed after a large mine building. Other structures and elements were designed to leave the rider feeling that they were indeed riding on an out-of-control mine train.

The ride has three lifts. This allows for up to five trains to run at a single time, since each area between two lifts is a separately controlled block of track. In addition, two trains can be in the station. The trains originally ran through a tunnel, behind a waterfall, and under a rock-grinder. Finally, the ride coasted peacefully through the interior of a period saloon, complete with

Mine Train on first lift.
Photograph by Author, 1985.

Mine train in action.
Six Flags' public relations photograph, 1972.

characters playing cards and a piano. The saloon was followed by the highlight drop straight into a 150-foot curving tunnel twelve feet below Lake Caddo. The underwater tunnel was a first for a roller coaster ride.

An element involving running the trains over a burning bridge was planned and pictured on some souvenir maps. This element was eventually abandoned.

Each of the trains have five cars, with six seats each, for a total of thirty riders per train. The three lifts are thirty-five, twenty, and twenty-five feet in height. The ride's original length was 2,484 feet and run time was three minutes and ten seconds. The trains travel at up to 26 mph, with guests experiencing up to 2 "g"s during the ride. With five trains running, capacity was 2,200 guests an hour. With four trains running, the hourly capacity is 1,850 guests.

Construction required 2,000 yards of concrete and 165,000 feet of reinforcing steel. Although the ride is a tubular steel coaster, wood is used for supporting the tubal steel rails, qualifying the ride as a hybrid coaster. The ride was built with 350 telephone poles and 110,000 square feet of redwood, cedar, and pine. In addition, 35,000 feet of electrical wire was installed.

The *Mine Train* is still operating today, although now it is considered a rather mild ride when compared to modern coasters. The word "Runaway" was to be dropped from the name beginning with the 1996 season to avoid confusion with the newly installed *Runaway Mountain* roller coaster in the

Confederate section. The change did not last. The name returned to "Runaway Mine Train" and the original name has remained since.

1966 Shows.   In the Texas section, a *Wild West Show* replaced the *Circus Show* in the *Texas Pavilion*. Featured in the show was the Peterson family of Ogallala, Nebraska. Other acts included Apache Indian dancers performing their traditional dances.

The show was produced by Frank Rush. Rush's daughter Suzy Self, and her husband Tom Self, also performed in the show. The family had previously produced Western shows in Oklahoma. Rush staged the show at Six Flags for the 1966 and 1967 seasons. In 1971, Frank Rush, his son Frank Rush, III, and Tom Self purchased the 126-acre *Sandy Lake Amusement Park* in Dallas. The park is now operated by four generations of the Rush family.

Campus Revue.   With 300,000 guests viewing the amphitheater show each year, the *Campus Revue* was again one of the most popular attractions in the park. The fifth annual show, again set at Gilchrist University, was *Let's Do It, (Let's Find a Cause)*. The show was performed by twenty-six college students. Claire Sissy King and Ventriloquist Jay Johnson were members of the cast. The revue ran only in the summer months.

Dolphin Show.   In June, the park's first dolphin show opened in a 25,000-gallon pool on *Skull Island*. The aquatic theater was located on Pirate Island near where the canoe dock was initially built. The single season show featured a dolphin named "Skipper" and his trainer Diane Langer. The show was removed at the end of the season. In 1969, a larger dolphin pool was built nearby.

In the Modern section, the refreshment stand was enlarged. The *Leather Store* in the *Mexican Bazaar* was replaced by a *Curio Shop*.

Every year was a record year as yearly attendance increased each season since the park opened. For 1966, attendance was just under the two million visitor mark with a record 1,915,720 visitors. On May 9, 1966, the park set a new daily attendance record, surpassing 25,000, with a total attendance of 25,184. The park estimated that by 1966, nearly forty percent of its guests were from out of state.

1967

On April 29, 1967, Miss Texas, Sharon Kay Logan, snipped the ribbon to open the park for its seventh season. Tickets prices increased for the first time in four seasons to $3.95 for adults and $2.95 for children under 12.

The season saw full operation of *The Runaway Mine Train*, which had only operated regularly for the last part of the season in 1966. In addition, 1967 saw the addition of two new mid-season rides. In August of the season, the *Spindletop* ride was introduced along with the *Jet Set Trainer* airplanes. The park spent a total of $250,000 for the two rides.

Spindletop Ride. The *Spindletop* was a standard carnival ride, typically known as a "rotor". The rotor consisted of a barrel shaped room housed above a motor designed to rotate the room at 28 to 33 revolutions per minute. Riders enter the round room through a side door. Once inside, the door is closed and the riders stand with their back to the round wall.

As the room begins to rotate, "g" forces are created sufficient to hold the rider to the wall of the barrel. Once sufficient speed was obtained, the operator hit a switch and literally "dropped the floor" three feet out from under the riders. The riders remained pinned in place by the force created by the spinning of the ride. Twenty-five to thirty riders could ride at a time.

After a few moments spinning, the operator raised the floor back to its original position under the feet of the guests and the ride slowed to a stop.

The name *Spindletop* had a double meaning. The name referred to the ride's action of spinning like a top. Historically, it also referred to the tremendous oil field in Beaumont, Texas. On January 10, 1901, a well drilled in the Spindletop oil field struck oil, producing the largest oil gusher the world had ever seen. The field was so productive that it brought in 100,000 barrels a day, starting the Texas oil boom.

For its first year, the ride was located outside the circle of the railroad tracks, in the southeast corner of the park. The ride was built on a new path that connected the Boomtown section with the Frontgate area, bypassing the Modern USA section. The location was near the site where the *Puppet Show* (*Majestic Theater*) was later built.

Spindletop (1967-1989) at its third location at the previous site of the Texas Astrolift Station in the Texas Section. Ride is cone shaped building near the middle of the image. Photograph by Author, 1984.

The ride was moved after one season to a spot near *Skull Island* where the small dolphin pool was located the year before. The move was necessary in order to make room for the puppet show to open the following season. This placed the ride at the end of the tower slide when the *Tower* was built in 1969.

The ride stayed near the *Tower* until the end of the 1982 season when it was relocated to the site of the former *Texas Astrolift Station* in order to make room for the *Roaring Rapids*. The ride was removed in 1989 in order to make room for the *Texas Giant* exit walkway.

The *Spindletop* and the *El Sombrero* ride are the only rides in the park to have been operated at three different locations, although the park has had different scrambler rides in three different locations in the park.

Jet Set.   Also introduced for 1967 was the *Jet Set* ride. The ride consisted of twelve ride units designed to look like jet airplanes. Two riders could sit in each unit in side-by-side seating. Each jet had a nine-foot wing span and was attached behind the seats to a fifteen-foot vertical steel girder.

The mounting of the planes allowed each Jet to move up and down along the length of the girder. In addition, they could rotate on the girder, so that the nose of the plane could be pointed in any direction in a 360-degree circle. The ride was controlled by the riders, who used a control stick to lift, drop, and rotate the plane in order to simulate the commands of an actual jet plane.

The *Jet Set* was the first ride of its type to operate in the nation. Possibly, it was the only one of its type ever installed anywhere. The ride was designed and built by Intamin, AG of Zurich, Switzerland. ("AG" is a German designation for a type of business structure.) Intamin is a ride manufacturing company founded to supply diverse rides to the new themed amusement park industry. The original focus of Intamin was the design and construction of amusement park observation towers. The name INTAMIN is taken from the phrase INTernational AMusement INstallations.

Intamin was officially formed in July of 1967, just shortly before the ride was built. The *Jet Set* appears to have been the first ride installed by Intamin in an amusement park. The *Jet Set*, however, was the first of many rides Intamin provided Six Flags, as Intamin replaced Arrow Development as the park's major ride supplier.

The ride was located in the south end of the USA section, near the current site of the small children's rides in *Looney Tunes Land*. Like the *Spindletop*, it was located outside of the railroad tracks along the new path between the Frontgate and Boomtown.

The rather low capacity ride lasted only four seasons. It was removed after the 1970 season to make room for the *Big Bend* roller coaster. The *Jet Set* was the first ride removed from the park that was installed after the first season.

Just south of the *Jet Set* ride, a new refreshment stand and food patio opened. On park maps the stand was simply referred to as a refreshment

Jet Set Airplane Ride (1967-1970).
Planes moved up and down, and rotated around a steal beam.
Sky Crane (1963-1968) in background.
Souvenir slide circa 1967.

stand. When the *Big Bend* opened in 1971, the stand became the "Big Bend Snack Shop".

Also in the Modern section, an *Animal Fair* store was added in the exhibit hall building. The *Waples Store*, located in the Texas section, was replaced by a *Country Store*. In Boomtown, an additional refreshment stand was added around the corner from the souvenir shop. This stand was formally named *Mustard's Last Stand* in 1972.

1967 Shows. The "*Numbers Games*" was the sixth and last *Campus Revue* show at the *Amphitheater*. Charles R Meeker, Jr., produced and directed the show in association with David Blackburn. The cast consisted of twenty-two performers, singers, dancers, and musicians. It was again set at Gilchrist University. The summer show ran for 12 weeks.

At the *Crazy Horse Saloon*, two separate casts alternated as the show's company. One entire cast was composed solely of members of the Kappa Kappa Gamma sorority at SMU.

In the Confederate section, after two downsizing in the length of its run, the *Butterfield Stagecoach* ride was completely removed at the end of the 1967 season.

Likewise, at the end of the season, the Indian dancers and their *Indian Village* were removed from the park. The trading-post souvenir store, with its exhibits of western artifacts, remained and was expanded the following season to include the *Cyclorama of the American Indian* display. The cyclorama, as well as parts of the new Flume II, filled the area vacated by the *Indian Village*.

Before the park opened in 1961, Marco Engineering had estimated that two million guests a year would visit the park. The park did not, however, reach two million visitors in one season until the 1967 season. Yearly attendance for the season was a record 2,037,000. On August 1, 1967, Mrs. H.W. Cost of Metairie, Louisiana, became the 10 millionth park visitor. A new daily attendance record was set on May 6, 1967, with 28,877 guests.

Six Flags Over Georgia.   This season is also notable for events outside of the park. Six years after *Six Flags Over Texas* opened, its first sister park, *Six Flags Over Georgia*, opened near Atlanta, Georgia. The opening of *Six Flags Over Georgia* officially made Six Flags an amusement park chain.

Six Flags Over Georgia was built on the same concepts as the Texas park. The new park included many of the same rides, such as a railroad, river adventure, log flume ride, antique cars, sky-lift, carousel, and mine train. The park was built for $12 million, two million more than the original Six Flags. Built on 276 acres, it opened in June of 1967. Randall Duell was the park's key designer. Gene Patrick served as the assistant art director in the design of the park.

Despite the earlier predictions of a multitude of general theme parks being built following the Disney model, *Six Flags Over Georgia* was the first new general theme park to open since *Legend City* amusement park opened in 1963. The only other parks built during that time were specialty and attraction parks, such Universal Studios Hollywood, animal parks, and sea life parks.

1968

The eighth season opened on Saturday, April 13, 1968. Multiple renovations and additions were made all around the park. Major new attractions included a second flume ride, as well as two theaters. In addition, the *Fiesta Train* underwent a major overhaul. Altogether, the park spent $2 million dollars on improvements and additions for the season. This was the largest amount spent on improvements for any season since the park opened.

The park was using the catch phrase "The Sound of Fun Surrounds You". Ticket prices were up to $4.50 for an adult and $3.50 for children under 12. Children under 3 were free. The park size was now shown as 140 acres, up from 115. Promotional materials indicated that the park's hourly ride and attraction capacity was now estimated at 29,000 guests.

Southern Palace Theater.   For the park's eighth season, the amphitheater in the Confederate section was enclosed to become the *Southern Palace Theater*. The new indoor theater cost $200,000 to construct. It was built in the same location as the amphitheater, with the stage and seating in essentially the same spot in both theaters. With 1,200 seats, it held the same number of guests as the amphitheater.

The *Southern Palace* continued the entertainment format established for the amphitheater. The air-conditioned theater was the new home of the *Six Flags Revue* variety shows. The theater was later named for David Blackburn, becoming the *David Blackburn Southern Palace Theater*. Blackburn went on to be Vice-President of Show Productions for Six Flags, Inc.

Crowd waiting to enter the Southern Palace.
Photograph by Author, 1998.

For its inaugural year, the *Southern Palace* featured not one, but two completely different shows, a daytime show and an evening show. The daytime show was *BC-TV*. This revue was a satire on modern television set in Rome during the time of Julius Caesar. It was a humorous show featuring the usual singing and dancing. Written by Jack Kaplan, the show was produced by David Blackburn and Michael Jenkins.

The evening show in the *Southern Palace* was the *Red, White and Blue Revue*. This show had a cast of ten, with a twelve-member orchestra. The 35-minute show capsulated the history of the United States. The show was later memorialized on a record album. Performed 695 times during the summer, the show was considered the most successful show to date.

Krofft Puppet Circus. The other theater to be added for the season was the *Sid and Marty Krofft Puppet Show*. In keeping with the nature of the theater, the original front facade featured numerous whimsical characters and shapes. The first puppet show was the *Krofft Brothers Puppet Show, "Circus"*, a show designed to entertain adults as well as children. The puppets used were of all forms, including marionettes, animated figures, and costumed characters. Like the Southern Palace, the new theater cost $200,000.

Six Flags Crazy Band in French Section in front of Pierre's Treasures.
The Crazy Band was a roaming street band that performed through the day.
Six Flags' souvenir slide, circa 1966.

The Krofft brothers produced puppet shows worldwide. Located in Georgia, they first became associated with Six Flags at the new Georgia park in 1967. They also sponsored a highly successful show at the *1964 New York World's Fair*.

The theater building still stands in the southeast corner of the park, although the front facade has been completely changed. The theater has had several names since the Kroffts' show left the park. Subsequent names included the "Good Times Square Theater" and the "Majestic Theater". As with the *Southern Palace*, the air-conditioned theater holds 1,200 guests.

In addition to the puppet show, puppeteers Sid and Marty Krofft influenced many of the other improvements around the park.

Fiesta Train Renovations. The Krofft brothers also completely redesigned scenes along the *Fiesta Train*. Almost all of the animations were removed and replaced with newer, larger scale scenes as part of the $400,000 renovations. The centerpiece of the ride was a sixty-foot tall volcano that "erupted" periodically with a "bang", followed by smoke rising into the air. In addition, "lava" constantly flowed down from the top of the volcano.

The trains for the ride were also changed. The charming sombrero hats, which covered the cars and which gave the train its nickname of the "Hat Train", were gone, replaced with square roofs. The trolley style engines were redesigned as well. One engine was reconfigured to resemble a dragon, influenced by the designs of the Aztec and Mayan Indians. The other appeared as a brightly painted orange diesel engine, with SFFR, for "Six Flags Fiesta Railroad" painted on the side.

A scene of children singing and dancing was in view as the trains loaded. The first scene was of a runaway bus, running in a constant circle. It was filled with riders and various farm animals.

A new Mexican village was also added to the ride's attraction. In sharp contrast to the ride's earlier sleepy town with villagers napping and riding on burros, this village included a cross fire between the town's people and desperados. The train went though the center of the town's square with guns blazing from both sides.

Fiesta Train, remodeled by Sid and Marty Krofft, with several new scenes.
Shown is the Volcano and runaway bus. The trains traveled through
the volcano, where guest viewed the volcano monsters and a puppet circus.
Postcard SF-T-6, circa 1968.

The trains also traveled through the volcano, where the riders were treated to a view of the "lava monsters". The end of the ride was a trip through a building containing a Mexican circus, with high-wire acrobats and other acts. The characters in the circus were puppets very similar to those used by the Kroffts in the puppet show on the other side of the park.

Also featured were a piñata village and a pyramid with a twenty-foot waterfall. Nearby were "dancing columns" which rocked back and forth on their bases.

The loading dock area for the ride is best remembered for the music which played their constantly. The music consisted of children singing the "Fiesta Song", with its ever-repeating verses.

Only a few of the original scenes remained on the ride. One element of the ride that was not changed was the track layout. The ride continued to follow the same route it previously traveled.

110

The dancing tamales, which danced for seven years next to the tracks of the *Fiesta train*, were moved to the "Mexican junction" of the *Six Flags Railroad*, where they continue to twirl and dance to this day. The men riding on the little burros also became a part of the railroad's "Mexican junction".

Flume Enhancements.   By 1968 the flume ride and *Mine Train* rides were the most popular rides in the park. Capacity of the highly popular flume ride was increased by adding a second flume next to the original. The rides share the same queue house. Guests can decide which one to ride based on which line that they enter. The total capacity of the two rides was estimated at 3,400 guests per hour.

Sid and Marty Krofft also exerted their influence on the flume ride. They designed and constructed giant animations for each of the rides. On the original flume, now designated as "Flume 1", a Snidely Whiplash type villain, complete with handlebar mustache, was mounted on the first lift. The logs went directly under the character as he sawed a log, which threatened to fall into the flume and onto the riders below.

Flume II with covered drop; Lumber Jack character on low lift.
Walkway at top of picture leads to the arena area.
Photograph by Author, 1976.

The new flume ride, designated as "Flume 2", cost $350,000. It featured a giant Paul Bunyan type lumberjack on the first lift, constantly swinging his ax towards the logs and riders, as they passed directly under him. In addition, a cover was built over the final drop on Flume 2, creating a tunnel. The second flume is the eighth oldest ride in the park.

Both the giant characters, as well as the covered drop, were duplicated on the two flume rides at *Six Flags Over Georgia*.

Left: Volcano "Lava Monster" designed for the Fiesta Train volcano.
Six Flags' public relations photo, 1968.
Right: Villain character sawing logs at the first lift of Flume 1.
Photograph by Author, 1976.

Cyclorama Museum. The *Cyclorama Museum of American Indians* was added as part of the *Indian Trading Post*. The cyclorama contained a life size depiction of Texas Indians in a natural setting, with Texas animals and a painted scenic background. The 90-foot long cyclorama curved around the back of the *Trading Post*. It was 28 feet deep and 14 feet high. One hundred and fifty guests could view the exhibit at a time.

On display around the diorama were Indian and Western relics. The relics, some of which were 150 years old, were part of the collection of the trading post's owner, Skeet Richardson.

The cyclorama was titled "The Coming of the Indian Traders". The life size scene depicted buckskin dressed Caucasians standing next to an Indian chief. Also included in the display were other Native Americans, including women and children, going about their daily activities.

The cyclorama display was built onto the back of the Indian trading post in an area that was previously used by the Indian dancers. The air-conditioned building, with its unique display, became a popular retreat from the heat. As always, cowboy, Indian, and western related souvenirs were sold in the front of the store.

The park layout was also changed. A new path was added connecting Boomtown to the Confederacy, next to the *Southern Palace*. The path traveled between the north side of *La Salle's River Adventure* and the south side of the lake on which the canoes traveled. The path now runs on the north side of the *Roaring Rapids*, between the *Tower* and Boomtown.

Portion of the Indian Diorama. Great Southwest Corp. postcard 39585-C.
Also on the back of owner Skeet Richardson's business card, circa 1968.

Also for guest comfort, three hundred and twenty-five more tons of air conditioning were added park-wide, increasing the park's capacity to 1,000 tons. Along with the air conditioning, additional lighting was added to enhance the appearance of the park in the evening.

The Six Flags Gazette. For eight seasons, 1961 to 1968, Six Flags published its own newspaper, the *Six Flags Gazette*. The *Gazette*, published on standard newsprint, was sold throughout the park. The paper was published in connection with the *Daily News Texan* and included free in its various local papers. The number of editions published during a season was reduced over the years. It started in 1961 as a weekly publication, but by its final season of publication, it was yearly. The Gazette articles covered activities behind the scenes at the park, park personnel, the history of Texas and the park, and new rides and attractions.

The home of the Gazette was an office located in the Confederate section. At the *Gazette* office guests could also purchase souvenir "wanted posters", newspapers and "playbills" with their own name printed as the subject of the poster. An antique printing press was on display in the building.

In 1969, the *Gazette* building was renamed to the "Newspaper Office". The post office moved into it in 1974. A tintype studio, allowing guests to buy antique stylized photographs, was added in 1975. The "Gazette" name was returned to the building in 1982. The store was renamed to "Professor Bloodgood's Antique Photos in 1984".

On *Skull Island*, a cannon shooting activity was added in the area that had previously been *Pirate Island*. Similar to the shooting gallery, guests could pay to shoot small air propelled projectiles from replica cannons. The shot went out over a small pond towards pirate themed targets, such as a pirate ship.

This addition on *Skull Island* was offset by other reductions in the island's activities. In August of 1968, additional portions of *Skull Island* were closed in order to make way for the construction of the *Texas Oil Derrick*. By the end of the season, the long suspension bridge to *Indian Island* was removed, as well as the three swamp tree slides located on the island.

In the Mexican section, the *Curio Shop* moved across the pathway. The space it formally occupied became a shop with a glass-blower creating souvenirs as guests watched. Glass blowing was featured at the shop until 1988.

The *Sky Crane* ride was removed at the end of the 1968 season and relocated to the newer *Six Flags Over Georgia*.

Total park capacity was up to 29,000 guests an hour. Attendance for 1968 was expected to reach two million yearly visitors as it had in 1967. Instead, however, the park saw only 1.7 million guests. The 1968 season became the first season since the opening of the park in which attendance declined from the previous season. In fact, yearly attendance was the lowest for any season since 1965.

Six Flags Over California.   In August of 1968, Great Southwest Corp. announced what was to be its third park, *Six Flags Over California*. Planned to open in Disney's home state, the park would be located at Pleasanton, in northern California.

The park was budgeted for construction at $20 million. Construction was set to begin in 1969 and be completed for an opening in 1971.

As with the other Six Flags locations, the park was to have a historical theme. Corporate officials announced that the park was to carry the "Six Flags" brand name even if California did not have six sovereign flags. The 140-acre park was to be built on 243 acres already purchased by Great Southwest. Initial plans called for twenty major shows and attractions.

In October of 1968, the corporation flew 160 local residents, media representatives, and city officials from California to Arlington to view the Texas park. In the party was the current Miss California, Sharon Terrill. Miss Terrill was herself a former Six Flags hostess, working at the frontgate in 1964 and 1965.

Despite efforts to promote the park, it faced zoning obstacles and objections from the local community and media. Community support was so negative that in February of 1969, Great Southwest completely abandoned the project. The Corporation did announce, however, that they were looking at other locations in California to build a new park.

In July of 1969, Great Southwest announced that its third park would instead be *Six Flags Over Mid-America*, near St. Louis Missouri.

*Late 1968 aerial picture. Tower is virtually complete, but slide lanes have not been added.
The ride did not open until 1969. The new Southern Palace is observable
in the middle of the picture, while the new puppet show is visible at the bottom middle.
The Texas Arena is shown in top left corner. Photo: US Geology Survey, 1968.*

In June of 1968, another major theme park, *Astroworld* opened in Houston, next to the Astrodome complex. The park was also designed by Randall Duell. At the time that it opened, *Astroworld* was not associated in any manner with Six Flags.

In California, *Knott's Berry Farm* officially converted its roadside attraction, which had been free to enter, to a paid amusement theme park.

1969

By 1969, Six Flags was well established as a regional tourist attraction. Business was consistent each season. Success, however, was not considered a reason to slow down and rest on yesterday's accomplishments. The last year of the sixties was another big year of expansion. Great Southwest reported that $19 million was invested in the park.

Despite a heavy rainstorm, the season started with opening ceremonies on Saturday, April 12. Angus Wynne was once again the master of ceremonies. The guests of honor were actors Mark Lester and Jack Wild, stars of the current movie *Oliver*. Jack Wild was also one of the lead actors in Sid and Marty Krofft's upcoming TV production, *HR Pufnstuf*.

This was the last opening ceremony at which the park released helium balloons containing free coupons to the park. Ticket costs remained at $4.50 for adults and $3.50 for children under twelve.

The Tower. The season's major new attraction was the *Texas Oil Derrick*, a 300-foot tall observation tower designed to look like a traditional oil derrick. The structure, also known as *The Tower*, was added at the north end of the park in an area that previously held part of the *Stagecoach* run and part of *Skull Island*.

The Tower opened on May 24, 1969. While the ride is billed as "the world's largest land-based oil derrick", it does not function in any capacity as an actual oil well. Although built on land that was previously part of Skull Island, the new attraction was promoted as being in the nearby Boomtown section.

The attraction was announced to the public on August 16, 1968. Work on the ride actually began in August of 1968, with most of the structure completed in two weeks. Erection of the entire framework took just over one month. The tower's 800,000 pounds of steel beams were designed and fabricated in Austria. They were then shipped to Texas for assembly. The ride was assembled like a giant erector set object using the prefabricated steel beams.

The ride cost $750,000 to construct. Although virtually complete in August of 1968, the ride could not open on the park's opening day in April of 1969 due to a long-shoreman's strike that held up the ride's high-speed elevators and twelve-lane slide in a ship sitting in the Port of Houston.

Nearly twice as tall as the sky crane ride, the *Tower* was the tallest structure in the park until the installation of the *Superman Tower of Power* in 2003. In addition, the guests' view was no longer limited to a specific ride time as it was with the *Sky Crane.*

Each of the two high-speed elevators lift approximately twenty-five guests to one of two observation decks. The lower deck is 255 feet high and is 1,490 square feet. The higher deck is 267 feet high and is 1,936 square feet. The two observation decks are connected by a staircase, allowing guests to move from one to the other.

The original elevators traveled at ten feet per second. Each elevator is lifted by eight cables and balanced by 62 weights totaling 3,100 pounds. They lifted 2,000 visitors per hour to the platforms.

Guest access to the observation areas is by the elevators only.

The 300-foot Six Flags Tower resembles an oil derrick and opened in 1969. Photograph by Author, 1985.

There are, however, 19 flights of stairs, with a total of 525 steps, which can be used in an emergency.

From the observation decks, the guests are provided a bird's eye view of the entire park. On a clear day, guests can see downtown Fort Worth to the west and downtown Dallas to the east.

For a quarter, telescopes provide close up viewing. At night, twenty-eight 1000-watt floodlights illuminate the ride. Painting the tower takes 950 gallons of International Orange, the same color as the Golden Gate Bridge.

In the 1980s, the shoulder high railing system on each observation desk was supplemented with a mesh fencing which caged in the entire observations deck. The ride was closed for most of the 1998 season while the then thirty-year old elevator system was modernized.

Tower Slide. Another 4,300 square foot platform was built on the structure's fifty-foot level. From the east side of this platform, a 180-foot long twelve-lane super-slide descended at a 35-degree angle. Guests rode down the slide sitting on burlap sacks. The super-slide level was accessible only by stairs; elevator service was not provided to the slide level. The slide's capacity was 2,000 riders an hour.

Superslides were very popular at the time, frequently found at carnivals and as standalone attractions on shopping center parking lots.

The slide was removed following the 1975 season. Although it is no longer open to the public, the platform and railing used by the slide are still visible at the fifty-foot level.

The Six Flags *Tower* was the first major attraction constructed by the newly formed Intamin company, and likely their second ride installation after the *Jet Set*. F. B. McIntire Equipment Company, which erected the *Astrolift*, was Six Flag's contractor for the tower.

Tower Slide installed on side of Tower. (1969–1975).
Photograph by Author, 1975.

Beginning in 1988, the *Tower* was decorated at Halloween with a 70-foot high giant ape scaling its side. He was later replaced with a giant spider. At Christmas, the *Tower* is frequently decorated with large stars on the observation desks.

The *Tower* has two sister towers, both constructed by Intamin. One is at *Kings Island*, in Kings Island, Ohio, and the other at *Kings Dominion*, just north of Richmond, Virginia. Although the towers at these two parks are designed to look like the *Eiffel Tower*, and not an oil derrick, dimensionally they are almost identical to the Texas *Tower*. The other two towers were built in 1972 and 1975.

Due to the construction of the *Tower*, nearby *Skull Island* was significantly reduced. For the 1969 season, it consisted of the original island with the original *Skull Rock* and slide, as well as the original tree slide. The tree house and slides, added in 1963, as well as the barrel bridge, were also still in place. They now connected *Skull Island* to the new *Tower* area.

Mini-Mine Train.   The *Tower* was not the only attraction added for 1969. A second roller coaster, the *Mini Mine Train*, opened next to the original mine train. The coaster, designed for younger children, is a smaller, milder version of the original. The original ride traveled on 810 feet of track. The ride was rebuilt in 1998 to accommodate the *Mr. Freeze*. The height of the lift is twenty feet and the trains travel at 20 mph. The ride lasts one minute and ten seconds.

Like the mine train, the *Mini Mine Train* was built by Arrow Development. The *Mini Mine Train* was the last attraction built for *Six Flags Over Texas* by Arrow Development. Arrow previously developed and built the park's flume ride, the river's track system, ride portions of the cave ride, and both the *Chaparral* and *Happy Motoring* cars. Arrow also installed several rides at the new *Six Flags Over Georgia*, which opened in 1967.

Its opening marked the first time that Six Flags had more than one operating roller coaster in the park at the same time. The *Tower* and the *Mini Mine Train* are tied for the ninth oldest operating ride in the park. Each was closed for the 1998 season.

Mini Mine Train and station house.
Photograph by Author, 2014.

The Chevy Show.   Across from the *Cave* ride, near where the *Stagecoach* queue house once stood, the *Chevy Show* opened. The show was named for its corporate sponsor, the Chevrolet Corporation. The show was a state of the art *Cinesphere* movie theater. It used a 180 square-foot curved circular shaped screen, with carefully placed bench seats, to create a realistic feel to the movies shown.

The movie shown did not have a particular story line. Instead, the film showed various scenes designed to maximize the effect of the theater and to promote the latest Chevrolet vehicles. Typical scenes were designed to simulate riding in various vehicles, such as a roller coaster; a helicopter flying through the Grand Canyon; a downhill run with an Olympic skier; a ride around a speedway in a racecar; and a glider sailing off a cliff. The effect could be so real that guests were known to sway forward when an on screen vehicle came to a sudden stop.

In order to keep the show entertaining, the various scenes in the movie were changed from time to time. The Chevy Show movie was featured for twenty-two years. The theater name was changed in 1984 to the *Chevrolet Theater* and in 1988 to the *Cinema 180 Theater*.

The theater building itself remains across from the *Gold River Cave Ride* and has hosted several other shows over the years since the *Chevy Show* movie was retired. It is now known as the *Lone Star Theater*.

The Dolphin Show. Another show was added for this season. A new *Dolphin Show* was installed next to the newly opened tower. The pool was 30-foot by 30-foot, nine-foot deep, and held 115,000 gallons. The new tank was much larger than the 1966 dolphin pool. The theater had seating for 1,500.

The *Dolphin Show* featured four dolphins performing various feats of skill, such as jumping over poles; chasing balls around the pool; jumping through hoops; and for a finale, jumping through fire. Only two of the dolphins performed per show. The pool area had space for two dolphins to rest while two performed.

Dolphin and trainer.
Six Flags' postcard SF-T-5, circa 1969.

During the show, the trainers were very careful to explain the differences between porpoises and dolphins, as well as how to identify each type of mammal. Over the years, however, the park management in its various press releases and souvenirs constantly used the terms as though they were interchangeably, referring to the theater as both a porpoise and a dolphin show.

The theater seated 1,000 guests. It was later transformed into a high dive show. The theater was reconfigured several times for various life action and stunt shows. The theater was torn down in 1992 to build the *Batman Stunt Show* at the same location.

The *Fabulous Flickers* was the musical revue at the *Southern Palace* with sixteen cast members. It featured songs from movie musicals.

The *Cavalcade of the Horse* was the western show in the arena. At the end of the 1969 season, the *Wild West* show closed.

Attendance for 1969 reached 1.835 million, bringing it back up above 1968, but still under the two million visitor record set in 1967. Single day attendance hit a new mark with 28,848 visitors on May 10, 1969.

1970

The park's tenth season opened on April 11, 1970. Guests of honor for opening day were Connie Haggard, Miss World, USA, and Sid and Marty Kroffts' character HR Pufnstuf. Angus Wynne hosted the opening ceremonies for the last time. There was an opening ribbon for cutting, which Pufnstuf ate instead. Ticket prices increased to $5.00 for adults and $4.00 for children under 12. The park was now billed as having 145 acres.

The first season of the seventies was marked with little in the way of additions or major improvements. In fact, 1970 was the first season since the park opened that a not a single additional ride was added. (While no totally new ride was added in 1968, a second log flume ride was built and the *Fiesta Train* was extensively remodeled.)

Los Voladores Show.   Although no new rides were added, the *Texas Arena* was remodeled so that the *Los Voladores*, the "Flying Indians of Mexico", could perform their acrobatic show. The Voladores are traditional Tontonacan Indians of the Veracruz area of Mexico, famous for performing their acrobatics at the Palacio Tropical in Acapulco, Mexico. Their show replaced the *Wild West Show*. The *Texas Pavilion* was remodeled to hold 2,000 visitors for each show.

As they performed above the arena, the Indians wore costumes representing eagles and other birds. One of the highlights of the show was performed by four of the Indians suspended by ropes from atop of a 100-foot pole. At the end of their routine, they spiraled down the pole in unison suspended by the ropes.

Texas Travel Exhibit miniature model of Six Flags.
Photograph by Author, 1976.

The *Los Voladores* also performed as Mexico's entry at the *1964 New York World's Fair* and the *San Antonio Hemisfair of 1968.*

Six Flags Model. An exhibit consisting of a miniature 1/16' scale model of *Six Flags Over Texas* was added in the *Travel Exhibit* in *Luther's Land Office* building in the Boomtown section. *Luther's Land Office* was named for Luther Clark, President of Six Flags and the park's construction supervisor.

The 10' x 10' model took fourteen months to construct at a cost of $20,000.00. It was constructed by Cost Systems Engineers Inc. of Fort Worth using the park's original building plans, color photographs, and ground measurement.

The entire park was featured in the scale model. Included were 3/8ths inch scale people. Many of the miniature rides on the exhibit were animated. A working "N" scale railroad circled the park while a working *Astrolift* ride crossed over the model park. The elevators traveled up and down in the tower, as the *Sombrero, Missilechaser, Carousel,* and *Flying Jenny* all slowly spun around.

The Travel Exhibit building in which the model was contained was also a tourist information center. In addition to the model, it featured large photos of Texas scenes, travel pamphlets, and Texas travel maps.

1970 Shows. During the spring, the *Southern Palace* show was *Sing-in-70*, a musical revue. The show featured contemporary music synchronized to slides projected on a stage screen. During the summer, *Sing-in-70* served as the day show, while *45 minutes from Broadway* was the evening show. The evening show was performed by a cast of nineteen.

In addition to the shows, HR Pufnstuf made personal appearances throughout the park during the summer time.

In the Modern section, Ralston Purina pet food company replaced Southwest Life as the sponsor of the *Animal Kingdom*. Southwest Life sponsored the zoo since the park opened.

Nearby, a new gift shop, the *Spectrum Mod*, opened. The shop sold some traditional souvenirs, but specialized in contemporary items, including popular posters and t-shirts that did not specifically relate to Six Flags. The name was shortened to the *Spectrum* in 1974.

The *Do-Nut* shop replaced the *Animal Fair* in the exhibits building. The *Do-Nut* shop was later renamed the *Sweettooth Bake Shop*.

In order to make room for the addition of the *Big Bend* roller coaster, the short-lived *Jet Set* ride was removed at the end of the season.

Six Flags was still rated the number one tourist attraction in the state, while the *Astrodome* in Houston replaced the Alamo as the number two choice. The park set a new single day attendance record on May 9 with 30,180 guests. That record was then broken one week later, on May 16, with 34,381 guests. Overall attendance stayed just under two million, with 1,970,000 visitors. Despite the lack of a major new attraction, attendance exceeded the previous season.

While there were few additions at the Arlington park, Six Flags, Inc. was completing efforts to construction the third, and final, general theme park built under the Six Flags name. The last original park, *Six Flags Over Mid-America*, opened the following season.

In August of 1970, the *Six Flags Mall* opened near to the park. At the time, it was the largest indoor shopping center in the Dallas Fort Worth area.

Glass blowers have long been a tradition at Six Flags, beginning as early as at least 1963.
While guests watch, they created unique and custom souvenirs.
Originally located in the Mexican Section, later moved to the Texas Section.
Photograph by Author, 2006.

5.

THE PENN CENTRAL BANKRUPTCY

1970

Ownership Background.   Six Flags was originally constructed and operated by the Great Southwest Corporation (GSW). The Great Southwest Corp. was a publicly held Texas based corporation whose original key stockholders were Angus Wynne; his uncle Toddie Wynne; his cousin T.L. Wynne; New York real estate developer William Zeckendorf, owner of the Webb & Knapp investment company; and the Rockefeller Center.

In 1964, some of the key stockholders decided to sell their interests in GSW. They negotiated a sale of their stock to the Pennsylvania Company, a holding company that owned the non-railroad interests of the Pennsylvania Railroad. At the time, the Pennsylvania Railroad was one of the largest railroads in the country.

In June of 1964, both the board of directors of the Pennsylvania Company, and the board of the Pennsylvania Railroad, approved the purchase of 49% of the outstanding stock of the Great Southwest Corp. at a cost of approximately $12 million.

Although concerned that key original stockholders of GSW were selling their interests, the corporate resolution of the Pennsylvania Company specifically noted that Mr. Angus Wynne was President and CEO of Great Southwest Corp. It further noted that he would continue to operate the company even after the purchase. Wynne enjoyed good working relations with the directors and officers of the Pennsylvania Railroad. Satisfied that Angus Wynne was fully competent to manage the company, the purchase went forward.

Confident in the company, the Pennsylvania Company continued to buy stock in GSW. By 1968, the Pennsylvania Company owned a large controlling interest in GSW.

In 1968, the Pennsylvania Railroad merged with the Central Railroad to form the Penn Central Transportation Company. Known as the Penn Central Railroad, the resulting railroad was the largest privately owned railroad in the world. Penn Central Transportation Company, in turn, owned 100% of the Pennsylvania Company.

At various points between 1968 and 1970, the Pennsylvania Company owned from 87% to 91% of Great Southwest Corp., owner of *Six Flags Over Texas* and *Georgia.*

After the merger, the new Penn Central Railroad was in dire need of additional capital to finance it operations and improve its balance sheet. Looking everywhere for cash, company officials came up with a plan to sell shares of the two amusement parks to a partnership. They would then enter into an agreement with the new partners to manage the parks. This plan raised capital for Penn Central, appeared to increase the Penn Central's book value, and allowed Great Southwest to maintain control of the parks.

As a result, in January of 1969, *Six Flags Over Georgia* was sold for $23 million to a limited partnership, referred to as *Six Flags Over Georgia, LTD.* A Great Southwest subsidiary became the general partner of the new limited partnership. The general partner is the partner that manages a limited partnership; the limited partners own investment interests only.

In a similar transaction finalized in June of 1969, Great Southwest Corp. sold *Six Flags Over Texas* to a second limited partnership, then named *Six Flags Over Texas Fund, LTD.* Great Southwest Corp. was paid $40 million for the park. The corporation received $1.5 million down, as well as a note for $38.5 million.

It is doubtful that these transactions were of any actual benefit to either Great Southwest Corp. or the individual parks. They were, rather, solely an attempt by Penn Central to obtain operating cash for the ailing railroad through its non-railroad businesses. In addition, the transactions were used to improve the railroad balance sheets through creative bookkeeping.

As general partner of both limited partnerships, Great Southwest retained operational control of the parks. Under the agreement, Great Southwest also received both management fees and a percentage of the parks' profits. The lack of ownership of the parks, however, was a legal entanglement that has affected the parks' value, and complicated the parks' management, ever since the partnerships were formed.

On June 21, 1970, a year after the sale of *Six Flags Over Texas* to the limited partnership, the Penn Central Transportation Company unexpectedly filed bankruptcy. The bankruptcy of the $6.85 billion business was at that time the largest bankruptcy ever filed in the United States. The fact that the country's sixth largest company, and the nation's largest railroad, was having financial difficulty had been obscured for years in its financial statements and public records. The sale of the Six Flags parks was just one of the many financial transactions its officers had manipulated in order to artificially improve the appearance of the company books.

The unexpected bankruptcy, combined with the less than candid book-keeping by railroad officials, led to a complete loss of faith in the top officers and directors of the Penn Central. Creditors and trustees of the bankrupt railroad insisted on new management. The Penn Central creditors wanted a clean sweep of the company's key management personnel. This was achieved by replacing the officers of the Penn Central.

Due in part to the drain of operating funds from the parks by the railroad, Great Southwest was in critical need of cash to complete and open *Six Flags Over Mid-America*, as well as to continue its day-to-day operations. The new Penn Central management arranged for an infusion of cash from several New York banks to help fund Great Southwest operations.

The banks, however, would not release the money without a complete change in the subsidiary's management. The banks' position was that anyone who was a part of the Penn Central management was considered suspect and must be replaced. Angus Wynne, through his business dealings with the Penn Central Railroad, was considered closely associated with the Penn Central's top officers and directors. The New York bankers wanted him replaced despite his experience and success in operating the warehouses, the land development company, and the amusement parks.

Accordingly, near the end of 1970, Angus Wynne, the founder of Six Flags, resigned as President of Great Southwest Corp. With Wynne's resignation, Penn Central took over management control of the corporation, installing its own officers and directors. From that point on, Wynne had no further involvement in the park and is said to have never again entered the property. For the first time since the park opened in 1961, Angus Wynne was no longer the man behind the scenes.

Victor Palmieri was installed by the Penn Central bankruptcy trustees as President and CEO of Great Southwest Corp. Bruce C. Juell was installed as the company's executive vice-president. By 1972, Juell replaced Palmieri as President.

6.

SEVEN SEAS
1972 - 1976

The bankruptcy of the Penn Central affected more than just Six Flags in Arlington. The bankruptcy also directly affected the City of Arlington's plans for a sea-life park. On May 12, 1970, the voters of Arlington overwhelming approved a ten million dollar bond package. As with other major developments in Arlington, Mayor Tom Vandergriff was a major force behind the proposal. Seven million dollars of the package was to fund *Seven Seas*, a new marine themed amusement park to open next door to Six Flags. The remainder of the funds were for enlargements to Turnpike Stadium, which city officials hoped would help attract a major league baseball team to the city.

Seven Seas was already several years in planning and fully designed when the bond package passed. It was designed by Mike Jenkins of Leisure and Recreation Concepts, Inc., an amusement park design firm organized in 1970. Jenkins had previously developed shows for *Six Flags Over Texas*.

The initial plan for the sea park called for 40 acres divided into seven sections, each representing a different aquatic area of the world's oceans. The park was planned to host seven major exhibits and twenty-six other attractions. Included were a pirate ship from which high divers dove into a pool; an Arctic sled ride; a 1,200-seat aquatic theater porpoise show; a 700,000-gallon killer whale tank and theater; and a large aquarium exhibit.

Rather than being a competitor to Six Flags, the new park was proposed and designed in cooperation with Angus Wynne and Great Southwest Corp. It was hoped that the new park would increase the total draw of tourists to the Arlington area. In this manner, the two parks would not compete, but rather would complement each other, as well as the other attractions in the area.

The original proposal called for Great Southwest Corp. to construct and operate the park. It was planned that Great Southwest Corp. would receive the income generated from the park and return to the city a fee for the use of the property. The expectations were that the receipts from the park

127

Seven Seas concept layout diagram.
Seven Seas postcard, circa 1971.

would be sufficient to reduced the debt on the seven million dollars worth of bonds as well as compensate Great Southwest for its participation.

The park was the first major non-coastal sea park in the country. By comparison, *Sea World of Texas*, the world's largest marine park, opened in San Antonio in 1988 on 250 acres of land at a cost of $170 million.

With Six Flags personnel participating, groundbreaking was held on July 8, 1970. Despite the recent bankruptcy of the Penn Central, Great Southwest Corp. was still the general contractor and was still planned to operate the park. In addition to groundbreaking, the city began a search for the various animals needed to operate the park.

In December of 1970, however, the Penn Central bankruptcy became an obstacle. Due to legal issues resulting from the unexpected Penn Central bankruptcy filing, the city council removed Great Southwest as the general contractor for the developing park. The city then took over as manager of the construction project. In addition, due to financial issues rising from the bankruptcy, Arlington and Great Southwest Corp. canceled the contract under which Great Southwest Corp. would lease and manage the park.

The new park was scheduled to open in June of 1971. So that guests could easily visit both parks, *Seven Seas* was planned to operate on the same schedule as Six Flags. The sole exception was the *Sea Cave*. The *Sea Cave* was a 200-seat seafood restaurant that would be open year-round. Daily capacity for the park was expected to reach 12,000 visitors. Total attendance of 675,000 was forecast for the first season, with $3 million in anticipated gross receipts.

On March 18, 1972, almost a year behind schedule, *Seven Seas* opened next to Six Flags. With a parade and a ribbon cutting, the park was up and running. With the city as the general contractor, the $7 million construction cost rose to $9 million. In addition, with no professional management company, the city was forced to undertake the day-to-day management of the park.

Initially, tickets were $3.75 for adults and $2.75 for children. By comparison, Six Flags tickets at the time were $5.74 and $4.75. When fully established, *Seven Seas* hoped to draw 850,000 visitors a year, more than a third of Six Flags attendance at the time. Actual attendance for the first year was under 500,000 visitors. Moreover, this would be the attendance high for all of the park's seasons.

While Six Flags had an all time high attendance year in 1973, attendance did not improve at *Seven Seas*. Yearly attendance fell to 422,464. This was less than the actual attendance of 470,811 for the year before and well below the target of 850,000.

Before the start of the 1974 season, Six Flags, Inc. was hired by the city to take over the management of the park. At the time, Six Flags, Inc. was under the control of the Penn Central Railroad bankruptcy trustee. Instead of the original plan which would have Six Flags taking all of the proceeds and paying Arlington a percentage, under the new agreement, Six Flags would be paid a management fee for managing the park.

The main difference in the two plans was loss allocation in the event that a season was not profitable. Under the original agreement, Six Flags would lease the park and would be liable for payments to the city, regardless of the profitability of the park. The risk of not making a profit during the season would fall on Six Flags. Under the 1974 agreement, however, Six Flags managed the park and received a fee for its efforts, regardless of the profitability of the park. The responsibility for a loss fell on the City of Arlington.

Seven Seas opened for its third season on May 3, 1974. Tickets were $3.75 for adults and $2.75 for children. With Six Flags, Inc. acting as manager, the sea park added live concerts by recognized performers to its attractions. These efforts proved insufficient to increase interest in the park and attendance dropped to less than 400,000.

By the end of the 1974 season, it appeared that the park could cover its costs of operation, but it would not be profitable enough to also reduce the bond debt. The city looked for another arrangement and attempted to rent the land to Six Flags, or any other company, to use as some type of tourist attraction.

In January 1975, Six Flags, Inc. announced that after thorough study, it had no interest in leasing the land used by *Seven Seas* for any other type of tourist attraction. Six Flags calculated that it would take four more years before the park was profitable.

For the 1975 season, ABC-Leisure Marine, Inc. contracted to manage the park. Leading the effort was George Millay, founder of both *Sea World* and *Wet 'n Wild*. Ironically, Vandergriff had originally attempted to interest Millay in managing the park before it was built. At that time, Millay was not interested in the park.

Millay's group refurbished and promoted the park. Attendance, however, did not improve, staying under 400,000. Part of Millay's agreement with the city was that his group would own the animals. At the end of the 1975 season, ABC-Leisure Marine ended its participation in the park and sold off all of the park's animals.

The city continued it attempts to salvage the park. For the 1976 season, they rented the park to J&L Enterprises, which renamed the park "Hawaii Kai". J&L brought in new dolphins and sea lions, as well as human performers. Despite the new spin, attendance barely broke 200,000, almost half that of the year before. J&L went bankrupt, ending its participation in the park.

Despite the city's efforts to make some type of attraction out of the park, it never opened again. Eventually all remains of the park were put to other uses. In the end, the park lost at least $8.5 million dollars. The City of Arlington taxpayers were left liable for repayment of the bonds.

The current Arlington Convention Center sits very near to where the park once stood.

7.

PENN CENTRAL MANAGEMENT
1971 – 1981

1971

A major milestone, the park's tenth anniversary season, was marked by the park's first change in management. Due to repercussions from the Penn Central bankruptcy, for the first time in the history of Six Flags, Angus Wynne was not involved with the park.

The season opened on April 3, 1971. Honorary guests for opening day of the tenth anniversary season were the three reigning beauty queens from each of the three states with a Six Flags park. These included Miss Texas, Bellinda Myrick, as well as Miss Georgia, and Miss Missouri. As in 1970, HR Pufnstuf, the park's defacto mascot, was also present to entertain the crowds.

During the year, Robert Freeman replaced Charles E. Pafford as the Vice President and General Manager of the park. Freeman served as the head of the park for the next four seasons.

Tickets were $5.75 for adults and $4.00 for children under 12. Children under three were free. The park's tagline was "Where in the World but Six Flags!"

The Big Bend. The new season did mark a major new attraction. Continuing the quest for unique new rides and attractions, in 1971 Six Flags introduced the *Big Bend Roller Coaster*. The name "Big Bend" was a clever play on words. It evoked the many "bends" felt by the riders on the curving, "bending", track. It also reflected a Texas theme, paying tribute to Texas' rugged Big Bend National Park, with its diverse rivers, mountains and deserts.

A Big Bend train starts to descend the first spiral lift hill as a second train enters the station area.
Photograph by Author, 1976.

Five years after the introduction of the *Runaway Mine Train*, Six Flags purchased the *Big Bend* from Schwarzkopf Industries Company of Germany at a cost of over $600,000. Schwarzkopf began manufacturing roller coasters in 1964. Beginning in 1974, Schwarzkopf was represented in the United States by the Intamin Company.

The coaster was not delivered for opening day and did not open to the public until June 20, 1971. The addition of the *Big Bend* brought the park's active roller coaster count to three. At the time, Six Flags claimed that the 52 mph train was the "fastest operating entertainment ride in the United States".

The *Big Bend* had many features that made it unique, even by today's standards. The roller coaster was what Schwarzkopf denoted as a "speed-racer" style coaster. Rather than the prevalent side-by-side seating, in which riders sit next to each other, the *Big Bend* cars had toboggan style bench seats. Riders straddled the seat, sitting in front and back of each other. With two car trains, each train could carry 12 riders. The trains were originally run with three train cars. The ride was designed for a capacity of 2,000 riders an hour.

The seats had side railings, calculated to negate any need for seat belts or other restraints. Although the ride could be safely ridden safely without restraints, they were added in 1974.

The ride was also different in that, unlike most roller coasters, it did not have any type of independent lift mechanism that pulled or lifted the units to the top of the lift hills. Instead, the *Big Bend* cars had motors in the train units themselves that "drove" the units to the top of the lift hills. The motors were activated by a third rail, situated in between the two track rails, much like an electric train.

Once over the top of the lift, the third rail ended and the trains were left to roll around the track at speeds of up to 52 mph. The track had banked curves of up to 78 degrees. The total ride lasted one minute and thirty-eight seconds.

The unique lift arrangements allowed the coaster to have spiraling style lift hills, rather than the straight up hills normally associated with roller coasters. These were both visually interesting and suspense building.

In keeping with its futuristic nature, the Big Bend was built in the Modern USA section. The dock and queue line were located along the same platform that had previously served the *Jet Set*, which was removed the previous season.

The ride had two spiraling lift hills. The first was eighty-one feet tall, significantly higher than the more established *Runaway Mine Train*. The second was fifty-one feet tall, also taller than the *Runaway Mine Train's* highest lift. The total track length was 2,876 feet, slightly longer than the *Mine Train*.

The ride was an immediate success and become extremely popular. The ride, however, was not without problems. The engines contained in the coaster cars were heavy, increasing the stress operating the ride exerted on the track and superstructure. In addition, the engines, like any other engine, required servicing, as did the electric supply to the third rail. As a result, the ride required more maintenance than was necessary with other roller coasters.

With the installation of the coaster, the refreshment stand to the south of the ride was renamed the "Big Bend Snack Shop".

Big Bend train units.
Six Flags' public relations photograph, 1972.

With the introduction in 1978 of the double loop *Shockwave*, the popularity of the *Big Bend* dropped somewhat. The ride was removed at the end of the 1978 season for various reasons.

Similar speed racers operated under the names of *Willard's Whizzer* (later "The Whizzer") at both of the *Marriott Great America Parks* and the *Zambezi Zinger* at *Worlds of Fun*.

Southern Palace.   At the *Southern Palace*, an elaborate production, *Sing Out! America* was presented. According to a *Dallas Morning News* review of the show, this was the park's "most ambitious [show] yet". During each show, the cast of sixteen dancers and singers wore 150 costumes. The show was enhanced with rear-projection slide-projectors showing related images. The show was produced by David Blackburn.

Texas Arena.   A new country western show, the "Six Flags Shindig" was presented at the *Texas Arena* as part of the changing entertainment offered at the outdoor theater. As part of the entertainment, guests could square dance with the performers during the show. This show replaced the *Los Voladores Indians* who performed in the arena for 1970.

The *Cattlemen's Exhibit*, located in the former bank building, was converted into the *Kachina Carving Exhibit*.

The 1971 season was the last in which an *El Chico* restaurant was located in the restaurant in Mexico. Beginning with 1972, the restaurant was simply referred to as the *Mexican Food Restaurant*.

In the puppet theater, Sid and Marty Krofft featured HR Pufnstuf in their newest production. In addition, their Saturday morning television show, *Lidsville*, featured scenes shot at *Six Flags Over Texas*.

Another Saturday morning show, Hanna Barbara's *Banana Splits*, also frequently featured clips filmed at the *Six Flags* parks. Although not a Krofft production, the costumes worn by the characters in the show were designed by the Kroffts.

Concerts.   The regular use of big name entertainers for concert appearances began at the park in 1971. The concerts were held in the *Texas Arena*, which was renamed as the "Texas Pavilion". In June of the year, *Three Dog Night* performed. In November, the park hosted, among others, *Tony Orlando and Dawn, Bread, Helen Reddy*, and *Paul Revere and the Raiders*. The park has provided a steady stream of popular concerts ever since.

Attendance for the season was estimated at just below two million guests.

In 1958, C.V. Wood predicted an imminent boom in the construction of amusement parks around the country. Instead, only a handful of parks opened between Disneyland's debut in 1955 and 1971. The start of the long predicted upsurge in amusement park construction was marked by the introduction of four modern theme parks in 1971. This started a surge in new amusement parks that would continue throughout the 70's.

Six Flags Over Mid-America.   Ten years after *Six Flags Over Texas* opened, *Six Flags Over-Mid America*, the third and final major theme park built as a Six Flags park, opened. Many other parks have acquired the "Six Flags" name, but they were opened under some other name and renamed as a Six Flags park after being purchased by the Six Flags parks system. *Six Flags Over Texas*, *Six Flags Over Georgia*, and *Six Flags Over Mid-America* remain as the only three major themed amusement parks constructed under the Six Flags name. (*Six Flags Autoworld* and *Power Plant* were exceptions, but they were small, short lived indoor parks.)

Now known as *Six Flags St. Louis*, the *Mid-America* park was built in what is now Eureka, Missouri, near St. Louis. The name "Mid-America" referred to the area around St. Louis and included both Illinois and Missouri. This larger area was selected as the theme of the park due to the fact that Missouri did not have its own six flags of sovereignty. The six themed areas were England, Spain, France, the states of Illinois and Missouri, and the USA.

The park was built at a cost of $50 million dollars, five times the original cost of *Six Flags Over Texas*. It included many of the rides which were favorites at *Six Flags Over Texas* and *Georgia*. These included versions of the flume ride, *Astrolift*, mine train, miniature cars, railroad, cave ride, riverboats, and a large theater. It also had some unique rides.

General Manager of the new park was Larry Cochran. Cochran began his amusement park career as a ride operator at the *Astrolift* when *Six Flags Over Texas* opened in 1961. Cochran was previously General Manager of *Six Flags Over Georgia*. He became president of the entire Six Flags chain of parks in 1987.

There were now three parks in the Six Flags amusement park chain. The company adopted the name of Six Flags, Inc. as the name of the

Aerial view of Texas section. Texas Astrolift Station shown in center. Train and railroad station to right. Chaparral Ride in lower right corner. Photograph by Author, 1976.

135

operating company that managed the parks. *Six Flags Over Mid-America* was not yet operational when the other two Six Flags parks were sold to limited partnerships. It has always been owned outright by the Six Flags chain.

As with *Six Flags Over Texas* and *Georgia*, Randall Duell was the park designer.

Three New Parks.   In addition to opening of *Six Flags Over Mid-America*, three non-Six Flags parks also opened in 1971. *Magic Mountain*, another Randall Duell designed park, opened in Valencia, California. This park was built with a budget of $20 million dollars, less than half of the budget for *Six Flags Over Mid-America*. *Magic Mountain* became part of the Six Flags chain of amusement parks in 1979.

Hersheypark, in Hershey, Pennsylvania, which had operated as a traditional amusement park for 67 years, reopened as a modern theme park in 1971. Randall Duell also created the design for the new park. The biggest amusement park event for 1971 was the opening of *Walt Disney World* in Orlando, Florida. The *Magic Kingdom*, a park very similar to *Disneyland*, was opened as the key attraction.

1972

The 1972 season's opening date was the earliest opening to date, March 25, 1972. This was the first season in which the park opened before April. The opening was scheduled for the first weekend after *Seven Seas'* grand opening weekend. *Six Flags* formally opened with special guests of honor Bobby Sherman (singer and actor) and Lassie (dog actor).

The preceding season, tickets prices were bumped up 75¢ for adult, bringing them to $5.75. In 1972, children's tickets followed, increasing from $4.00 to $4.75 for children under 12. Children under three remained free.

Following the installation of the *Big Bend* roller coaster, 1972 was a year of little change for the Texas park. The season did not see the addition of any major attraction.

The only new ride added during the year was the *"Rugged Buggy"*, the park's first "off the shelf" children's ride. It was introduced in the *Petting Zoo* area. The ride was a small turntable style ride with six cars modeled to resemble off-the-road vehicles. Each buggy held four to six small children. The ride later became part of the set of small rides that comprised *Looney Tunes Land*.

Will Rogers Show.   While a major ride was not added, a new show opened during July. The *Will Rogers Show* was built behind the puppet show. Similar to Disney's talking *Mr. Lincoln*, the *Will Rogers Show* pushed animations and robotics to the technical limit in an attempt to recreate a comedy show performed by a life sized robotic Will Rogers.

*Rugged Buggy introduced in 1972. Six Flags Over Texas first "off the shelf" children's ride.
Photograph by Author, 1998.*

Will Rogers was a highly popular cowboy comedian in the 1920s and '30s. He was known for telling jokes while performing rope tricks. He is famous for the line "I never meet a man I didn't like". Rogers passed away in a plane crash in 1935.

The Will Rogers figure used sixty precision air cylinders to create 360 different types of movements. The figure's lips were synchronized to the show's sound track.

The short-lived show was replaced for the 1975 season by the *Fun Guns of Dry Gulch*. In 1976, the building used for the shows became a queue-house for the *Texas Chute-Out*.

Having no new ride for the season, Six Flags continued to promote the *Big Bend* as the "fastest ride in the United States".

The *Southern Palace* musical was *Gotta Sing! Gotta Dance!*. It was noted in local reviews that the show had more of a plot than the other park revues of recent years. *Follies* was presented at the Krofft Puppet Theater.

The *Hash House* in the Boomtown section was renamed as *Dry Hole Charlies*. A dry hole is an oil term for a well that does not produce oil. The phrase "Steak on a Stake" was added in 1974. The other refreshment stand in *Boomtown* became *Mustard's Last Stand*.

The park's first electronic shooting gallery was added in the boomtown section, across from the *Caddo Canoes*. The weapons in the electronic shooting galleries fired a light beam that triggered animated targets. The gallery was named *Roughneck Range* in 1979.

Some changes were made at the entrance mall, with the addition of a large ball fountain in the center of the plaza where the star landscaping had once been. At night, lights changed the color of the fountain's water. The fountain cost $25,000.

New Frontgate design with Fountain Ball in center of mall.
Dancing waters and flags to the back.
Photograph by Author, 1985.

The last exhibit in the exhibit halls, the *Texas Electric* exhibit, was closed after the 1972 season.

Despite the lack of a new major attraction, 1972 was a record attendance year, breaking the two million mark with 2,062,000. This was the second season to pass two million visitors. The first was 1967. In addition, May 13, 1972, set a new all time daily attendance record of over 36,670 guests. This surpassed the previous all time high of 34,481 set on May 16, 1970.

May Saturdays are traditionally high attendance dates due to the numerous school end-of-year field trips. Attendance is also increased due to the several band and music contests held in connection with the park. The band contests started in 1964 and are now attended by thousands of band, orchestra, and choir students from around the country.

In January of 1972, Flagship Hotels, a subsidiary of American Airlines, purchased the *Inn of Six Flags*, as well as the golf course. Flagship Hotels had managed the hotel since 1965.

Approximately three miles from Six Flags, *Lion Country Safari*, a drive through wildlife preserve, opened on 485 acres in Grand Prairie. The new park was part of the area's growing entertainment district.

Nationally, two more Duell designed theme parks opened. One, *Kings Island*, opened near Cincinnati, Ohio. The other, *Opryland USA*, opened at Nashville, Tennessee. The park was themed on country music and featured several country music shows. *Opryland* closed in October of 1997.

1973

Six Flags Over Texas opened even earlier than 1972, moving from the last Saturday in March to March 17, 1973. HR Pufnstuf was again on hand at the front gate for the opening ceremony. Ticket prices increased slightly to $5.95 for adults and $4.95 for children. Seasons passes were offered, allowing access to the park for the entire season. Six Flag's tagline was the "Entertainment Capital of Texas".

Good Time Square. In contrast to the lack of expansion in 1972, the 1973 season saw significant additions. For the first time since 1963, the park management debuted an entirely new section. The new section, which opened on March 31, was named "Good Time Square". The new five-acre section, located east of Boomtown, cost $1.5 million to construct. Somewhat ironically, *Good Time Square* was a themed version of a traditional carnival or fair midway. Technically, the new section was another subcomponent of the USA section.

There was some inconsistency regarding the exact name of the section. The 1973 map listed the new train station as the "Goodtime Square Depot". The next year, however, park materials, including the large sign located in the section, carried the name "Good Time" for the depot, theater and shirt shop. Over the years, maps and other materials have used the names "Good Time Square", "Good *Times* Square" and "*Goodtimes* Square".

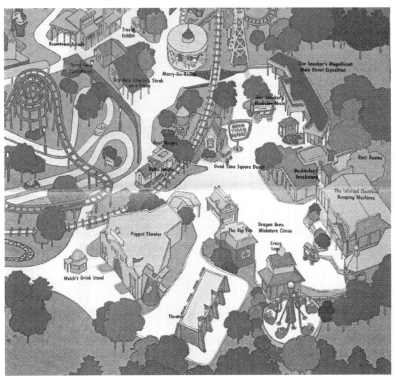

Good Time Square from 1974 souvenir map.

Above and Below - Good Time Square games.
Photographs by Author, 1998.

The section included *Doc Snooker's Magnificent Main Street Exposition* games area, which consisted of carnival games; the *Infernal Electrical Bumping Machines,* a bumper car ride; a miniature circus exhibit; and the *Crazy Legs* monster ride.

The sixteen carnival style games that originally composed the *Doc Snooker's Magnificent Main Street Exposition* were a first for Six Flags. The games provided the park a midway section, with game barkers and large prizes to attract the unwary. They tested such skills as tossing a ring on to a glass soft-drink bottle; filling balloons by hitting a target with a water gun; and tossing a basketball through a hoop.

Angus Wynne never allowed carnival games in the park due to his feelings that they distracted from the themes of the park and created more of a carnival atmosphere.

Good Time Square Rides.   The section was home to two new rides and a new *Good Time Square Railroad Station*. The railroad station replaced the *Boomtown Railroad Station* and was located directly across the tracks from the *Boomtown* station's former location.

The railroad engines were also turned around for the first time. They now left the Texas station heading south towards the Mexican section, whereas for the first twelve years of operation they left the station heading north. They have since been turned again and now leave Texas facing north as they did originally.

New to the park was the *Infernal Electric Bumping Machines*, a traditional bumper car ride. The fifty cars were powered by electricity running through the roof of the building and reaching the cars through a rod on the back of each vehicle.

The other new ride was the *Crazy Legs* ride, a standard "monster" or "octopus" style ride. Its six arms each held four pods, which in turn held two riders each, for a total of forty-eight riders. The ride operated in the park for ten years. It was removed from the park in 1982, when it was replaced by the *Texas Tornado*. The name "Crazy Legs" was also used on a different ride added in 2006.

Bumper Cars (1973-2007) in the new Good Time Square section.
Photograph by Author, 1998.

Good Times Square Games at top, Carousel, lower left, Railroad train, mid-right.
Photograph by Author, 1976.

The *Dragon Brothers Circus* was a miniature circus located in a small building next to the *Crazy Legs* ride. The scale model depicted a three-ring circus, with acts, crowds, animals, and sideshows. It contained 4,000 miniature people, along with 2,000 miniature animals. The model represented more than 10,000 hours of construction by PK Schmitter. The exhibit was removed at the end of the 1976 season. The building in which it was housed was then converted into a souvenir shop.

There was also a small bandstand for musical performances. To complete the section, a restaurant, *Doubleday's Triple Play*, was added.

The Passing Parade was featured at the Southern Palace with a sixteen member cast and a fourteen piece orchestra.

In the Modern section, a computer horoscope stand and a jewelry shop were added in the former corporate exhibit building. The *Big Bend Snack Shop* refreshment stand to the south of the ride was renamed to the *Prospect Point Snack Shop*. The Modern refreshment stand was named the *Pit Stop*, a name it had until it was renamed *Mother Morton's Snack Stand* in 1977.

In the Confederate section, *Abigail's Gift Shop* became *Sherman's Flame*, a candle store. The *Emporium* became *Miss Abigail's Emporium*.

In Texas, the *Depot Café* became the *Iron Horse Snackshop*. The former bank building, which held the *Kachina Carving Exhibit* since 1971, became *Sneaky Water's Antiques*.

La Terraza Snack Stand (the Terrace) in the Mexican section was renamed as the *La Cantina Snack Stand* (the Canteen).

GT (Happy Motoring) cars (1961-1986). In order to keep a current look, the 1961 vehicles were updated to these sleeker and more modern looking vehicles in 1973. Photograph by Author, 1985.

On May 19, 1973, a new daily attendance record was set with 40,742 guests for a single day. A new seasonal attendance record was also set. A record 2,267,000 guests visited the park during 1973. This was over 205,000 more than the previous season. The previous high attendance season was 1967. The year was also the highest revenue year since the park opened.

At the end of the season, the cannon shooting range was removed. The space on which it was located was used to construct the *Skeeball Palace* in 1974.

The park held a Halloween event, with seasonal shows at the *Chevy Show Theater* and the *Southern Palace*. There were also costumed monsters throughout the park and a monster parade.

Continuing the growth in the amusement park business, two more Randall Duell designed parks opened during the year. One, *Worlds of Fun* amusement park, opened in Clay County, Missouri, at a cost of $10 million. The 235-acre park was built by Lamar Hunt. The second, *Carowinds*, opened on the border of North and South Carolina. *Carowinds*, a 398-acre park, was built at a cost of $70 million. Both parks are now part of the Cedar Fair Entertainment Company park system.

Circus World, a circus themed park, opened in Florida. The park closed in 1986.

1974

Grand opening for the 1974 season was held in the *Southern Palace* on March 16, although the season's actual first day of operation was Friday, the 15th. The weather was chilly, reaching down into the low 50s. Bob Freeman, the park's general manager, dedicated the season to the park's young host and hostess. The opening was followed by a performance of the new *Southern Palace* musical *Great to Be Here*.

Tickets for the season were $6.50 for adults and $5.50 for children under 12. Children under three were free.

Gasoline shortages were a major concern throughout the booming amusement park industry as the 1974 season began. The shortages kept many guests from driving to parks from distant locations. On the other hand, the shortages made Six Flags an attractive alternative to local residents who may have otherwise taken vacations at more remote locations.

The Music Mill. Seeing the success of outside performers in augmenting the park's other attractions, for the 1974 season, Six Flags built a larger amphitheater, the *Music Mill Amphitheater.*

The *Music Mill* is located outside the train tracks in the northwest corner of the park. Originally built to seat 4,500 concert-goers, the theater was specifically designed to host popular singers and performers.

The *Texas Pavilion (Texas Arena)* was still open in 1974, providing the park two outdoor venues for the season. The design of the *Texas Pavilion* with its stadium seating, and large arena area, was suited for big production events, such as the rodeo and circus attractions of seasons past. The *Music Mill*, with its performance stage, was designed more for musical concerts and similar performances. The *Texas Pavilion* closed after the 1974 season.

Part of Figure 4 in Patent #3,899,848 (1975).

During the early '70's, closed circuit TV's were installed in the queue houses of several of the major rides. The TV's featured the antics of the aniform "Archie". Aniforms are a form of "live animation" using line puppets controlled by sticks invisible to the viewer. Similar to the talking bird that occupied the hotel in the Texas section, Archie's operator used a two way closed circuit TV system and hidden microphones to interact with guests waiting in line in the queue-houses. Shown is a Diagram for an Aniform similar in appearance to the Aniform that appeared at Six Flags.

Above: Concert at Music Mill Theater after expansion. Six Flags' public relations photo, circa 1986.
Below: Music Mill theater after 1986 expansion. Photograph by Author, 2002.

Also new was the *Skeeball Palace*, which opened near the base of the *Tower*. Skeeball is a game in which players attempt to roll balls down an alley and into target holes. It was invented in 1909. In 1977, the rights to the game were acquired by the Philadelphia Toboggan Company. The *Skeeball Palace* featured multiple lanes, as well as a prize center.

In the Modern section, a giant poster studio replaced the computer horoscope store. The candy store became *Crazy Confections*. A cotton candy stand was added across from the *Pit Stop*.

Souvenir Shop located in the Texas section next to Casa Magnetica and the Flume Ride. Built when the park opened, the building was originally the Six Flags Post Office. In 1974 it became the Hanging Tree. The store has since had several different names and sold various types of product. Photograph by Author, 2008.

The souvenir store in Boomtown was named *Gusher Gertie's Souvenirs*. This was modified to *Gusher Gertie's Leather Crafts* in 1976 and *Justin Leather Crafts* in 1977.

The *Texas Bank & Trust Company* building, which had held several exhibits since 1965, was converted to a restaurant, the *Sandwich Emporium*.

In Texas, the *Post Office* and *Country Store* both became the *Hanging Tree* gift store. The *Western Shop* became *Peco's Belle's Tumbleweed Tokens*.

The *I.C. Fizz Soda Fountain Specialties* replaced the meat market. *I.C. Fizz* became *Rose's Cantina* in 1980. The cantina has also been known as *Rose's Cantina* and *Rose's Cantina Nachos*.

At the end of the season, the *Flying Jenny*, was removed from the park. The small mule drawn carousel had been in the park since opening day, first appearing in the Confederate section as the *Lil' Belle Carousel*.

Attendance was again over the two million mark for the season, but was still down slightly from the previous season. Guest visits for the year were reported at 2,204,571. This was only the second season to that date in which attendance did not exceed the year before, with 1968 being the first.

Another new theme park, *Great Adventure* of Jackson, New Jersey, opened on July 1, 1974. Six Flags, Inc. purchased the park three years later.

Skeeball Palace (1974-1991) games building in Tower area.
Photograph by Author, 1986.

1975

Grand opening date for the 1975 season was March 15, with a
preview opening on March 8 and 9th. Tickets went to $7.00 for
adults and $6.00 for children under 12, with children under three free. Parking
was still 50¢ a car.

Daniel P. (Dan) Howells was the park's new Vice-President and
General Manager, a position that he held for the next three seasons. Howells
started with Six Flags in 1972. After he left *Six Flags Over Texas*, he became
the General Manager of *Six Flags Magic Mountain*. He went on to become
President and CEO of Six Flags Corporation from 1982 to 1985.

Cyrus Cosmos.   During its course of development, Six Flags had
never created a mascot character with a strong identity to the park. There
had been some characters developed from time to time, but none was used
in any major way to promote the park. One previous character, *Fun Man*, was
depicted with a hooded mask and cape. *Fun Man* was featured on some souvenirs, but was not part of any major PR promotions. For a time, HR Pufnstuf
served as the park's most famous costume character, but no major advertising
campaigns were built around him.

For 1975, Six Flags developed a new mascot, *Professor Cyrus Cosmos*. A
rather tall, brown haired man dressed in white and blue, Professor Cosmos
was promoted as "part time inventor, part time illusionist, and full time
showman". The park promoted the opening of new rides introduced in the
next few seasons as his "inventions". Cyrus Cosmos was promoted in TV and
print ads along with Six Flags current slogan "*Six flags - It's what you wish the
world would be*". (There were several variations of the slogan including "what
you wish the world *can* be" and "what you wish the world *could* be".)

147

One of the Professor's contributions in 1975 was the *"Cyrus Cosmos Incredible Electric Light Brigade Parade"*, a light parade featured ever night just prior to the park's closing. Other characters included Captain Dynamo, King Electro, Father Light, and the Electrophant. Cyrus Cosmos also performed the *Cyrus Cosmos Wonder Show, a* magic show at the *Music Mill* during the 1975, 1976, and 1977 seasons.

Rotoriculous.   One of the first new theme rides promoted as a Cyrus Cosmos invention was the *Rotoriculous*. The *Rotoriculous* was built at the back of Good Time Square between the *Bumper Cars* and the *Crazy Legs* ride. The ride opened on May 10, 1975. The *Rotoriculous* was designed by the Six Flags staff from a typical *Himalaya* or *Musik Express* style ride. The ride is a turntable type ride with a chain of seats strung together to form a circle around the edge of the ride.

Rotoriculous (1975-1988) building after being renamed the Rotodisco.
Photograph by Author, 1986.

The thirteen speed *Rotoriculous* differed from other *Himalaya* style rides, however, in that it operated completely indoors. It was housed in a small building with just enough room for the ride and control station. In addition to the ride, the room was equipped with special audio and visual effects, including an icon of the seventies, a large disco mirror ball.

As the ride started, the cars slowly moved in a circle around the track. As the ride slowly started forward, a recorded narration began, telling the story of the invention (the ride) and its intended purpose.

Within a few moments, however, the narrator announced that something had gone wrong, at which time the ride began to rotate backwards, slowly at first, then at much greater speed. Simultaneously with the ride changing directions, the sounds became more chaotic and random, while slides and lights were flashed on the walls around the ride. As the riders traveled in a circle, they were overwhelmed with a seemingly random display of lights, images, and sounds. Eventually the problem was solved, things were

148

brought back to "normal", the ride slowed down and the bizarre lights and sounds terminated.

As the years past, the slides and lights where used without the opening narration. In 1979, the ride was renamed the Roto-disco and the disco ball became the centerpiece effect. The ride was removed at the end of the 1988 season in order to make room for the *Flashback* roller coaster.

Red Baron Flying ride located in the Modern section. Originally the C. Cosmos Flying Machines, later Bugs Bunny's Spirit of St. Louie. Photograph by Author, 1998.

C. Cosmo Flying Machine Co.   Also new for the year was the *C. Cosmo Flying Machine Co.*, the park's second small children's ride. The ride features small biplanes in which younger guests travel around in a circle. Riders could cause their individual planes to travel up and down by pulling and pushing the flight stick at their seat. In keeping with the idea that Cyrus Cosmos designed the ride, the ride was originally named for him. A small statute of Cyrus Cosmos in flight gear stood in the center of the ride.

The ride was originally placed near the entrance to the *Speelunker's* cave, at the former site of the *Flying Jenny*. In 1976, as Cyrus Cosmos was slowly phased out, the planes were painted red and the name was changed to the *Red Baron*. In 1983, the ride was moved to the Modern section and became a part of the children's attractions assembled for *Pac-Man Land*. In 1985, the name was changed to the *Tasmanian Devil Flying Aces*. The ride was renamed again in 2001 and is currently known as *Bugs Bunny's Spirit of St. Louie*.

Fun Guns of Dry Gulch.   In the small theater at Good Times Square, the short-lived *Will Rogers* show was replaced by the also short-lived *Fun Guns of Dry Gulch* show. This show was based on a series of prop guns that provided the basis for humorous tales and stories told by the attendant.

The *Fun Guns of Dry Gulch* was removed in 1976 and the building used for the theater was pressed into service as a queue house for the *Texas Chute-Out*.

Shows.   In perhaps one of the most unique performances in Six Flags' history, Bob Gordon and Curt Nevin performed an acrobatics show on thirty-foot sway poles mounted on top of the 300-foot *Six Flags Tower*. The two acrobats, who billed themselves as "America's Champion Daredevil Aerialists", did various routines, including hanging by their toes and standing on their hands. They did not use any safety nets or harnesses.

The performances, which could be viewed anywhere in the park with an unobstructed view of the top of the tower, were done four times a night from June to August 10. This routine is considered possibly the highest sway pole routine ever performed. The show was reminiscent of the *Los Voladores* who performed on 100-foot poles in the Texas Arena in 1970.

In the Southern Palace, the show *Jukebox Jubilee* was performed.

Yearly attendance was once again up over the year before with 2,277,006 guests. On May 17, 1975, thirteen-year-old Sheri Jones became the 25th million visitor to enter the park. By the end of the season, an estimated 26,788,000 guests had visited the park.

In contrast to the ongoing success of Six Flags, *Astroworld* in Houston operated for its first seven years with less than stellar attendance. The park was seeing only a million visitors a year and needed to increase revenues. During 1975, the Six Flags corporation entered into a twenty-year lease of the park. Before the 1976 season, Six Flags exercised an option in the lease to purchase the park, making it the first amusement park added to the Six Flags park chain that was not built as a Six Flags park.

Elsewhere, another Randall Duell park, *Kings Dominion* opened in Virginia. *Kings Dominion* is a sister park to *Kings Island* in Cincinnati, Ohio, which opened in 1972. Both parks are now part of the Cedar Fair Entertainment Company.

In June of 1975, *Old Chicago* opened in Chicago, Illinois. The complex was a combination shopping center and amusement park. Promoted as "The world's first indoor amusement park", the park shut down in 1980 after five less than successful seasons.

1976

America's bicentennial year was a year of major celebration through-out the country. It was a double celebration at Six Flags, in that it was also the year that Six Flags celebrated its 15th anniversary. The season opened on March 20, 1976, with just under 14,000 guests. This was nearly double the opening day attendance of the previous year. Preview weekend was March 13 and 14.

Tickets were $7.50 for all guests. Children under two, however, were still free. Season passes were $25.00.

New for the bicentennial year was the *Texas Chute-Out*, the world's first "modern" parachute drop ride.

The Texas Chute-Out. Opening on April 10, 1976, the ride was located to the east of the puppet show theater. The ride consisted of an eight-foot wide tube structure that was two hundred feet tall. Twelve arms, each forty feet in length, were mounted on the top of the structure. The ride was a total of 85 feet in diameter from the end of one arm to the end of its corresponding arm.

Cables on each arm pulled a small bench seat straight up 175 feet above the ground. The ride then stopped for a brief moment, long enough to give the riders a bird eye's view of the surrounding areas. The seats were then released, allowing the riders to free fall thirty-five feet towards the ground. At that point, the ride's braking mechanism engaged and the thirteen and a half foot diameter parachute deployed above the riders. The riders then "floated" down another one hundred and forty feet to the surface.

Each chute had three guide cables and four control cables. The ride was driven by twelve motors and winches located in the engine room at the top of the ride. These controlled the two and a half miles of steel cable used by the ride. Access to the motors was through a two-man elevator located

Left: Texas Chute-Out ride unit over roof of Majestic Theater.
Right: Texas Chute-Out (1976-2012).
Photographs by Author, 1998 and 1983.

inside the eight-foot tube structure. The tube also contained counterweights for each of the ride seats. The electronics room was in the base of the structure.

Each ride lasted twenty-eight seconds and was billed by the park as similar to jumping off of a three-story building. The design capacity for the ride was between 1,500 and 1,600 riders per hour. Depending on size, two or three guest could ride on a single seat.

Built by Intamin AG, in Berne, Switzerland, the $1.5 million ride was known as the "first modern" parachute ride due to the fact that it was based on earlier rides of a similar style, but with less sophisticated technology. The most famous of these earlier rides was the *Parachute Jump* built for the *1939 New York's World's Fair* and moved to Coney Island in 1941. This amusement park icon operated at *Steeplechase Park* at Coney Island until 1964.

Southern Palace cast honoring America's bicentennial with Celebrate!
Photograph by Author, 1976.

The ride weighed an estimated 368,868 pounds and required 3,040,000 pounds of concrete to construct on the site. It was estimated that the ride used 28 miles of electrical wiring.

A second parachute ride was open the same year as the *Great Gasp* at *Six Flags Over Georgia*. The *Great Gasp* closed and was demolished in 2005. A third, the *Sky Chuter*, opened at *Six Flags Over Mid-America* in 1978. It closed in 1982, a mere four years later.

The *Chute-Out*, along with the *Flashback*, closed in September of 2012 to make room for the *Texas SkyScreamer* to open for the 2013 season. The *Chute-Out* operated in the park for thirty-seven seasons. It served the park for more seasons than any other ride which has been removed from the park.

American Pie! Jamboree, billed as a "puppet show, people show, and picture show all rolled into one" was held at the *Good Times Square Theater. Celebrate!* was the new musical revue at the Southern Palace.

In the Texas section, the *Doggie Hotel* was converted to an apple-cider drink stand. The next season, the same stand was converted into a lemonade stand.

The bicentennial and fifteenth anniversary turned out to be a good year for *Six Flags* as the park nearly reached 2.5 million guests. The park had a seasonal attendance record of 2,429,532, up over 1975, which was also a record year. Total attendance since 1961 was 31,760,000.

By Six Flags' fifteenth anniversary, the theme park industry was firmly established. It was estimated that more than $1 billion was invested in theme parks since 1970. A survey by C.S. McKee & Co. indicated that 55 million guests visited 22 major theme parks during 1975. Theme parks were the third most attended tourist attractions, behind horse racing at number one and the national parks at number two. It was estimated that theme park attendance was nearly twice that of professional baseball, football and basketball combined.

The theme park boom continued as more new theme parks were built around the country. For the Bicentennial, the Marriott Corporation opened two sister theme parks, each named *Marriott Great America* park. One opened in Santa Clara, California, and the other in Gurnee, Illinois. Like the unsuccessful *Freedomland,* the Great American parks were themed on the history and development of the United States.

Each park cost $50 million to develop and construct. Both of these parks were designed by Randal Duell's firm, *R. Duell and Associates.* A third Marriott park was set to open in the Washington DC area. This park, however, was scrapped over concerns for historical properties near the proposed site.

Sid and Marty Krofft, having worked closely with the Six Flags chain of parks for years, decided to open their own park in 1976. Like *Old Chicago* that opened the year before, *The World of Sid and Marty Krofft* was located totally indoors. The $14 million park was housed on eight levels of the Omni International Center in Atlanta, Georgia.

Capacity was limited to 6,000 visitors. Due to the limited capacity, tickets were sold in advance. The key attraction was a giant pinball machine ride. Riders rode in vehicles designed to look like a giant pinball as it bounced its way around the pinball table.

The Kroffts planned that the small indoor amusement park would be the first of several built around the country. The indoor park suffered from operational problems, including difficulties efficiently moving guests around the eight levels. The park closed after only five months of operation and 330,000 visitors.

1977

March 19th, 1977, was opening day for the 1977 season, with a preview opening on March 12th and 13th. Ticket prices for the season went up 45¢ to $7.95 for both adults and children. Seasons passes were $29.95. Parking was up to 75¢.

The entrance mall and the pathway into the Mexican section were expanded by removing the covered canopied walkway into the Mexican section. A new gift shop, *Mercado De La Plaza*, the "Market Square" was added between the Mexican section and the Frontgate. A gazebo was added between the new store and the section's other major shop, *Casa de Regalos*, the "House of Gifts". *Mercardo* still operates at the same location.

The Spinnaker. New for the season was the *Spinnaker*, an Enterprise style ride built by Schwarzkotf and sold by Intamin. Located just south of the *Tower*, the ride was located on a spot that at one time was part of *Skull Island*. The name was another play on words, as it refers both to the spinning action of the ride and to a type of sail on a sailing ship. The sailing reference coincided with the pirate ships associated with *Skull Island*.

The ride was composed of twenty-one gondola units mounted on arms arranged in a circle around a base. Each could hold up to two guests. The ride sat parallel to the ground, with the gondolas suspended from the ride. The ride then started to spin, gradually increasing speed. As the ride spun at

Left: Spinnaker ride, (1977-1995). Six Flags' public relations photograph, circa 1977. Right: Shockwave train. Six Flags' public relations photograph.

a faster rate, the capsules rotated until they no longer hung down, but were forced straight out, parallel to the ground.

At that point, an arm on the side of the ride lifted the ride up to a 90-degree angle, so that the riders were now spinning around like a Ferris wheel. Unlike a Ferris wheel, however, when the gondolas reached the top of the circle, the riders were turned completely upside down.

The ride was very visually entertaining to spectators, especially at night when its many spinning lights created attractive patterns in the dark. The *Spinnaker* was removed at the end of the 1995 season.

Nearby, a pirate ship outdoor theater was added on *Skull Island*. *Captain LaFeet's Flagship Follies* was staged on the thirty-foot pirate ship. The small show featured various pirate related characters including singing cannon-balls.

In order to refresh the *Chute-out*, stand-up baskets replaced the bench seats on several of the units. With the baskets, riders could opt to ride the parachute ride standing up.

In the Modern section, the poster shop was removed from the old exhibit hall building. The building now held the *Solar Circuit*, *Crazy Confections*, and *USA Hat Shop*.

The *Pit Stop* refreshment stand in the Modern section was renamed "Mother Morton's Snack Stand" in 1977. The name was returned to "Pit Stop" in 1981.

Aerial view of Mine Train and Good Times Square Area.
Carousel is shown under oil derrick. Photograph by Author, 1976.

Next door, Kodak dropped its sponsorship of *The Kodak Exhibit and Store*. The store was renamed as the "Camera Shop". The *Animal Fair* moved in with the camera shop. The *Animal Fair* became the "Toy Store" in 1974 and "Fuzzie Farm" in 1983.

After seventeen years in the park, the original *Missilechaser* was removed at the end of the 1977 season.

Six Flags saw another daily attendance record on July 3, 1977, when *KC and the Sunshine Band* performed at the *Music Mill*. A total of 45,596 guests visited the park in a single day. The season also broke a season record with the park hosting over 2,549,000 guests, breaking 2.5 million guests for the first time.

In 1977, Six Flags purchased *Great Adventure* of Jackson, New Jersey, bringing the number of amusement parks in the chain to five.

1978

For one of its earliest opening to date, the park opened on March 11, 1978. Ticket prices increased 55¢ to $8.50 for both adults and children.

By 1978, numerous theme parks were operating around the county. In order to attract as many guests as possible, each park competed to see which could provide the most thrilling and exhilarating roller coaster ride. It was estimated that nineteen new major roller coasters were built during 1978 in parks around the nation. An official with the Arrow Development Company called it the "year of the coaster".

One innovation that roller coaster designers sought was a design of a coaster that could safely turn riders upside down during the ride. Early roller coaster designers had attempted such inversions using vertical loops. The problem with their designs was that they utilized nearly perfectly round loops. These loops turned out to be too dangerous; resulting in up to 12 g's being exerted on the riders. These forces were not safe and presented an unacceptable ride.

Arrow Development, pioneer in the development of tubular steel roller coasters, developed a solution. Arrow discovered that they could avoid the high g's associated with vertical inversions by using a twisting corkscrew shaped track instead of a vertical loop. In 1975, they introduced their first corkscrew looping roller coaster at *Knott's Berry Farm* in California. The ride was simply named the "Corkscrew".

Shockwave. German manufacturer Schwarzkopf came up with a different solution to the inversion problem. Designer Anton Schwarzkopf discovered that the g-forces exerted on the rider were significantly reduced if the loops were not made round, but rather in a teardrop shape.

In 1976, Schwarzkopf installed the first modern vertical (non-corkscrew) looping roller coaster incorporating his teardrop loops. The coaster, *The Revolution*, was installed at *Magic Mountain*, California. The ride was featured in the 1977 movie *Rollercoaster*.

Deep into the roller coaster competition, *Six Flags'* management authorized Schwarzkopf to build a ride similar to the *Revolution* at *Six Flags Over Texas*. They would up the ante, however, by having not just one, but two loops.

The second loop would immediately follow the first. The ride was dubbed the "Shockwave" and was an immediate hit, so much so that queue lines had to be run out the queue house and throughout the area in front of the ride. At times, guests had to wait hours to ride the state of the art coaster.

The ride was billed as the "tallest, longest, fastest, double-looping roller coaster in the world". The ride was installed by Intamin, AG of Zurich, Switzerland and cost $2.5 million dollars to construct. Intamin was still acting at the time as the business representative for Schwarzkopf.

The ride was installed in clear view of the Dallas Fort Worth Turnpike on ten acres of previously unused land on the north side of the park. (The turnpike is now I-30). This placement caused traffic slowdowns, as passing drivers would slow to a near stop to watch the coasters speed through the double loops.

The ride features an initial 116-foot lift, followed by a 36-degree drop into the two seventy foot loops. The one minute, fifty-eight second ride travels through 3,500 feet of track. The trains travel at up to 60 mph, with banks up

Shockwave approaching top of lift.
Six Flags' public relations photograph, circa 1978.

Shockwave famous double vertical loops.
Photograph by Author, 2008.

to sixty degrees. Riders pull up to 5.9 g's. The three trains have seven cars each and can hold up to 28 riders. The ride capacity is 1,800 an hour. A computer controlling the ride resides in an airtight climate controlled room.

At the *Southern Palace*, the new show *Jazz Crazy!* was directed and choreographed by Cissy King, former Six Flags and Lawrence Welk Show performer. It featured the songs, dance, and costumes of the roaring '20s.

In the Confederate section, *Sherman's Flame*, a candle shop, was converted into a snack shop. The snack shop was later named the "Carmel Corn Snack Shop".

At the end of the 1978 season, the *Cyclorama of the American West* was removed from the back of the *Indian Trading Village* to make space for a small theater. The *People Mover Show* opened in the theater the next season. On *Skull Island*, the giant skull for which the island was named was removed from the park.

After running for a year along with the *Shockwave*, the *Big Bend* roller coaster was removed at the end of the season.

The year was a record attendance season for the park. With the opening of the *Shockwave*, the park had a record breaking 2.78 million guests visit the park during the season. This was the highest attendance year for the first twenty-six years of the park and was a record that would not be exceeded until the 1987 season.

The "American Coaster Enthusiasts" (ACE), a non-profit organization dedicated to roller coasters and roller coaster riding, was formed in 1978. Their first convention was held that year in *Busch Gardens* in Williamsburg, Virginia. For more information, visit www.aceonline.org.

1979

The park opened the season even earlier than in 1978, opening the first Saturday of March: March 3, 1979. Ticket prices increased 75¢ to $9.25. Dan Howells was still Vice-President and General Manager of the park on opening day. He was replaced, however, by Errol McKoy in June of the year. McKoy rose through the ranks, beginning his career as a ride operator when the park opened in 1961. He was General Manager of the park until November when he was again promoted.

Rather than one single new attraction, three attractions were added for 1979. These were a virtual reality theater, the *Sensational Sense Machine;* a magic show, the *People Mover Theater;* and a retheme of *Casa Magnetica* as *The Lost Temple of the Chisos.* General Manager Dan Howells noted that the emphasis for the season was on the family audience.

The idea of virtual reality theaters became very popular in the 1970's. Ride designers wanted to develop an attraction that blurred the distinction between a theater and a ride, allowing guests to experience a thrill experience, without leaving a theater.

Six Flags' first offering of this nature was the *Chevy Show.* With its curved screen and high-speed film, it created an artificial feeling of motion on the part of the viewers.

The next generation of such attractions was based on the concept of actually moving the viewers' seats. This was accomplished by designing either the seats, or the entire theater, to rock from side to side and front to back, in synchronization with scenes riders viewed on a movie screen.

Two versions of Six Flags bumper stickers, with older version on top. While guests visited the park, attendants placed Six Flags bumper stickers on all of the vehicles on the park's parking lot. Guests that did not want the free stickers on their cars were advised to leave their visors down. Six Flags ended this practice at the end of 1979, after distributing ten million bumper stickers.

Sensational Sense Machine. The *Sensational Sense Machine* was *Six Flags'* effort at a state of the art virtual reality ride. The *Sensational Sense Machine* was located in the Modern section, at the former site of the *Missilechaser* ride.

The ride was a small theater which held 50 guests. The room was built on a hydraulic platform that allowed the whole room to shift up and down and from side to side. Using computer controls, the room moved in sync with the action of a movie shown at the front of the room.

The first planned movie, created by Ed Hansen and Associates, consisted of an animated voyage into our solar system. A later movie consisted of scenes from other rides, many from the Texas park. So, the ride simulated the ride experience on other rides within the park.

The attraction was designed by Intamin, A.G., in cooperation with Six Flags.

The ride opened on April 7 and lasted through the 1984 season. In later seasons, just the movie was shown without the building moving. The area in which it was installed is now closed to guests.

People Mover Show. A new show, the *People Mover Show,* was opened in a 400-seat theater built behind the *Indian Trading Village.* The theater was built at the previous location of the *Cyclorama of the American West.* The show was a small one-man magic and light show. The message of the show was love and understanding. It was open for the 1979 and 1980 seasons.

Lost Temple of the Chisos. In addition to the show and virtual ride, *Casa Magnetica* was rethemed to become the *Lost Temple of the Chisos.* Like the original *Casa,* the attraction was walk through. The entrance, however, was moved near the Flume 2 exit, allowing for a longer entrance path. The *Casa* building was redecorated to resemble an ancient Mayan temple. Guests viewed animations and special effects based on this new theme.

Rather than a live tour guide such as *Casa Magnetica* used, the new attraction used a recorded spiel that commented on the various affects on display. The change was open only for the 1979 season. After that, the attraction was returned to the original *Casa Magnetica* theme and spiel.

The puppet show was *The World On a String,* featuring more than 200 puppets.

Several changes were made in the Texas section. Across from the *Red Schoolhouse,* a second electronic shooting gallery, the *Buckeye Gallery,* was installed at the site of the lemonade stand. This is next to where the *Hotel* and *Tonsorial Parlor* were located. Next door, a new arcade building replaced the original sheriff's office and jail building. A two-story hotel façade, the *Silver Spur Saloon,* was added to the front of the arcade. In 1983, it was named the *Roaring Springs Gameroom.*

The *General Store* tobacco shop was converted to the *Roaring Springs Bath House.* This building was also used as an arcade. The building also contained a ring shop. The original arcade, which sat next to the Texas Shooting Gallery, was converted to a souvenir store.

160

*Targets in Electronic Shooting Gallery. Each target was activated by a light shot by a rifle.
Photograph by Author, 2005.*

Further down Texas Street, the *Hanging Tree* souvenir store was converted into *Texas Triple T,* a tee-shirt shop.

In the Modern section, the *Dog Tags* store was added in a new building next to the *Spectrum. Prospect Point Snack Shop* was renamed to the "Kooper Kettle", also referred to as the "Kooper Kettle Kookie Kitchen". It was later called the "Kooper Kettle Cotton Candy Palace".

Los Amigos Souvenirs, located in the Mexican section, became a hat store named *Los Amigos Hats.*

In Boomtown, a sign shop was added behind the *Boomtown Arcade.*

In Good Times Square, the *Rotoriculous* was renamed the *Rotodisco.*

The 1979 season was the last season during which *Cyrus Cosmos* was featured on the large souvenir maps. He last appeared on the park's seasonal brochure in 1977. Although there was no formal announcement of his demise, by 1980, *Cyrus Cosmos* was no longer employed as the park mascot, or in any other capacity. He simply faded into amusement park history.

The end of the season saw the removal of two of the park's original attractions. The original *Happy Motoring* miniature car track was closed. The second track, which was added in 1962, remained as the sole track. The queue house for *Happy Motoring Freeway* was converted to a hot dog stand named *Happy Hotdogs.*

The second original attraction removed was the *Fiesta Train.* After its removal, its queue house was used for the *El Sombrero,* which was moved next to the building. A new larger employee canteen was built at the *El Sombrero's* old location.

During the season, the park saw about 2.6 million guests. An attendance decrease of 5% was attributed to gasoline shortages. Still, by the end of the ninetieth season, the park has been seen by 37 million visitors.

In 1979, *Magic Mountain* in California was acquired by the Six Flags chain of parks and became the sixth theme park to join the Six Flags amusement park family.

On March 12, 1979, Angus Gilchrist Wynne, II, founder of *Six Flags Over Texas* and the Six Flags chain of amusement parks, passed away at the age of sixty-five years.

1980

Twentieth Season.   Six Flags opened for its twentieth season on March 1, 1980. Special guests were the Apache Band and Belles dance team from Tyler Junior College. Ticket prices were $9.95, with two-day tickets at $14.95. The ticket price increased in July to $10.50. This price surpassed $10 a ticket, which was considered by industry experts to be a psychological buyers' barrier that entertainment centers should not exceed.

Ray (Raymond C.) Williams was appointed the new General Manager of the park in November, 1979, a position he held through the 1983 season. Williams began his amusement park career as a ride operator on the *Six Flags Over Georgia* riverboat ride during its first season in 1967. After his term of General Manager of *Six Flags Over Texas*, he became the General Manager of *Six Flags Great America* in Chicago and then *Six Flags Great Adventure* in New Jersey. He would later serve as President of ride manufacturer Arrow Dynamics, a successor company to Arrow Development. Williams replaced Errol McKoy, who was promoted to Executive Vice President of the Six Flags System. McKoy went on to serve as the President of the State Fair of Texas for twenty-five years.

In an effort to keep gasoline shortages from deterring attendance, Six Flags built its own gas station on the park's parking lot. The station was open around the park's hours of operation and helped to assure visitors that gasoline shortages would not interfere with their day in the park.

This was the first season that individual costumes were not used at each ride. Instead, individuals in each department wore western style outfits. The outfits were different colors between departments.

Up to 1980, *Six Flags Over Texas* had never hosted a wooden roller coaster. While the modern metal coasters provide a high tech experience, they never match the rugged rough and tumble feel of the traditional wooden coaster. Six Flags' corporate management was aware of the appeal of the wooden coasters, having successfully built *The Screaming Eagle* at *Six Flags Over Mid-America* and the *Great American Scream Machine* at *Six Flags Over Georgia*.

Judge Roy Scream.   In order to bring the appeal of the wooden coaster to the Texas park, the *Judge Roy Scream*, "*Awe West of the Pecos*", was

Judge Roy Scream train and station house, built in 1980.
Photograph by Author, 2012.

installed next to the entry lake on property south of Good Time Square. This property had previously been totally outside of the park proper. This was the land Angus Wynne originally planned for the *Great Southwest Sports Center*, including the proposed shooting range.

The *Judge Roy Scream* was one of the few major new attractions to have its grand opening on the same day that the park opened for the season.

To create the *Judge Roy Scream*, the park hired William "Bill" Cobb and his Dallas, Texas, firm William Cobb & Associates. Cobb participated in the design of at least fourteen wooden coasters, including the *Screamin' Eagle* and the *Texas Cyclone* at *Astroworld*.

Since the ride is outside of what had always been the park proper, an access route was created through an eighty-foot long tunnel that travels under the park's entry driveway. The eight-acre ride runs parallel to the large pond located outside the front gate. Construction of the ride increased the size of the park used for attractions to 200 acres. It was billed as the "biggest addition" in the park's history.

The first official riders on the new coaster were Theresa Pool, the first official guest into the park in 1961, and Lex Ann Haughey, the then current Miss Texas.

The ride supports two trains of four cars each, with a total of twenty-four riders per train. The trains travel up to 53 mph. The ride's main lift is 65 feet, with a 50 degree, 60-foot drop. The trains travel a total of 2,480 feet of track in approximately one and a half minutes. The designed ride capacity is 1,200 passengers an hour. Riders feel 2.5 gs during the ride.

Judge Roy Scream with Chute-out in the background.
Notice stand-up baskets on right side of Chute-out.
Six Flags' public relations photograph, circa 1980.

The ride's name is derived from the name of the famous Texan, Judge Roy Bean. The sign at the top of the lift hill, just before the first drop, reads "Appeal Denied".

The ride is constructed from 323,800 board feet of Douglas Fir produced in Washington state. Construction also required 20,075 bolts and 400,000 nails. The trains were manufactured by the Philadelphia Toboggan company. *The Judge* cost $2.1 million dollars to design and construct.

While not as large as its sister "scream" coasters, the *Great American Scream Machine*, at Georgia, and the *Screaming Eagle*, at Mid-America, the *Judge Roy Scream* was immediately popular. The coaster brought the park's operating coaster count to four.

For a time in 1994, some variety was created by turning the trains around, allowing the riders to ride backwards as they traveled around the track.

The park also revamped *Caddo Lake* for nightly fireworks during summer months of the 1980 season. One of the lake's two islands was removed. The adjacent sidewalk was widened by fifteen feet to allow room for guests to stand and watch the fireworks.

An outdoor "miniature village" display was added in the Modern USA section in the area of the removed Happy Motoring car track. The miniature village included a small pond with coin operated remote control boats. Remote control boats were also located on a small pond near the entrance to the *Spinnaker*.

The *Six Flags Follies*, with music of yesterday and the old west, played at the *Southern Palace*. *Sing and Laugh with the People Mover Man* was the show at the *People Mover Theater*.

In the Mexican section, the *Los Amigos Hats* was converted into a Mexican refreshments stand. A new hat stand was opened across the path closer to the Frontgate.

Employee sews guests name onto a hat at one of the many Six Flags hat shops. Photograph by Author, 1976.

In the Texas section, after one season, *Texas Triple T* became *Texas Boots*. The *Iron Horse Snackshop* became the *Jimmy Dean Café*. Two new catering picnic pavilions were built at the location of the old *Texas Arena*. Each pavilion holds 500 people. The *Titan* roller coaster was later built to the south of the pavilions, and the *Texas Giant* to the east.

The *Astrolift* cable car ride was removed from the park at the end of the 1980 season. The *Astrolift* was an original attraction from the park's first season.

The summer of 1980 was by far the hottest summer on record since the park opened. The season saw 69 days of over 100 degree temperatures, with 42 such day in a row. The heat affected the park in many ways, from discouraging attendance to threatening plants. A heat wave of similar severity was not seen again until 2011. The impact of the heat was felt on attendance, which fell for the second year in a row. The number of guests decreased to 2.4 million for the season.

Approximately thirty major theme parks had opened around the nation in the twenty years since *Six Flags Over Texas* first opened its gates. It was calculated that over a 100 million Americans visited theme parks a year. The Six Flags chain was represented with six of these parks, *Six Flags Over Texas, Georgia*, and *Mid-America*, as well as *Astroworld, Great America*, and *Magic Mountain*.

1981

The park celebrated its twentieth anniversary season in 1981. The season opened on March 7 and saw the introduction of one new ride. In addition, two million dollars was spent renovating and improving the park for the season. Ticket prices for both adults and children remained at $10.50.

El Conquistador. For this major anniversary, *El Conquistador*, *"the Flying Ship of Spain"* was introduced. While technically themed as a Spanish attraction and situated near the exit to *Flume II*, the ride was physically located within what had before been the Mexican section. In fact, the ride was located very near to the spot at which the *Fiesta Train* volcano was located. This placement created a blurring of the Spanish and Mexican sections to the extent that they are now sometimes referred to as if they are one section.

The ride is a traditional swinging ship ride in which riders sit facing the center of the boat. The ride is suspended from a frame that allows it to swing back and forth like a pendulum. When operating, the eight-ton boat slowly starts to rock back and forth, until it reaches the point where it seems as if it will go completely upside down. Each time the ride reaches its maximum height on either side, the riders experience a moment of weightlessness before the ride changes directions. At the peaks, the boat swings 150 degrees, taking the riders fifty feet into the air. A typical ride lasts three minutes.

The boat holds fifty riders and has an estimated capacity of 1,200 riders an hour. It is powered by 150-horsepower electric motors and is computer controlled. It was built in Switzerland by Intamin and is classified as a "Bounty" swing ship. The *Conquistador* cost the park $500,000.

The Conquistador, "Flying Ship of Spain", introduced in 1981.
Photograph by Author, 1984.

Shows.   For the 1981 season, the show in the *People Mover Man Show* was changed to the *County Critter Revue*. The show featured computer controlled animated farm animal characters. The technology was similar to the animations that were then appearing at pizza theaters, such as *Showbiz Pizza* and *Chuck E. Cheese's*.

John Hardman's *Stars 'n Strings Puppet Show*, with a cast of big name star puppets, was featured at the *Good Time Theater*. The *Six Flags' Follies* was the hold over performance at the *Southern Palace*. The *Crazy Horse Saloon* featured *That good ole Texas Opry*.

As a special event, every night during the summer, the *All American* fireworks show, *Rockets' Red Glare*, could be viewed over the park's lagoon.

The *Sandwich Emporium*, located in the Texas section, became the *Pony Express Pizza*.

In the Mexican section, a new building replaced the outdoor market that housed the *Plaza De Flores*, formerly the *Flower Market*. The cotton candy stand and glass blower already at the site were moved into the new building, along with a sign shop.

In Boomtown, a snack stand was added next to *Dry Hole Charlies*. It was renamed to the "Smokehouse Sausage Stand" in 1983.

Attendance fell for the third year in a row, with 2.3 million guests in attendance.

Left: The Conquistador, installed in 1981. Photograph by Author, 2010.
Right: The Cliffhanger (1982 – 2007). Right Stuff sign shown at top.
Photograph by Author, 1998.

8.

SIX FLAGS EMPLOYEES

The one constant that has made Six Flags a success over the last fifty years is the dedication of the enthusiastic workers that take on the responsibilities of staffing the park.

Angus Wynne knew that one of the keys to a successful park was a staff of cheerful responsible youths. He did not refer to this staff as "employees". Instead, the park workers were "hosts and hostess". Employees in turn were trained that the park's visitors were not customers, rather they were the park's "guests". This philosophy has continued throughout the life of the park.

Over the years, these youthful workers have performed tasks as diverse as operating roller coasters; guiding canoes; reciting ride-spiels; operating steam engines; selling ice cream; directing parking lot traffic; making paper flowers; issuing and cleaning thousands of costumes; cooking millions of hot dogs, hamburgers and other dishes; barking carnival games; stocking prizes, postcards, maps, t-shirts, and numerous other souvenirs; singing; dancing; and reenacting gunfights and firing squads.

When the park first opened in 1961, the park's policy was that individuals had to be twenty-one years of age to apply for a job. Over the first few years, the number of students required to properly operate the park quickly increased. As it did, the required minimum age decreased. For the second season, the age was lowered to 18, and for 1963, it was 17. By 1966, the minimum age was 16. Now, 15 year olds are allowed to hold some positions. In 1961, most of the park's seasonal employees were college students, whereas now most are from area high schools.

In 1961, the park required nearly 600 seasonal employees. The next year, the number of seasonal hosts and hostess employed increased to 915. Nearly two-thirds of those returned after working in the park the year before. When it was time to hire for the 1963 season, the park received 8000 applications for 1,250 seasonal positions.

By 1967, the park was receiving 8,000 to 10,000 yearly applications to fill 1,500 seasonal positions. This number increased to 2,500 employees by 1980. In 1985, there were 3,200 seasonal employees, with an average age of 16. In order to reduce costs in a more competitive environment, the number of seasonal employees decreased in the late 1980s, dropping back to 2,400 by 1988.

In 1994, the park had 2,500 seasonal employees and 225 full time workers. During this time, the park also started hiring more senior citizens and teachers on summer break. The park was holding at 2,500 seasonal employees by the year 2000.

In 1961, base pay was a dollar an hour. By 1985, it had increased to $3.50 an hour. In 1998, the base rate was $5.00 an hour. In 2001, it was $5.15 an hour.

For years, yearly auditions were held at colleges around the state to locate talented performers for the live shows. Auditions of singers and dancers would be held in as many as fifteen locations, with final auditions in the Fort Worth-Dallas area.

For decades, Six Flags personnel told newly hired employees that Six Flags supplied everything they needed to work in the park, they only had to bring "tennis shoes and a smile". From their first day of training, each employee was taught the value of smiling at the guests.

Pages from 1974, 1975 and 1976 Employee Manuals. These manuals provided employees with park policies, procedures and information and were distributed to seasonal employees each year. The manuals trace back to Freedomland USA and other Marco parks.
From Author's Collection.

Originally, each employee wore a costume representative of the particular attraction or section of the park at which the employee worked. In fact, an employee working at more than one location during the day was required to return to the wardrobe area and change into the appropriate costume before changing assignments.

Eventually, Six Flags abolished the use of individual costumes for all employees. There were a few exceptions, such as performers, as well as specialized positions, such as security guards and railroad engineers. The remainder of the host and hostess now wear the same generic outfits. These outfits are the property of the employees and not supplied by the park.

Over the last fifty years, it is estimated that well over 100,000 individuals have been seasonally employed at the park.

Notable Employees. The park's shows were the starting place for many successful performance careers. In 1964, at the age of 16 years, Betty Buckley performed at the *Amphitheater*. Buckley later was a star of TV's *Eight is Enough*, as well as numerous Broadway shows. She is a significant contributor to area theaters and a major supporter of high school musicals.

Steve Calloway, park General Manager from 1996 to 2006, speaks at former employee event. Picture by Author, 2001.

Ventriloquist Jay Johnson was a member of the *Amphitheater* cast in 1966, before becoming a member of the cast of the TV Show *Soap*. In the 1970's, ventriloquist *Jeff Dunham* performed in the park.

Cissy King performed with Jay Johnson at the *Amphitheater* in 1966. She later became a regular dancer on the *Lawrence Welk Show*.

John Denver, one of the most popular singers of the early 70's, worked at Six Flags in the early 60's. He was a ride operator, however, and not a performer. Apparently, his voice and style were not quite what the park desired for its shows at the time.

Actor Dennis Burkley, who portrayed characters for forty years on numerous TV shows, including *King of the Hill*, was also a former performer in the park.

The winner of the first season of *American Idol*, Kelly Clarkson, was formerly a singer in the *Southern Palace*.

Sandra Brown, bestselling author of over seventy books, was also a Six Flags' employee. She met her husband, former TV reporter and news anchor, Michael Brown, in 1967 when they both were performers at the park.

As noted through-out the book, many leaders in the amusement park industry started out as seasonal employees at Six Flags Over Texas and the other Six Flags parks.

Former Employee Association. In 1997, prior to the creation of Facebook and other social media sties, former ride operator Alan Reynolds started a website designed to allow former employees to reconnect and share their Six Flags memories. His site evolved from a small site, which he had to update manually, into a more sophisticated discussion board. His website resulted in the organization of several reunions of former employees.

Bruce Neal, Six Flags PR representative for thirty years, addressing the 1999 former employee event. Photograph by Author, 1999.

In 1999, the former employees formed their own non-profit organization, the *Six Flags Association of Former Employees*. This organization has sponsored reunions and picnics for former employees for the past fifteen years.

In cooperation with the park's management, the group sponsored its first reunion in 1999. The group also sponsored reunions of former employees in 2001, in connection with the park's 40th season; 2006, for the 45th anniversary; and in 2011, for the park's 50th anniversary.

Information about the association, as well as prior and upcoming activities can be found on the organization's website www.sfafe.net.

9.

BALLY MANUFACTURING CORP.
1982 – 1987

In December of 1981, Bally Manufacturing Corp. announced the purchase of Six Flags Inc. from Penn Central. The purchase, which was finalized in January of 1982, included six amusement parks, *Six Flags Over Texas, Six Flags Over Georgia, Six Flags Over Mid-America, Astroworld, Magic Mountain* in California, and *Great Adventure* in Jackson, New Jersey. Also included were two wax museums and a chain of approximately forty electronic game arcades. Bally already owned approximately 250 arcades, including the *Aladdin's Castle* arcades.

Bally was the leader in pinball and slot machine manufacture and was well known as a leader in video game entertainment. In addition, Bally owned the license to the *Pac-Man* game. At the time, game arcades were booming, appearing anywhere people congregated. Located in pizza parlors and arcades around the country, *Pac-man* was one of the first blockbuster video games. Bally was also experienced in the travel and entertainment business due to its ownership and management of a chain of hotel casinos.

The initial sales price was structured between $75 million in cash and a three-year $65 million note, for an estimated total of $140 million dollars. The exact sales price was finalized based on the net worth of the park chain as of the end of 1981. The price was an average of approximately $22 million per park, depending on the value attributed to the non-amusement park assets.

The purchase only included the rights to manage *Six Flags Over Texas* and *Georgia*, as both of these parks were still owned by separate limited partnerships.

As a result of the purchase, the Six Flags chain became known as *Six Flags Corporation.*

1982

With a variety of competitive rides being installed in theme parks around the country, *Six Flags Over Texas* kept up by installing new and innovative attractions. The 1982 season was no different. The park opened on March 6, the first Saturday of the month. For the new season, the world's first free fall ride, the *Texas Cliffhanger*, was introduced.

For the second year in a row, ticket prices increased by one dollar, to a total of $11.95. In addition, during this time period, the park was charging a $2 upcharge for some of the concerts held on the park's parking lot.

Cliffhanger. Designed by Intamin, the *Cliffhanger* was a 128-foot tall "L" shaped free-fall tower. A Six Flags' press release for the ride notes that when riding the *Cliffhanger*, "the sensation is the same you would feel if you stepped off the roof of a ten story building". (In some publications, the drop was compared to falling from a "nine story" building.) The ride was also billed as "the world's only free fall ride".

Although the ride was not as tall as the *Chute-Out*, the free fall drop was longer. By comparison, the *Chute-Out* was billed as creating the same feeling as stepping off of a "three" story building.

The rides' padded gondolas each contained four seats. The gondolas were lifted by an elevator mechanism to the top of the tower's 128-foot structure. There they moved forward, onto an outside track. Once properly positioned, the units were released for a free fall of approximately sixty feet, or ten floors, straight down the side of the tower.

Near the bottom, the track curved gradually, changing directions by 90 degrees, so that it ran parallel to the ground. The car then ran down an 86-foot long braking track. The units rotated with the track so that riders rode on their backs along the braking section. An array of 103 sensors were used to capture the weight and speed of each individual gondola. Using this information, a computer determined braking pressures for each unit.

During the fall, riders reached 55 mph in less than 2.5 seconds and experience a 3.5 g force. As with the flume and mine train, *Cliffhanger* style rides were immediately adopted by amusement parks around the country. The first of its kind ride cost the park $2.1 million.

In 1995, the Modern section was rethemed as an "Air Force base and astronaut training center" in connection with the addition of the *Right Stuff Theater*. At that time, the *Cliffhanger* was renamed as the "G-Force" and themed as an astronaut training apparatus.

Even later, the ride was renamed as the *Wildcatter* and themed with the Boomtown section. The ride was not, however, physically moved. Rather than moving the ride, the Boomtown section was simply expanded into the area around the Cliffhanger. The size of the Modern USA section was reduced accordingly.

Above: Cliffhanger (right lower corner) and Modern Section, 1986.
Happy Motoring track is at bottom.
Shockwave and Air Racer are in the upper right.

Below: Similar view from 1991.
Splashwater Falls has replaced Happy Motoring track.
Texas Giant is visible in background. The train is visible in the lower left.
The area which was used for Snow Mountain at Holiday in the Park
is shown in the lower right hand corner.
Both Photographs by Author.

The *Cliffhanger* was imploded at the end of 2007 season.

Nearby to the newly installed *Cliffhanger*, the *Happy Motoring Cars* were renamed as the *GT Cars*.

A children's Ferris wheel was added in the Modern section. Originally simply referred to as the *Kiddie Ferris Wheel*, the ride was a small wheel with six small round enclosed units. Each unit held four children. The *Rugged Buggy* ride was moved from the petting Zoo area and placed next to the new Ferris wheel. The two rides were placed near the former location of the *Big Bend* queue house and track. Additional children's rides would be added at this location over the following seasons.

Also in the Modern section, a game room was added in the old exhibits' hall, which now housed the modern shopping area.

In Boomtown, the leather souvenir store became the *Airbrush Artist shop*. This shop lasted until 1991, when it became a caricatures stand. *Dry Hole Charlies* sold hamburger platters. *Mustard's Last Stand* was renamed to *Gold Miner's Hotdogs and Pizza*.

America - Saluting American Music was the new musical at the Southern Palace. Fireworks continued from Caddo lake.

In order to start construction on the *Roaring Rapids* ride, the last voyage on *La Salle's River Adventure* was taken after the park closed on August 15, 1982. On board were park employees and former employees of the ride. The very next day, demolition on the ride, as well as the last remnants of Skull Island, was begun to make way for the *Roaring Rapids* ride set to open the next season. The riverboat ride had been in the park for twenty-two seasons.

Some of the riverboats were sold to nearby *Lion Country Safari* in Grand Prairie to be used in their river attraction. That park closed in 1992. Some of the boats made their way to Jefferson, Texas, where they are used as *Touring Basin Riverboats*. After being outfitted with steerable gas engines, and otherwise brought to Coast Guard compliance, the boats are still in service, providing tours on the *Big Cypress Bayou*. Another was spotted docked with the glass-bottom boats at *Aquarina Springs* in San Marcus, Texas.

The *Spindletop* was moved from its spot near the *Tower* to the former location of the *Astrolift* station in the Texas section. This change was also in order to accommodate construction of the *Roaring Rapids*.

In addition to the riverboats, three other long time park attractions were removed after the 1982 season. One was the petting zoo. Over the years, it had been significantly reduced in size from the *Animal Kingdom* that opened in 1961. The last remnants of the attraction were removed at the end of the season.

Nearby, the red caboose that had served as the Lost Parents location since the 1964 season was also removed from the park. Both the *Petting Zoo* and the *Lost Parents* caboose were removed so that a new *Pac-Man Land* children's section could be built for the 1983 season.

Finally, in Good Times Square, the original *Crazy Legs* ride was removed.

Attendance was down at amusement parks around the country. The decline was attributed to nationwide bad weather, an unfavorable economy, and competition with the *World's Fair* in Knoxville, Tennessee. *Six Flags Over Texas* was an exception, with attendance up slightly to 2.38 million visitors for the season.

On October 1, 1982, Disney opened *EPCOT Center* in Florida. The 300-acre park was the second park in its *Walt Disney World Complex*. Construction costs were estimated near one billion dollars.

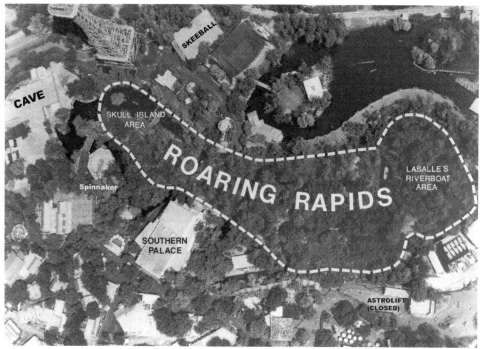

Pictured above is the area consumed by the Roaring Rapids. Construction of the ride resulted in a major transformation of the park. Both LaSalle's River Adventure and the last remaining portions of Skull Island were removed, while the Spindletop was moved. Elsewhere in the park, Crazy Legs, the Lost Parents Caboose, and the Petting Zoo were removed (not pictured).
Six Flags' public relations photograph, 1982. (some labels added).

1983

The 1983 season started on March 5, 1983. The new season brought two new major attractions. One, *Pac-Man Land*, was designed for the younger guests. The other, the *Roaring Rapids*, was targeted at the rest of the family. A swing ride was also added.

Ticket prices started the year at $11.95 for both adults and children. By summertime, however, they increased to $12.95.

Roaring Rapids.   The *Roaring Rapids* was constructed for the 1983 season. The large artificial river used for the ride extended over much of the area that had once contained *Skull Island* and *LaSalle's River Adventure*.

The ride was designed by Bill A. Crandall, a Six Flags executive at *Astroworld*. Crandall's idea for the ride was inspired by the 1972 Olympic Kayak races. The ride was intended to simulate a whitewater rafting trip on a raging river. Instead of the inflatable style river rafts popular for whitewater rafting, guests ride in round twelve seat solid rafts.

It was somewhat ironic that the new ride replaced the *Skull Island* section, as *Skull Island* was the very place that Crandall started his amusement park career as a ride operator for *Six Flags Over Texas*.

Built by Intamin AG, of Zurich, at a cost of $4.2 million, the ride was at the time the most expensive built in the park. The ride's reservoir holds 1.5 million gallons of water. In order to keep the river flowing, the ride's two 400

Roaring Rapids ride lift at loading dock.
Photograph by Author, 1983.

Roaring Rapids (1983), with Spinnaker (1977-1995), and Southern Palace (1968).
Remote control boats are shown in upper right corner.
Photograph by Author, 1983.

Roaring Rapids rafts and one of the ride's three waterfalls.
Photograph by Author, 1983.

horsepower pumps propel 167,000 gallons per minute. Other pumps create the ride's three waterfalls.

Creation of the riverbed required 11,100 tons of concrete. It contains four sets of rapids, with three lakes in between each. Two of the lakes have wave machines to create turbulence and artificial rapids. In addition, two of the lakes contain waterfalls. The tallest waterfall is 36 feet high, with a flow of 10,000 gallons of water per minute.

The ride supports twenty rafts, each capable of carrying twelve passengers. Ride capacity is 2,000 riders per hour. The river is 1,440 feet long, with four stretches of rapids. The total water level drops 14 feet from the start of the ride to the finish. Generally, the water travels at 16.6 feet per second. With a maximum speed of 15 mph, a typical ride lasts four minutes and forty-five seconds.

Directed high-pressure water nozzles and carefully designed dips in the bottom of the artificial waterway are used to create the whitewater effects.

While portions of the ride are physically located in sections of France, the Confederacy, and Boomtown, the entrance is located near the base of the *Tower.*

For a time in the late 1990's, the entrance to the ride was moved to the French section, near the former location of the entrance to *LaSalle's River*

Longhorn Game Room located in the Texas section next to the Courthouse. Built when the park opened, the building was originally a general merchandise store and pottery shop. In 1963, it became the Tobacco Store. It was the Tobacco Store until 1979. It later became a game room. Photograph by Author, 2010.

Adventure. At the time, the name of the ride was changed to *LaSalle's River Rapids.* None of the rides' apparatus was changed for this conversion. The park simply routed a new queue line to the ride from an area in the French section that already bordered the ride. The name and entrance were later changed back to the original location.

The first river-rapids ride opened at *Astroworld* in 1980. The new ride proved so popular that Six Flags theme parks installed a version of the ride at all of the chain's parks at the time. It has since become a standard attraction at most modern amusement parks.

Texas Tornado.   In addition to the major attraction added, an "off-the-shelf" flat ride, the *Texas Tornado* swing ride was introduced in Good Times Square at the site of the former *Crazy Legs* ride.

The Texas Tornado in its original location in Good Time Square. This was the site of the original Crazy Legs. Behind the ride is the Texas Chute-Out.
Photograph by Author, 1983.

The *Tornado* is a standard swing ride, in which riders sit in swings suspended in a circle around a motorized midpoint. As the ride starts, the center axis extends upwards, pulling the swings higher into the air. As it does, the swings start to rotate around the axis. As the ride speed increases, the swings travel further and further out from the center of the ride. A typical ride last one minute and forty seconds.

The ride was manufactured by Chance Manufacturing Company. In 1989, the ride was moved to the original site of the carousel in the Boomtown section. It was renamed the "Gunslinger" in 2005.

Pac-Man Land entrance (1983 - 1984).
Photograph by Author, 1983.

Pac-Man Land.   Bally's presence as the new park owner was most felt in the Modern section where a new themed section designed for small children was opened as *Pac-Man Land*. Named in honor of *Pac-Man*, Bally's best known character, the new section occupied most of the area that had previously held the *Petting Zoo*.

In the new children's section, Bally added several children's "soft play" attractions. The new activities were named after various elements from the Pac-Man game. They included hand powered "go-carts"; a play area with an obstacle course; small slides designated as "Blinky Boppers"; a ball pit named the "Power Pill Plunge"; a small inflatable hill, designated as "Pac's Peak"; an inflatable bounce area known as the "Pac-Man Pillows"; and a maze, called "Pac-Man Passage".

South of the railroad tracks, across the path from the *Rugged Buggy* and Ferris wheel, a set of small buildings were constructed to resemble a railroad train. The buildings were designed after a steam engine, railroad cars, and a caboose. These were the new home to the lost parent's area, a party room, and a diaper changing area.

The *Red Baron* ride was moved to the new section from its former spot near the cave. This gave the new section three children's rides, the Ferris wheel, Rugged Buggy, and Red Baron. The construction of the Pac-Man area cost the park an estimated $500,000.

Also as a sign of Bally's presence, the show in the *County Critter Revue* theater (previously the *People Man Mover Show*) was changed to the "Pac-Man Magic Show".

The Pac-Man Land train buildings. The caboose was for lost children, the middle car was a diaper changing area, and the other a private party car. Chute-out is in view in the background.
Photograph by Author, 1983.

One of the "soft-play" areas in Pac-Man Land.
Photograph by Author, 1983.

In the Texas section, the arcade building next to the electronic shooting gallery was renamed the "Roaring Springs Gameroom". *Jimmy Dean Café*, next door to the Texas train station, became "Fletcher's Hot Dogs". Near the Flume entrance, *Texas Boots* became the "Gilded Unicorn".

In Boomtown, the snack stand next to *Dry Hole Charlies* was renamed to the "Smokehouse Sausage Stand".

The Spirit of Olympics show was presented during the summer in the *Good Time Theater*. The 22-minute show featured over 4,500 images portraying the highlights and history of the Olympics. Twenty-seven projectors presented the images on three different screens.

The dolphin show was removed at the end of the season, although it would return in 1989. The *Caddo War Canoe* ride was removed at the end of the 1983 season to make room for the *Great Air Racer*. Likewise, the placement of the *Great Air Racer* required the termination of fireworks on Caddo Lake.

A three-day Christmas event was held in the park over the Thanksgiving weekend. The event featured characters from the then popular Hanna-Barbera children's show *Shirt Tales*, as well as holiday themed costume characters.

The 1983 season again saw increasing attendance, with 2.5 million visitors for the season.

In Arlington, *Wet 'n Wild* water park opened across I-30, a short distance from Six Flags. The *Wet 'n Wild* chain was founded by George Millay, with the first water park opening in Orlando in 1977. The chain eventually grew to ten parks. Six Flags purchased the Arlington park in 1995.

In Arizona, after a bankruptcy and several different owners, *Legend City* closed it gates and was torn down. It operated for twenty years.

1984

Opening date was not held the first Saturday of March, but rather the second, March 10, 1984. The season saw the introduction of both a major new ride and a new show. The new ride was *The Great Six Flags Air Racer*, which was introduced along with the *U.S. High Diving Team* show.

This was the final season that all tickets were sold for one price, with both children's and adult tickets starting the season at $12.95.

Great Air Racer. The *Great Air Racer* was a high swing ride with twelve ride units shaped to look like barnstorming biplanes. Each plane could hold up to six adult guests, two each in three rows of seats, for a total of seventy-two riders. Each ride cycle lasted approximately three minutes.

The planes were each connected by cables to a circular structure mounted above them on the ride's round tower. After loading, the structure

Above: Great Air Racer (1984-1999) planes in flight.
Below: Air Racer plane painted with American Flag scheme.
Both photographs by author, 1985.

began to rise up the tower. As it rose into the air, the planes also rose up in unison. As the planes rose, they began to spin around the tower. Eventually, the force of the spinning sent each plane circling further and further from the tower. At their highest, the planes "flew" nearly 100 feet off of the ground.

The planes reached a spin rate of roughly 36 miles per hour. After a few minutes of spinning, the rotation slowed and the planes began their descent back to the tarmac below.

The planes were painted in various schemes. Originally, they were painted to represent the six flags of Texas, with each flag represented by two different planes painted with the colors and icons of the flag.

The ride, built by Intamin, cost $2 million dollars to build. It was removed at the end of the 1999 season after sixteen years of operation. A sister ride was installed at *Six Flags Over Georgia*.

US High Diving Team Show (1984–1988).
Diver performing at Tower Theater. Photograph by Author, 1985.

Diving Show. At the *Tower Theater*, the *US High Diving Team Show* replaced the *Dolphin Show* in the large pool. Little was done to convert the theater to the new show, other than the addition of the diving platforms and the removal of the dolphins. The diving show consisted of trained divers performing acrobatic dives from various platforms high above the pool. The show was designed to be dramatic, visually interesting, and humorous. It featured thrilling high dives, synchronized diving, and comedic routines. The show was staged until 1989.

Coca Cola and 7-up sponsored a second season of the *Spirit of the Olympics Show* at *Good Time Square Theater*. *Star Struck* was featured at the Southern Palace and *Gonna have a Party* was featured at the Crazy Horse Saloon. The *Pac-Man Show* was in its last season at the Pac-Man Theater.

Spring Breakout. *Spring Breakout* began in 1984. While the park had previously been open over spring break week, the *Spring Breakout* event added attractions and activities designed to attract college age students to the park. *Spring Breakout* is now a yearly event.

The popularity of high tech souvenirs was reflected by the conversion of the *Los Amigos*, located in the Mexican section, into a computer portrait stand. At the stand, guests purchased pictures of themselves drawn by a computer using a video camera and dot-matrix printer.

After two seasons of increasing attendance, the park saw a slight decrease to 2.3 million visitors for the season. This was down from the numbers that the park was seeing in the mid and late seventies, but near the figures that the park had seen for the last three or so seasons.

During the year, the seventh amusement park was added to the Six Flags chain with the purchase for $113.2 million of Marriott Corporation's *Great America Park* near Chicago, Illinois. This purchase split the ownership of the two *Great America* sister parks between different park chains.

On July 4th, 1984, *Six Flags Autoworld* opened as an indoor park in Flint, Michigan. The park, billed as "the largest indoor entertainment complex in the world", was themed on automobile manufacturing. Six Flags managed the park for an ownership group consisting of a local government and a group of investors. The park was constructed with an investment of $70 million dollars. It closed early in its first season. It went bankrupt after a failed attempt to reopen the next year.

1985

The park opened on March 2, 1985, the first Saturday in March, without any major new attractions planned for the season. In fact, it was the first season since 1979 that did not feature a new ride attraction. The season, however, brought major changes in the theming of the park with the introduction of the Warner Brothers' Looney Tunes characters.

Robert D. (Bob) Bennett began an eleven-year run as the Vice President and General Manager of the park. Bennett had been with the Six Flags chain for 10 years, starting his career in the amusement park business as a sales representative.

Separate children's tickets were reinstated at $7.95 each, ending the policy of one ticket price for all guests begun in 1976. This resulted in a seven-dollar drop in children's ticket prices. The park promoted the new children's price to encourage families and increase attendance. The decrease in the children's tickets was offset by an increase in adult tickets to $14.95. Guests also now had to pay sales tax on park tickets due to the implementation of a sales tax on amusement park tickets authorized by law in 1984.

Unlike the original children's tickets, the new children's tickets were based on guest height, rather than age. Children less than 42 inches in height

Pac-Man land was converted to Looney Tune Land. Shown is the new entrance.
Photograph by Author, 1985.

qualified for the reduced ticket price. This policy is logical given that ride restrictions are based on height and not age. In addition, height of the child is easier than age for ticket attendants to verify. Children under two were admitted free, as they had been since 1982. Prior to that time, children under three were free.

Parking was $3.00 per vehicle.

Looney Tunes Land.   Beginning in 1985, Bugs Bunny, Sylvester, Daffy Duck, and their Warner Brothers' cartoon pals became the park's official mascots. Several attractions were renovated to feature the various characters. The most notable change was in *Pac-Man Land*. The entire children's section was rethemed to become the more child friendly *Looney Tunes Land*. Looney Tunes costume characters presided over the opening of the converted section.

The park's use of the Looney Tunes characters stemmed from the Six Flags chain's purchase in 1984 of **Marriott's Great America** park. *Great America* held a license to use the Warner Brother's Looney Tunes characters in the park since it opened in 1976. After the purchase of the Illinois park, Warner Brothers expanded the license with Six Flags to include its other six parks, including *Six Flags Over Texas*. Six Flags now had access to a wealth of well-known and established characters to use within the parks.

In 1990, Warner Brothers purchased an interest in the Six Flags chain. Use of the Warner Brother characters in the Six Flags parks, however, predated any Warner ownership investment in the parks by five years.

While there was little change in the attractions available, there were changes in the names of the attractions. In the soft play area, the air pillows became the *Porky Pig Play Pen* and the ball pit was renamed as *Tweety Bubbles*.

Daffy Duck Lake Boats (1985–2000) in Looney Tunes Land.
Porky Pig Magic Wheel (1991–2001) in background.
Photograph by Author, 1998.

The children's Ferris wheel became the *Elmer Fudd Fewwis Wheel*; the *Rugged Buggy* became the *Roadrunner Runaround*; and the *Red Baron* became the *Tasmanian Devil Flying Aces*. A fourth ride, a small boat carousel, was added and designated as *Daffy Duck Lake*. The other rides were relocated a small distance in order to make room for the boat ride.

The shopping area located in the Modern section now housed the *Six Flags Recording Studios*, a *Cover Photo* shop, *Six Flags Hallmark*, *Looney Tunes Gifts*, and the *USA Hats*. The *Hallmark* was removed in 1987.

The park's shows also reflected the new characters. The name of the *Good Time Square Theater* was changed to the *Looney Tunes Theater*. The theater hosted the *Bugs Bunny Story*, with Bugs Bunny and the other popular Looney Tunes characters. The show told the story of how Bugs became a famous star. In addition, Warner Brothers' costume characters strolled through the streets greeting guests throughout the park.

Some of the theaters hosted more traditional shows. *The Southern Palace* show, *Celebrate America!*, featured fourteen performers in a tribute to American holidays. *The Crazy Horse Saloon* featured the six character *Texas Heartache*.

There was also a nightly fireworks show with patriotic music. A puppet show featuring *Argyle the Snake* was performed from a show wagon. The *Chevy Show* continued to feature its wide screen special effects and the high divers continued to perform at the *Tower Theater*, now referred to as the "Aquatic Theater".

In Boomtown, the *Six Flags Carousel* was removed from the park in order that it could be remodeled for the park's 25th anniversary in 1986. Renovations took longer than anticipated and the ride did not return to the park until 1988.

Next to the Texas Depot in the Texas section, *Fletcher's Hot Dogs* became *Newman's Corndog Café*.

Holiday in the Park. While there was no major attraction added for the season, *Holiday in the Park* was held for the first time in 1985. The new event, held during the Christmas holiday, transformed a portion of the park into a winter wonderland. For the first year, all of the rides and several entire sections were closed during the event. The park, however, was, elaborately decorated with Christmas lights and other decorations. The stores were stocked with Christmas and holiday related items. The emphasis of the event was on the shows, all of which were staged with a holiday related program.

The decorations included lighting in 600 trees. A 30-story high star, 50 feet by 34 feet, was mounted on the side of the top of the *Tower*. The *Chute-Out* was transformed into a Texas sized Christmas tree with 7,500 lights running from the ground to the top of the ride. In total 325,000 lights we used to decorate the park.

Original artificial snow sledding mountain created in Modern USA section of park for Holiday in the Park. Later a new hill was built at a location near the Music Mill Theater.
Photograph by Author, 1990.

Ice Skating Show at Music Mill Amphitheater during 1990 version of Holiday in the Park.
Photograph by Author.

The three shows were the highlight of the event. A fourteen-person musical, *A Jolly Holiday,* was presented at the *Southern Palace.* The *Crazy Horse Saloon* featured a *Country Christmas.* The *Bugs Bunny Merrie Holiday Revue* was staged at the *Looney Tunes Theater.*

In addition, small bands, strolling singers, and area choirs performed in outdoor settings throughout the park. Horse drawn carriages provided romantic rides through the park. Seasonal foods were also available to guests.

Special attractions included a petting zoo and *Snow Mountain.* Located in the Modern section, *Snow Mountain* allowed guests to test their skills at snow sledding on an artificial snow mountain. A large model train layout was also on exhibit. Of course, Santa was there to greet the crowds. A Christmas parade topped off the evening. Several stores sold holiday related items. A children's only shop was available for the little ones to do their gift shopping.

Tickets for the event were $4.50. Children under 2 were free. The first *Holiday in the Park* ran from November 29 to December 31.

Holiday in the Park was a large success and has been repeated every year since. It has expanded until now it includes most of the park's rides and attractions. With the addition of the *Holiday in the Park* event, the park's season ended much later. December 31, 1985, was the last day of the season.

By 1985, the park had expanded to 205 acres. Despite the lack of a new thrill ride, attendance for the year reached 2.6 million visitors. This was 300,000 more guests than the year before and up over the last four years. This includes 101,000 visitors during *Holiday in the Park.* Sometime near the start of the season, the fiftieth million guest entered the gates. By the end of the first twenty-five seasons, nearly 52 million guests had visited the park.

East side of Park, 1985. Air Racer is to the left. Diving show is in lower left corner.
Roaring Rapids is to the right. Cliffhanger is mid-top.
Photograph by Author, 1985.

A year after the opening of the doomed *Autoworld* park in Michigan, another small industrial themed indoor park opened with the Six Flags name. *Six Flags Power Plant* opened in the Pratt Street Power Plant in Baltimore, Maryland. The park operated through 1989 before closing.

1986

*S*ix *Flags Over Texas'* twenty-fifth anniversary was celebrated in 1986. The park opened on March 1, 1986. In celebration, the park was set to add a new type of roller coaster, the *Avalanche Bobsled Ride*. National advertising used the slogan "It's Showtime".

Ticket prices for both adults and children remained the same as the previous season. The prices were actually $15.92 and $8.47 after inclusion of the new sales tax. The was a $4.00 extra charge for some of the events held at the *Music Mill* theater.

La Vibora sled, (Bobsled ride) unit with yellow, red and black track.
Photograph by Author, 2006.

Avalanche Bobsled.   The *Avalanche Bobsled* ride is situated in the Mexican section, in an area that extended from the flume ride to the parking lot and included an area that formerly held a portion of the *Fiesta Train*. The ride is a unique type of ride in that it does not run on a traditional roller coaster track. Instead, the cars ride in a curved structure, more like the flume of the log ride than a traditional roller coaster track. The result of this configuration is that not every ride is exactly the same as the one before it. It also creates the illusion that the cars could leave the flume area, creating an apprehension of danger.

The main lift is sixty-four feet high and the ride track is 1,490 feet long. The sleds travel at up to 32 mph for a ride of approximately one and a half minutes. The ride track banks up to 70 degrees. Each bobsled holds up to six riders, for an hourly ride capacity under 1,000 riders per hour. Seventy sensors along the track monitor both the speed and location of each unit. This data is then sent to the ride's computerized control and safety system.

Built by Intamin Co., the ride is an AG Bobsled style ride. While the ride was new to *Six Flags Over Texas*, it was not new to the Six Flags park system, having operated at Six Flags *Magic Mountain* during 1984 and 1985. The ride is estimated to have cost over five million dollars when first constructed at *Magic Mountain*.

Aerial view of Bobsled ride track layout in original blue paint.
Photograph by Author, 1990.

The ride track was originally painted light blue. In 1996, it was renamed the *La Vibora*, Spanish for the "Viper". This name change brought it more closely into the theming of the Mexican section where it resides. The outside of the track structure was repainted in red, black, and yellow sections to resemble the strips of a snake. The *Avalanche Bobsled* increased the park's roller coaster count to five.

As part of the anniversary celebration, the park held a parade each evening from July 4 to Labor day.

In Texas, *Newman's Café* next to the *Texas Depot* became a funnel cake stand. In Boomtown, the name of the *Smokehouse Sausage Stand* was returned to "Boomtown Snack Shop".

In order to draw even larger crowds to more well known performers, the *Music Mill Theater* was expanded to hold 10,000 people, up from the original 4,500 guests.

At the end of the season, the remaining *GT Car* track, originally the *Happy Motoring Freeway*, was removed to make room for the *Splashwater Falls* to open the next season. The track, which was the second one installed, had been in the park since 1962, serving a total of 25 seasons.

The year saw the second highest attendance since the park opened, with 2.74 million visitors. The number includes 170,000 guests that attended the second *Holiday in the Park*. This number was just under the 1978 record of 2.78 million.

1987

The park opened on March 14, 1987. Adult ticket prices were up a dollar, to $15.95 for adults. Prices for children jumped two dollars to $9.95.

By 1987, the park was hosting 2.5 million guests a year and over 55 million guests had visited the park. The park's second quarter century began with the addition of the spectacular water ride, *Splashwater Falls*. In addition, during the summer months the park presented a special attraction, *The Incredible Acrobats of China*.

Splashwater Falls.   Both the *Log Flume* and the *Roaring Rapids* established that crowds in the Texas heat appreciate a ride that gets them wet. *Splashwater Falls*, built in 1986, and opening on May 15, 1987, was designed as the simplest ride that could accomplish this task. The ride sits on approximately two acres in the Modern USA section in an area that had once been occupied by the *Happy Motoring Freeway*.

The ride's track is an 800-foot long oval shaped waterway. The ride's six boats are twenty-feet long and are each designed to hold twenty riders sitting in five rows of bench seats. The ride starts with a large lift hill on which the boats travel over fifty feet into the air at a twenty-degree angle. The boats then float onto an elevated waterway where they travel through a 180-degree curve. Once the boats finish the curve, they slide down a 45-foot drop at a 35-degree angle into a quarter million gallon splash pool.

Highlight splash of Splashwater Falls (1987), now known as the Aquaman Splashwater. Six Flags' public relations photograph, circa 1987.

The boats travel 30 mph during the drop. At the bottom of the drop, all of the riders experience some degree of splash. Some riders are likely to be totally soaked. In addition, after disembarking, riders can wait on the exit bridge that crosses over the splash zone for the next boat to fall. Doing so, they experience the full impact of the boat's 20-foot splash, virtually guaranteeing that they will be soaked through and through.

The ride lasts three minutes and thirty seconds and has an hourly capacity of 1,800 riders. The ride uses 250,000 gallons of water, circulated around the ride by an 180-horsepower pumping station. The ride was constructed by O.D. Hopkins Associates Inc. of New Hampshire. Hopkins originally manufactured sky rides. They began specializing in water rides and transport systems in 1980. Estimated cost of construction is just over $1 million.

The ride is a modern version of the *Shoot-the-Chute* rides of the early 1920s. In these rides, boats would drop down a slide or waterway into a pool of water. Prior to opening the *Splashwater Falls* in Texas, similar rides were installed at *Six Flags Over Georgia* and *Great America.*

The ride was later renamed the "*Splashdown Reentry Test Simulation*" in 1995 to correspond with the retheming of the modern section as an astronaut training center. In 1999, the name was changed back to *Splashwater Falls,* sometimes indicated as just *Splashwater.* In subsequent years it was also listed as *Splashdown* in some publications. In 2007, it was renamed to "Aquaman Splashwater", based on the DC Comic character of the same name.

Shows. Highlighting the shows for the season was the *Incredible Acrobats of China* held at the *Southern Palace.* The cast were members of the *Shanghi Acrobatic Troupe.* Each evening during the summer months the acrobats performed their feats of daring. Also on stage at the *Southern Palace* was the Six Flags' Musical *Stars & Stripes Salute!* Billed as a full-scale musical production, the show was performed during the afternoons by fourteen performers.

The *Crazy Horse Saloon* presented *Country Express,* a country music show with a six person cast. The *USA High Divers* again performed at the pool next to the *Tower. The Bugs Bunny Story* with Bugs Bunny and other popular Warner characters continued at the *Good Time Theater.*

In the Texas section, *Annie's Notions and Dry Goods Store* became *The Ole Woodcutter* custom woodcrafts store. *Pony Express Pizza* became *Newman's Corn Dog Café.*

In the Mexican section, the high-tech computerized portraits studio was converted into a much lower-tech balloon stand.

A new yearly attendance record was set with 2.8 million visitors for the year. This broke the previous record from 1978 by approximately 20,000 guests.

A Six Flags' press release from 1987 estimated that there were thirty other modern theme parks then operating in the US.

9.

WESRAY CAPITAL
1988 – 1991

Wesray Capital Corp., a private investment fund, purchased Six Flags Corp. from Bally Entertainment in a leveraged buyout in April of 1987 and took the chain private. The chain of parks then included seven major parks, up from six when Bally purchased the chain in 1981.

It was reported that Wesray paid a total of $617 million for the parks, approximately four times the amount paid by Bally for six major parks six years earlier. The breakdown for the purchase was reported as a net $350 million in cash and provided for the assumption of $250 million in Six Flags related debt carried by Bally. The remaining $17 million was not detailed.

In addition to the two parks managed for limited partnerships, *Six Flags Over Texas* and *Georgia*, the chain owned *Six Flags Over Mid-America*; *Astroworld*; *Magic Mountain* in California; *Six Flags Great Adventure* in Jackson, New Jersey; and the most recent acquisition, *Six Flags Great America* near Chicago, Illinois. The park system also owned two water parks, *Six Flags Atlantis* in Florida and *Six Flags Waterworld* in Houston. *Six Flags Atlantis* was sold in 1988 and permanently closed in 1992 after Hurricane Andrew. The company also owned one animal park, *Six Flags Wild Safari Animal Park* next to *Six Flags Great Adventure*.

Allocating half the value of a park to the water and animal parks, Wesray paid an approximate average of $72 million per park, whereas in 1981, Bally paid an average of $22 million per park. As this was a leveraged purchase, Wesray borrowed heavily to raise the purchase price. Although the parks were profitable, the interest payment on the debt began causing an overall loss to the corporation. By 1990, interest payments alone were $80 million. Problems servicing the debt would haunt the corporation during the upcoming years.

One of Wesray's first corporate acts was to move the corporate headquarters for Six Flags Corporation to the Dallas-Fort Worth metroplex. In 1971, the corporate offices were relocated to California and later moved to Chicago.

At the time, nationwide seasonal attendance at the Six Flags' parks was estimated at nearly 20 million guests.

1988

Instead of a new ride for the 1988 season, the featured attraction was the return to the park of the *Six Flags Carousel*, which was rebuilt over the previous three years. The season opened with an increase in adult ticket prices of two dollars, for a total of $17.95. Prices also rose two dollars to $11.95 for children under 48 inches.

Silver Star Carousel.   The *Six Flags Carousel* was removed from the park after the 1985 season for renovations. It was planned that the ride would return for the park's twenty-fifth anniversary in 1986. Instead, the refurbishing of the ride took much longer than expected and the ride did not return until after three years of painstaking restoration. After refurbishment, the ride was renamed the *Silver Star Carousel*. The carousel was returned to the park in mint condition.

Over 30,000 hours of labor were spent to restore the ride. Each horse was completely rebuilt and repainted. New body parts were created as needed. Coatings of fiberglass, as well as old layers of paint, were stripped off the animals before repainting. Gold leaf paint was used on parts of the harnesses of the horses. The stirrups of the sixteen outside horses were gold plated.

The ride structure was restored in addition to the horses. The original top of the ride, known as the "rounding board", was restored for the ride. It is decorated with 3,000 tiny light bulbs. Two of the horses that were originally part of the ride when it was installed in 1963 were missing and were replaced.

Silver Star Carousel at its new home at the Frontgate.
Photograph by Author, 2006.

Instead of returning to Boomtown, where it had resided for twenty-three years, the carousel was relocated to a place of prominence inside a structure built specifically for the ride at the park's Frontgate. It is now located amidst the park's signature Frontgate six flags. Entrance to the ride is by a set of stairs that cross over the *Dancing Waters* pond.

After it was completely refurbished, the ride was valued at over five million dollars. Individual horses are worth between $50,000 and $100,000.

Other minor changes were made around the park. The *Chevrolet Theater* was renamed as the *Cinema 180 Theater*. In the Modern section, the USA food court was rebuilt with indoor seating and air conditioning. In Boomtown, the *Boomtown Snack Shop* became the *Blue Ribbon Fixin's*.

In Texas, *Peco's Belle's Tumbleweed Tokens* became *Texas' Best Souvenirs*. The *Gilded Unicorn* souvenir store became *Yosemite Sam's*.

At the end of the season, the *Rotodisco* was removed from the park in order to make room from the *Flashback* roller coaster. The *Texas Tornado* was moved for the same reason. Also leaving the park were the high divers. They performed at the pool next to the *Tower* for their last season.

Attendance appears to have dropped nearly 300,000 guests from the record levels of 1987, with 2.5 million guests visiting the park for the 1988 season.

Frontgate "Fright Night" decoration. Fright Fest" began as "Fright Nights" in 1986 and expanded into a major yearly event.
Photograph by Author, 1988.

Frontgate Ball Fountain turned into Halloween Pumpkin.
Photograph by Author, 1998.

Fright Nights. Originally named "Fright Nights", *The Fright Fest Halloween* celebration began in 1988. It was an immediate success, with a new park attendance record of more than 45,000 guests on the first day. One of the featured elements was a 70-foot tall, 2,000-pound, balloon gorilla climbing up the side of the Tower.

In May of 1988, *Sea World of Texas,* now known as *Sea World San Antonio,* opened in San Antonio. Built at a cost of $170 million dollars, the park is the largest marine life theme park in the world. Another theme park, *Boardwalk and Baseball,* was planned to open next door to the sea park. This park, however, was never built. The *Boardwalk and Baseball* park would have been a sister park to the original *Boardwalk and Baseball* in Florida.

1989

The park opened on March 4, 1989. Ticket prices were $19.16 for adults and $13.08 for child and seniors. For a new attraction, the park opened its second roller coaster in three years.

Flashback Roller Coaster. The *Flashback* roller coaster brought the park's roller coaster count to six. The ride, which cost $2 million to install, was located in Good Times Square. Both the *Rotoriculous* and the *Texas Tornado* were removed to make room for the new coaster. The *Rotoriculous* was retired from the park, while the *Tornado* was moved to the former location of the carousel in the Boomtown section. The Flashback is a *boomerang* style roller coaster built by the Vekoma Ride Company of the Netherlands.

The boomerang style roller coaster is quite popular in amusement parks due to the large number of elements squeezed into a very small operating space. There are over twenty similar operational coasters.

The ride starts with the sole train being pulled backwards out of the station house up a one hundred and twenty-five foot incline of 45 degrees. Once the back of the train reached the top of the lift, it was released, at which time it traveled back through the station house, into a loop, through a roll, into a second loop, through a third loop and up a second 45 degree, one hundred and twenty-five foot incline. The train was then pulled to the top of the second lift and released, at which time the ride repeats the track, this time with the riders traveling backwards. The track wraps around so that the second lift hill is positioned next to the original lift.

Flashback roller coaster (1989-2012).
Photograph by Author, 1998.

The train traveled up to 50 mph along the 875 foot track. The ride turned riders upside down a total of six times in the one minute and fifty second ride. Riders experienced a maximum of 5.2 g's. The single train held up to 28 riders in seven four person cars, for a capacity of 750 riders an hour.

The ride was removed during the 2012 season to make room for construction of the *Texas SkyScreamer*.

In keeping with the addition of the *Flashback*, Good Time Square was rethemed as a 1950's style midway. The section restaurant was renamed *Chubbie's Dinner*, serving hamburgers and malts 50's style. The diner seats 200 inside.

As a tie-in to the new ride, the *Southern Palace* show was *Flashback, the Musical*. The fourteen cast members performed numbers based on the high school days and music of the 50's.

The *Crazy Horse Saloon* show featured music based on a Texas theme, with songs such as *The Eyes of Texas* and *Yellow Rose of Texas*. An ice show, *Honor of Bugs,* was featured at the Good Times Square Theater.

In addition, the park's dolphin and sea lion show returned to the *Aquatic Theater* next to the *Tower* after an absence of five seasons.

In Boomtown, *Gold Miner's Hotdogs and Pizza* was renamed as *1/4 Lb Specialty Hotdogs* and *Blue Ribbon Fixin's* became *Turkey Legs and Smoked Sausage.*

At the end of the season, the *Spindletop* was removed after twenty-three years in the park to make way for the exit walkway for the *Texas Giant.*

Attendance changed little from the previous season, with an estimated 2.5 million visitors in both 1988 and 1989.

In Florida, Disney opened its third *Disney World* park, *Disney-MGM Studios,* now known as *Disney Hollywood Studios.* It is estimated that the 135-acre park cost in excess of $500 million.

1990

For its thirtieth anniversary session, Six Flags management opened the largest *roller coaster* in the history of the park. *Six Flags Over Texas* launched the record setting *Texas Giant* on the season's opening day, March 17, 1990.

 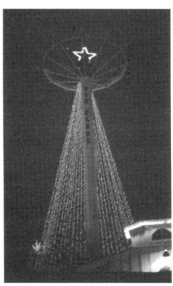

Left, Flashback (1989-2012) in action, 1998.
Right, Texas Chute-Out (1976-2012) with Holiday in the Park Lights, 1985.
Both rides were removed in 2012 to make room for the Texas Skyscreamer.
Both photographs by Author.

Adult tickets increased slightly to $19.95, staying just under the $20 barrier. Children's ticket prices, however, dropped from $13.08 to $9.98.

During the season, the entire Six Flags system of parks celebrated the 50th anniversary of Bugs Bunny.

The Texas Giant.   The *Texas Giant* was the park's seventh operating roller coaster and the parks' second wooden roller coaster. The ride was built at an estimated $5 million. Like the park's other wooden coaster, the Judge Roy Scream, the *Texas Giant* opened on the opening day of the season in which it was installed.

At the time that it was built, it was the world's tallest wooden roller coaster. Another amusement park, *Dorney Park*, challenged Six Flags' claim to the tallest roller coaster based on the fact that *Dorney Park* had a wooden coaster with a longer initial drop. The lift hill on their coaster was, however, lower than the *Giant*. The first drop on the other coaster was longer due to the fact that the ride was built on a hill. As a result, the first drop went below the initial track level, making a longer drop from a lower lift hill. A lawsuit brought against Six Flags by Dorney Park ended with an agreement that Six Flags could claim the "highest lift" and Dorney Park could claim the "longest drop".

Both coasters were constructed by the Dinn Corporation. The original ride was designed by Curtis D. Summers.

The *Giant* is located on 2.9 acres of the park in the Texas section, across the railroad tracks from the Texas railroad station. This area of the park

Original Texas Giant (1990-2009) as viewed from the Six Flags Tower.
The Titan is in the background.
Photograph by Author, 2008.

Texas Giant Train.
Photograph by Author, 2002.

was not previously developed for attractions. The ride was equipped with a state of the art computerized safety system.

The trains of the original *Giant* traveled up an initial lift of 143-feet, which was followed by a 53-degree drop of 137-feet. The trains traveled the 4,920 feet of track in two minutes and fifteen seconds. The trains traveled over 21 drops during the trip. The trains went up to 62 mph and averaged speeds of up to 39 mph. Riders felt positive "g" forces of up to 2.7, with a maximum turn bank of 60 degrees.

The ride required more than 900,000 board feet of pressure treated Southern Yellow pine lumber to build. In addition, 10 tons of nails and 81,370 bolts were used to construct the ride. The ride's three trains were built by the Philadelphia Toboggan Company. They carried up to 28 guests for a capacity of 1,800 riders per hour.

The ride closed on November 1, 2009, for a year-long renovation. The *New Texas Giant* reopened in the 2011 season as quite a different ride. [See the "2011" subchapter for information about the *New Giant*.]

At the time the Giant opened, the Six Flags system operated nine wooden roller coasters and twenty-nine steel coaster in its seven parks. An estimated eighty wooden roller coasters and 144 steel coasters were operated in North America.

Shows.   Six Flags continued the park's dolphin show for the year. Three dolphins were made available to the park due to the closing of *Sea-Arama Marineworld* in Galveston. *Sea Arama* had been in operation for 25 years. The dolphins performed in the *Aquatic Theater* next to the *Tower*. This was the last season for a dolphin show at Six Flags.

Likewise, 1990 was the last year for the *Cinesphere* style movie in the *Cinema 180 Theater,* originally known as the *Chevy Show Theater.*

A new ice show, *Bugs Bunny Celebration on Ice,* opened at the *Good Times Theater.* The show was a celebration of Bugs Bunny's fiftieth anniversary.

Next to the *Texas Depot,* the funnel cake stand became *Texas BBQ* and eventually, *Bubba's Texas Giant Hotdogs. Yosemite Sam's* gift store became *"Giant Souvenirs".*

Craft Festival.   The *Texas Heritage Crafts Festival* was first held in 1990. *The Crafts Festival,* held in the fall, featured numerous skilled persons demonstrating such crafts as wood carving, pottery making, soap making, and doll making. Seasonal snacks were cooked and sold. In addition, folk musicians performed traditional works at various places around the park. The festival continued through the end of the 2009 season. Beginning with the 2006 season, the name was changed to the *Best of Texas Festival.* A summer long event held in 2002 was also named the *Best of Texas Festival.*

With the introduction of the *Texas Giant,* the 1990 season set a new attendance record of 2.9 million visitors, 400,000 more than the season before. This was the highest seasonal attendance in the thirty year history of the park.

Giant Ape climbing the Six Flags Tower as part of the Fright Fest Decorations. Photograph by Author, 1988.

This was also one of the last seasons for which official attendance records were released. In the early 1990s, the management of Six Flags Corporation stopped publishing actual yearly attendance records for each park. Public attendance figures after that time are based on estimates calculated by industry specialists.

Circus World, located in Florida, which had been converted to *Boardwalk and Baseball Park* in 1987, became another causality of the competitive theme park business, closing permanently. The park was owned at the time by Harcourt Brace Jovanovich (HBJ). HBJ also built the *Sea World* parks.

In April 1990, Time Warner purchased a 19.5% share in Six Flags Corp. from Wesray Corp for $19.5 million dollars. The purchase would eventually lead to Time Warner's ownership of the amusement park chain.

10.

THE WARNER YEARS BEGIN
1991 & 1992

1991

The 30th anniversary season of the park was a little less dramatic than the preceding 30th season. Opening on March 9, 1991, no new major rides or attractions were added for the year. Tickets prices were $20.95 for adults. After dropping $4 the year before, children's ticket prices increase nearly $5 to $14.95.

While there was no major additions, the park did renovate the children's area and produced several new shows. A total of $5 million was spent improving the play area. Another $2 million was spent parkwide on improvements and renovations for the season.

Loony Tunes Land. Instead of a major ride addition, *Looney Tunes Land* underwent a major remodeling. As a part of the renovation, four new rides replaced activities in the soft play area. One was the *Martian Escape*, a mini-swing ride manufactured by Zamperla, a ride manufacturer that specializes in smaller rides. The *Martian Escape* was a child's version of the *Texas Tornado* swing ride. The ride was installed in the middle of *Looney Tunes Land*. In 2000, the name of the ride was changed and it was moved south of the railroad tracks.

The second new ride was a small train ride named *Sylvester's Jr.'s Train*. The train was a Zamperla *Rio Grande* style train. Guests could ride in the engine cab, the tender, a gondola, or a passenger car. The ride was located under a covering to the east side of *Looney Tunes Land*.

The *Convoy* was the third new ride. The *Convoy* is a Zamperla *Convoy* truck style ride. The ride units resemble semi-trailer trucks, with cab seating for two children and an open back seat for an adult and child or two children.

Martian Escape, a mini-swing ride was installed in 1991 as part of the revitalization of Looney Tunes Land. In 2001 it was moved to a different location in the section and renamed Michigan J. Frog's Tinseltown Parade.
Photograph by Author, 2012.

Sylvester Jr.'s Train added to Looney Tunes Land in 1991.
Photograph by Author, 1999.

Convoy Trucks, (1991) later renamed as renamed
Speedy Gonzales' Truckin' Across America in 2001.
Photograph by Author, 2012.

Porky Pig Magic Wheel (1991–2001).
The park's second Ferris Wheel style ride.
Photograph by Author, 1998.

The trucks are connected to each other to form a train. It was installed in an open area on the west side of *Looney Tunes Land*. The *Convoy* is still located in the park at its original location. It is now known as *Speedy Gonzales' Truckin' Across America*.

The forth new ride was *Porky Pig's Magic Wheel*, an Eli Bridge Company standard small Ferris wheel with twelve bench seats. *Porky Pig's Magic Wheel* was larger than the park's current *Elmer Fudd Fewwis Wheel*. It was added south of the railroad tracks, near the location of the section's current four children's rides. The ride was removed in 2001.

In addition to the new rides, a small jumping water fountain was placed at the north entrance in the section. The fountain was removed in 2006 and replaced with the *Looney Tunes Gazebo* stage.

As part of the Looney Tunes theming, the *Kooper Kettle* restaurant was renamed as *Wascal's Burgers and Fries*.

Hollywood Stunt Show. At the *Tower Theater*, the *Hollywood Stunt Show* replaced the *Dolphin Show*. There was little change in the theater. The pool itself was covered to create a large performance area, with a western town façade added at the back. The show featured trained stunt-men performing various action scenes. One featured a character using a zip line to enter the arena from the fifty foot platform of the tower.

Unending action at the Hollywood Stunt Show at the Tower Theater (1991).
The large sand stage area covered the former dolphin and diving pool.
Photograph by Author, 1991.

The Hollywood Stunt Show was produced by Benros Worldwide Entertainment and was staged for one year. Benros later produced *Gunfight After the OK Corral* and *Bad Day at the Backlot* stunt shows in the Texas section of the park. In addition to producing shows in numerous other parks, Benros staged the *Colossus* show for Freedomland in 1961.

The *Southern Palace* show was *PIZZAZZ!* The *Bugs Bunny Celebration on Ice* was held over for another season at the *Good Times Theater*. A new magic show started a two season run at *The Lone Star Theater*, the new name for the former *Chevy Show*.

A special show, *The Moscow Circus - Cirk Valentin* was performed in the park on weekends in the fall. The show was not a traditional circus, but one that emphasized dance, special lighting, music, and special effects. The show featured 45 performers, including acrobats, jugglers, and high-wire walkers.

In order to provide a smoother ride, renovations were made to the *Texas Giant* roller coaster. This would be the first in a series of on-going renovations designed to keep the wooden ride running as smoothly as it did when it first opened.

At the end of the season, the Speelunkers were removed from the cave to make way for a total refurbishing of the park's only dark ride. The Speelunkers occupied the attraction for twenty-eight seasons.

In addition, the *Skeeball Palace*, located near the tower, was removed to make room for the *Batman Stunt Show* to open the following season.

The balloon stand in the Mexican section became *Funamis Puppets*.

The season ended with approximately 2.7 million guests visiting the park, down slightly from the preceding season.

Ownership. During the year, Wesray Corporation sold its entire interests in the Six Flags parks. Time Warner Corporation purchased additional shares of Six Flags from Wesray, increasing its ownership interest in the park system from 19.5% to 50%. Two investment interests, The Blackstone Group and Wertheim Schroder, bought the second half-interest in the park system from Wesray Corporation. Time Warner and the two investment companies paid an estimated $710 million for seven theme parks, the animal park and one water park.

Time Warner contributed $30 million to purchase another 30% interest in the parks, while the two other firms paid $100 million for their interests. The remaining $570 was borrowed by the three firms together to complete the purchase. The money was used by Six Flags Corp. to reduce debt of $610 million from the 1987 leveraged buyout by Wesray Capital Corp.

Counting the water and animal park as a half park each, and factoring in Time Warner's current ownership, the price averaged to nearly $100 million per theme park. Under the new ownership, Six Flags Corporation continued to manage the Texas park for the limited partnership that owns the park.

1992

The 1992 season opened on February 29, the first time that the park opened in February. The season was highlighted by a major ride overhaul and a new show. The overhaul was of the *Cave* ride, although the new version did not open until June. The new show was the *Batman Stunt Show*. Ticket prices were $22.95 for adults and $16.95 for children 48 inches and under.

Yosemite Sam and the Gold River Adventure. Having removed the banana-head shaped Speelunkers from the cave, the ride reopened for the 1992 season as "Yosemite Sam and the Gold River Adventure". Also known just as the "Gold River Adventure", the new version of the ride featured Bugs Bunny and the other Looney Tunes characters.

The ride depicts the story of Yosemite Sam's robbery of "the payroll". "Sheriff" Bugs Bunny and his friends are responsible for seeing that the gold is returned and that the perpetrator is locked up for his misdeeds. As might be anticipated, the story ends happily for everyone but Sam.

The ride animations and features were designed by R & R Creative Amusement Design. The twenty-four ride scenes were built by Sally Dark Rides, a ride and animation company. According to the company, the redesigned ride contains twenty-nine animated characters as part of a total of 125 animations and other special effects.

All of the inhabitants of the cave were removed and replaced. In addition, most of the original special effects, such as the storm and rotating barrel were also removed or disabled. The ride structure itself, however, remained the same. The 3 ½ minute ride consisted of the same waterway through the same 20,000 square foot area as the original Speelunker cave.

The make-over cost $5 million dollars and opened in June of the year.

Batman Stunt Show. Also new for the season, the *Batman Stunt Show* was built at site of the *Hollywood Stunt Show*. The former arena and western set were removed. A larger theater was built in front of a three story set designed to resemble an industrial site in Gotham City, home to Batman and the villains that he battles. The newly renovated amphitheater could seat 2,500.

The show portrayed Batman's battle with the Joker. Explosions and fires augmented the action stunts. An appearance was also made by a twenty-one foot long Batmobile, which rolled onto the action area. The show corresponded with the release of the Time Warner movie *Batman Returns*. The renovations, sets, and props cost $3 million, with $63,000 alone spent on the Batmobile.

In addition to the Looney Tunes characters entertaining the crowds, the season saw the addition of a new Looney Tunes themed gift shop. The 6,300 square foot store, located north of the Looney Tunes rides and play

Yosemite Sam and the Gold River Adventure.
Photograph by Author, 2005.

Gold River Adventure scene, Bugs Bunny and Elmer Fudd recovered the Gold.
Six Flags' public relations photograph, circa 1992.

Batman and Batmobile in Batman Stunt Show (1992–2000) at the Tower Theater.
Photograph by Author, 1995.

area, was the largest store in park history. The store was located in the building that originally held the park's exhibit halls.

We are the World, also referred to in some materials as *Do You Hear the People Sing*, was staged at the *Southern Palace Theater*. *One More Payment and its Mine* was performed at the *Crazy Horse Saloon*. *Bugs Bunny Goin' Hollywood* was the show in *Looney Tunes Theater*. The magic show was held over at the *Lone Star Theater*.

Special events included *Fright Nights*, with Arania, the Black Widow Bride, widow of 13 husbands. *Texas Heritage Crafts Festival* was held again, as was *Holiday in the Park*, which featured a major ice production.

The park set a new yearly attendance record that was the highest for the first forty-five seasons and possibly the highest in the history of the park. With attendance up 22% over the 1991 season, park officials announced that over 3 million guests visited the park.

In March 1992, *Fiesta Texas*, the third major theme park in Texas, opened in San Antonio, Texas. It was built by USAA Real Estate Company and Gaylord Entertainment Company. Gaylord also owned *Opryland USA* theme park in Nashville, Texas.

In Bloomington, Minnesota, the Mall of America opened with its indoor amusement park, *Knott's Camp Snoopy*. The park has changed ownership and names, but is still operating. Its current name is *Nickelodeon Universe*.

In March of 1992, C.V. Wood passed away at age 71 and in December, theme park designer Randall Duell passed away at age 89.

11.

TIME WARNER II
1993 - 1995

1993

Time Warner purchased the remaining half of Six Flags, Corp. in 1993 and became the sole owner of the chain of seven amusement parks. Warner paid $70 million for the remaining interest in the park system. The purchase likely also required Warner Brothers to take on responsibility for the existing investment debt of the three owners. The seven parks then managed by the chain were the original *Six Flags Over Texas, Georgia,* and *Mid-America,* as well as *Astroworld, Magic Mountain, Great Adventure,* and *Great America.* During the changeover in ownership, no new rides or major attractions were added to the Texas park.

Ticket prices went up two dollars to $24.95 for adults. Tickets for seniors and children under 48 inches tall remained at $16.95.

The park opened on March 6th, 1993. Although no new attractions were added to the park, there were still some improvements. A complete facelift was performed on the Frontgate area. In addition, the Texas Giant was once again fine tuned between seasons to make it smoother and faster. Work was done to improve a banked section of track to give an extra boost of speed in the last 1,000 feet of the track. The changes made the ride slightly faster and trimmed a few seconds off of the ride time.

The *Southern Palace* hosted an ice skating show produced by Dick Foster Productions called *Ice Express.* This was the first time an ice show was hosted at the theater. Previous ice shows were at the Good Times Square Theater. *Now that Country* was the musical at the *Crazy Horse Saloon.* Next to the *Tower,* the *Batman Show* was expanded to include the Penguin and Catwoman characters.

Special events included *Spring Break-out* and *Fright Fest,* with the return of Arania the Black Widow Bride, and her new partner Dr. Blood. *The Texas Heritage Crafts Festival* and *Holiday in the Park* were also continued.

213

Attendance for the year is estimated to have fallen just under the 3 million mark and below the record set the year before.

In December of 1993, MGM *Grand Adventures Theme Park* opened in Las Vegas. The Hollywood themed park closed permanently in 2002.

The amusement park chain's official name was changed during 1993 from "Six Flags Corporation" to "Six Flags Theme Parks, Inc".

1994

The park opened for the season on March 5, 1994. Adult ticket prices went to $25.95, with $19.95 for kids and seniors. As always, children under 2 were free. The park was up to 205 acres, of which 100 were for entertainment.

For the first time in the history of the park, no major attraction was added for two consecutive seasons. Instead, the *Judge Roy Scream* was reenergized by running the trains backwards to provide a new ride experience.

As Warner Brothers continued to manage the park, additional shows were scripted to feature Warner Brother's characters and works. Music from the Warner Brothers movie *Pure Country*, staring George Strait, was featured in the *Lone Star Theater*.

The *Warner Music Rock Revue* was featured in the *David Blackburn Southern Palace Music Hall*. The show featured hits by Warner Brothers top recording artists. *Miss Lillie's Red Garter* was on stage at the *Crazy Horse Saloon*. For variety, the show featured a knife thrower.

A Hollywood animal act was also featured in the *Good Time Theater*, which was renamed to the *Animal Action Theater*. The audience saw demonstrations of the methods used to train animals for parts in movies and television. Animal actors included dogs, cats, and a pot bellied pig. Dogs and cats used in the show were rescued from local animal shelters. The show ran for five seasons before being replaced by *Illusionaria*.

The *Batman Show* continued in the Tower Arena.

The *O.K Corral Shoot-out Backlot* show was an outdoor action-comedy stunt-show featured in the Texas section. Rather than in front of the Courthouse and Jail, where the gunfights had typically been held, the show was performed in the area around the *Jersey Lilly*. For the stunts, additional sets and facades of western buildings where added. The show was tied into the release of the Warner Brother's movie *Wyatt Earp*.

Attendance for the year was estimated to have exceeded three million guests for the second time, ending just under the 1992 estimate. If accurate, this season was the second highest attendance year in the history of the park. In addition, sometime during the year, it is likely that the seventh-fifth millionth guest entered the park.

1995

The first day of operations for 1995 was Friday, April 28. This was the latest opening since 1967, and nearly six weeks later than recent openings. Admission increased two dollars for both adults and children tickets, reaching $27.95 for adults and $21.95 for children under 48 inches and seniors. Children under 2 were free.

In 1987, Disney opened *Star Tours*, a cutting edge virtual reality ride based on the highly successful *Star Wars* movies. In turn, Universal Studios opened its *Back to the Future* virtual reality ride in Florida in 1991 and in Hollywood in 1993. The success of these simulator rides increased interest in developing new virtual reality rides.

Right Stuff Theater. For 1995, Six Flags once again offered a virtual reality theater. Unlike the previous *Sensational Sense Machine*, this theater did not feature a building that rolled and turned. Instead, for the *Right Stuff Theater*, the seats themselves were mounted on mechanisms that allowed them to pivot and rotate individually based on the action on the screen. The action of the seats gave the rider the sense that they were participating in the action depicted on the screen. With perhaps a little bit of overstatement, the attraction was billed as "the most spectacular ride experience in the 34-year history of *Six Flags Over Texas*".

Hanger and F-104A Starfighter at the Right Stuff Theater, (1995–1998).
Photograph by Author, 1998.

The theater seats moved in sets of two. This design allowed for precise fine tuning of each seat for a more realistic experience. Controlled by computer, the seat movement could easily be reprogrammed to move in sync with different films.

The first movie shown in the theater was the four minute *Right Stuff*, for which the theater was then named. The *Right Stuff* simulated flight through the sound barrier in a jet aircraft. The rider experienced the flight from takeoff to landing.

The attraction was named after Warner Brothers' Oscar winning feature movie. The feature film traces the early history of the manned space program from experimental jet fighters through the flights of the first seven Mercury astronauts. The movie was in turn based on Tom Wolfe's book of the same name.

The theater featured a "preshow" area in which the guests waiting to enter the theater could view a short movie on video monitors. For the *Right Stuff*, the preshow monitors briefed the guests on the history of the first flights through the sound barrier.

The attraction opened on April 28, 1995, with four of the original seven Mercury astronauts on hand as guests of honor. Present to test out the ride were Alan Shepard. Aboard the *Freedom 7,* he became the first American to fly in space. Also present were Scott Carpenter, astronaut of the *Aurora 7*; Walter "Wally" Schirra, who flew in *Sigma 7*; and L. Gordon Cooper, who flew the longest Mercury mission in *Faith 7*.

The movie and seats were developed by Iwerks of Los Angles, California. Iwerks later became a part of SimEx ! Iwerks Entertainment. The film itself was conceptualized by Six Flags. The theater was a clone of the *Right Stuff* theater that was installed at *Six Flags Great Adventure* the season before.

The attraction was expected to entertain 1,100 visitors an hour. Although specific installation costs were not released, the ride was billed as a "multimillion" dollar ride.

In order to create atmosphere for the film, the theater building was designed to resemble an Edwards Air Force Base hanger. Edwards Air Base was the site of the events in the *Right Stuff* book and movie. An F-104 jet fighter was parked in front of the hanger, not far from where a jet fighter was displayed in the park's first season.

The versatility of the theater was the fact that the movie shown could be easily changed from year to year. As the movies changed over the years, there was no reason to continue to refer to the theater as the *Right Stuff* theater. The theater later became generically known as the *Adventure Theater* and the *3D Adventure Theater*.

In keeping with the addition of the theater, the entire modern section was rethemed to resemble an Air Force base used for astronaut training. Accordingly, the Cliffhanger was renamed as the *G-Force Anti-Gravitational*

Test Facility. Splashwater Falls' name was changed to "Splashdown Reentry Test Simulation", also referred to as "Splashwater Reentry Test Simulator".

The Chameleon.   Six Flags also offered a new upcharge ride for 1995. An upcharge ride is one that requires a separate payment, above the admission ticket. Such attractions are generally extra due to the extremely low capacity at which they can operate. The *Chameleon Virtual Reality Ride* was added in the Good Time Square area, near the train station. The attraction opened on July 14. Riders paid $5.00 to experience the system.

The Chameleon was another virtual-reality attraction. The ride was also a virtual game, with state of the art graphics. The ride consisted of six arms that rotated around a central hub. At the end of each arm was a two person capsule. The capsules could also rotate on the end of the arms. The small ride units moved in sync with the action displayed on a screen inside the units.

The ride was the first of its type operating in the United States. Graphics were generated using the same system used to create the dinosaurs for the movie *Jurassic Park*. The original game was *Labyrinth Rangers*, a space travel themed game in which the participants fought to save the universe. Since the ride was computer controlled, it was capable of running other games as well.

The ride was open in the park for four seasons. It was removed after the 1998 season.

The musical *Hot Rockin' Country*, a high-tech tribute to country music, began a four season run in the *Southern Palace. Miss Lillie's Red Garter Revue* continued a second season at the *Crazy Horse Saloon*.

In the Texas section, *Giant Souvenirs* became *Six Flag Kids*.

At the end of the 1995 season, the *Spinnaker* was removed from its location south of the *Tower* in order to make room for *Runaway Mountain*. The *Spinnaker* was later installed at *Six Flags Fiesta Texas*, where it was dubbed the *Wagon Wheel*.

During the year, Time Warner sold 51 percent interest in the park system to Boston Ventures for $1 billion. An investment group lead by Boston Venture paid Time Warner $200 million in cash and assumed $800 million in Time Warner debt. The deal was a part of a larger effort by Time Warner to reduce its corporate debt. The deal included purchase of five parks and the management of the partnership owned parks. These were the same seven parks operated by the chain since 1984. System wide attendance was estimated at 22 million guests a year.

Nationwide, the amusement park industry saw one of its largest single season increases, with estimated attendance rising to 280 million from 267 million. At the Arlington park, it was estimated that the season's attendance mark dropped just under the elusive 3 million mark, with 2.9 million visitors for the year.

12.

WARNER BROTHERS & BOSTON VENTURES
1996 & 1997

1996

The thirty-fifth anniversary of the park was celebrated in 1996. The park opened on March 2, 1996. During the opening weekend, anyone born the month the park originally opened, August of 1961, was allowed free admission to the park.

Steve Calloway took over as the General Manager of the park, replacing Bob Bennett, who retired after serving as the head for the park for the past eleven seasons. Bennett worked for Six Flags parks for 22 years. Calloway started as a seasonal employee at *Six Flags Over Georgia* in 1968, before working his way up the Six Flags' management ladder.

Tickets prices again rose two dollars, increasing to $29.95 for adults and $23.95 for children under 4 feet, with children under three free.

Runaway Mountain Roller Coaster. The *Runaway Mountain* roller coaster was added for the 1996 season. The ride brought the number of roller

Runaway Mountain (1996) ride units.
Six Flags' public relations photo,
circa 1996.

218

coasters operating in the park to eight. The ride was billed as "the Coaster that Dares the Darkness".

Runaway Mountain is located in the Confederate section next to the *Southern Palace*, in an area once occupied by the *Skull Island River Raft* ride and more recently by the *Spinnaker*.

The ride was built by Premier Rides of Maryland. Premier Rides would also build Six Flags' next roller coaster, the *Mr. Freeze*. Premier Rides is a different company from Premier Parks, the amusement park company.

Runaway Mountain's key feature is that the entire ride is contained inside a 14,000 square foot building. The darkness of the interior prevents the riders from knowing where they are heading. This lack of knowledge makes the ride more thrilling, even though it is not as tall as some of the other major coasters.

The ride's three passenger trains reach speeds of up to 40 mph and maximum g-forces of up to 3.6 g's. Each train holds twelve passengers in three cars, each of which seat four guests. The ride includes drops of nearly 90 degrees, banked turns at 82 degrees, and two high speed horizontal spirals.

The ride is 53-feet high and the track length is 1430 feet. The ride lasts one and a half minutes and can entertain 950 guests an hour. The ride cost an estimated $5 to $6 million dollars to develop and construct.

The publicity for the ride resembled the story line for the original skull island. As with the Skull Island, which was located in the same area, the mountain was said to contain gold left by the famous pirate Jean LaFitte.

Runaway Mountain ~ The Ride that Dares the Darkness (1996).
Photograph by Author, 2008.

The riders are on a search for the gold as they explore the mysteries of the mountain.

The ride was designed using the most current computer aided design techniques. It incorporates a "heart-line design", meaning that the rider's heart was used as the center of gravity. The ride also employs state-of-the-art computer controls, as well as a chainless lift that provides much quieter operation.

To add to the theming of the new roller coaster, *Granny's Chicken Restaurant* was renamed to *Gator McGee's Mountain Grill*. This was the location of the original *Naler's Chicken Plantation*. Gator McGee was a character created for the ride's backstory.

Dive Bomber Alley.   Six Flags' second major up-charge ride was also added in 1996. The ride is a *Skycoaster* style ride, installed and managed by Skycoaster, Inc. The ride swings riders suspended by cables through the air. It consists of two towers. One is a 173-foot tall arch tower. Behind it is a 153-feet launch tower. Riders are suspended from the arch tower by cables attached to a harness. A cable system connected to the towers pulls riders up towards the top of the arch as well as back towards the launch tower. When in position, the launch cable attached to the harness is released. The riders then swing out over Caddo lake suspended by the cable attached to the arch tower.

The two Dive Bomber Alley towers are shown above.
The tower which raises the riders into the air is shown in the middle of the picture.
The second, "V" shaped tower, is behind the Adventure Theater to the right.
Photograph by Author, 1995.

The ride was a development of the "bungee cord" era in which various attractions were designed to allow riders to feel the sensation of flying or controlled free falling. The ride has a $25 up-charge fee. The ride can accommodate approximately 36 riders per hour. A nearly identical Skycoaster, the *Caribbean Swing*, operates at *Six Flags Hurricane Harbor*.

At the *Crazy Horse Saloon*, the *Wild West Revue* began a three season run. *Bugs Bunny Wacky World Games* was on stage for a season at the *Lone Star Theater*. In addition, the *Texas Backlot Stunt Show* featured a new show.

In the Mexican section, the *Mexican Restaurant* was more formally named *Casa de Las Banderas*. The name translates to "House of the Flags".

The new Boomtown Station built after the Good Time Square Depot was removed to make room for the Mr. Freeze. Photograph by Author, 2007.

At the end of 1996, the Good Time Square train station was removed to make room for the upcoming *Mr. Freeze Roller Coaster*. A new Boomtown station was opened at the same location on the other side of the tracks. The new Boomtown station was different in design from the original station that stood at nearly the same location. The new station does not have any actual station building and consists instead of a loading platform and queue area

Estimated attendance at the park for the season was 3.1 million guests, again taking the park past the 3 million mark.

In January of 1996, Six Flags Theme Parks, Inc. took over the management of *Fiesta Texas*, with a ten year lease and an option to purchase the park. This was the first full amusement park added to the Six Flags system since the purchase of *Six Flags Great America* in 1984, twelve years earlier. It brought the number of Six Flags parks to eight and put Six Flags in control of three of the major amusement parks in Texas, *Six Flags Over Texas*, *Astroworld*, and *Fiesta Texas*.

Fright Fest character with guest in Looney Tune's Land.
Photograph by Author, 1996.

In 1995, Six Flags also purchased *Wet 'n Wild* in Arlington. Six Flags operated the park in 1996 under the *Wet 'n Wild* name. The name was changed to *Six Flags Hurricane Harbor* in January of 1997.

The International Association of Amusement Parks and Attractions designated 1996 the "International year of the roller coaster".

1997

The park opened on March 1, 1997. For the 1997 season, tickets prices were up two dollars to $31.97 for adults and $25.99 for children. The season saw little change, due to delays in opening the park's new attraction, the *Mr. Freeze* roller coaster.

Mr. Freeze Roller Coaster. The *Mr. Freeze* roller coaster was constructed in 1997 by Premier Rides, Inc. Named for the Mr. Freeze villain from the Batman universe, the ride's opening was set to coincide with Warner Brother's 1997 release of *Batman & Robin*, starring Arnold Schwarzenegger as Batman's arch villain, "Mr. Freeze". Due to technical difficulties with the new ride technology, however, the ride did not open until 1998, leaving the park without a major new ride for the season.

Most of the theaters continued their current productions. One exception was the *Lone Star Theater*, which started a two season run of *Warner Brothers Behind the Scenes*, a look behind the scenes at the making of a movie.

At the end of the season, the smaller of the park's two Ferris wheels, the *Elmer Fudd Ferris Wheel*, was removed from Looney Tunes Land.

Despite much higher than average rain fall and the failure to open the new cutting edge ride, Six Flags reported that 1997 was the Texas park's third highest season for both attendance and revenue. Attendance for the year was estimated at 3.1 million.

New theme parks were no longer being built at the rate at which they were constructed in the 70's. Although new theme park construction was down, existing theme parks continued to expand. It was estimated that fifty new roller coasters were built worldwide. Although many were expanding, one modern theme park, *Opryland USA*, closed in 1997 after twenty-six years of operation.

Outside the park, *Wet'n Wild* in Arlington, now owned by Six Flags Theme Parks, Inc. was renamed to *Six Flags' Hurricane Harbor*.

In December of 1997, a fifteen mile section of Highway 360 was designated as the "Angus Wynne Freeway" in honor of Angus Wynne and his economic contributions to Arlington and Grand Prairie.

By 1997, Six Flags was referencing *sixflags.com* in public relations materials.

Indian Village Trading Post, opened with the park in 1961 and is still in operation.
Originally, part of the Indian Village, Native American dancers performed in an area
behind the building. The building's roof line was raised in approximately 1966. In 1968,
the Indian dances ended and the back of the building was expanded to house the Cyclorama
of the American Indian, later converted to the People Mover Show, Country Critter Review,
and the Pac-Man Magic Show. The area in the back is no longer a guest area.
Photograph by Author, 1998.

13.

PREMIER PARKS
1998 – 2004

Premier Parks Ownership.   Separate limited partnerships
owned *Six Flags Over Georgia* and *Six Flags Over Texas* since 1969
and 1970, respectfully. The limited partnerships each contracted with the Six
Flags park chain to manage the parks. The management agreements between
the limited partnerships and the corporation were set to expire in December
of 1997. During 1997, the two partnerships each began negotiations to renew
the management agreements.

In March of 1997, the partners in the *Six Flags Over Georgia* partnership
entered into a new agreement with Six Flags Theme Parks, Inc. The new
agreement provided for a renewal of the lease of the park with an option for
the partners to sell their shares to the corporation over the next thirty years.
Under the agreement, all shares of the limited partnership would be purchased
by the Six Flags corporation by no later than 2027. At that time, the Georgia
park would be owned by the Six Flags corporation.

Negotiations with the partners in the Texas partnership, however, did
not proceed so smoothly. The partners in the limited partnership could not
reach a new agreement with the Six Flags management. Negotiations continued throughout 1997. Reportedly, the limited partners were making plans to
take over control of the park in the event that negotiations fell through.

During the negotiation period, Premier Parks, an amusement park
company based in Oklahoma City, made its own effort to reach an agreement
with the limited partnership members to manage the Texas park. In October
of 1997, Premier Parks announced that the parties had reached an agreement.
As part of the deal, Premier Parks would enter into an option to purchase the
park after 30 years for $315 million.

Faced with the prospect of losing control of the original Six Flags
park, Six Flags Theme Parks redoubled its efforts to reach its own deal with
the limited partnership. In November of 1997, Six Flags Theme Parks, Inc.
managed to outbid Premier Park and reached an arrangement with the Texas
limited partnership similar to the agreement reached with the Georgia partner-

ship. It was estimated that the Six Flags chain would purchase the park from the limited partnership over a time period for $350 million to $375 million.

Four months later, however, in a major surprise for the amusement park industry, Premier Parks entered into an agreement to purchase the entire Six Flags chain of twelve parks for $1.86 billion dollars.

At the time, the parks were owned or managed by Six Flags Theme Parks, Inc., a Time Warner subsidiary. Time Warner owned 49% of the subsidiary and Boston Ventures, a venture equity group, owned the remaining 51%. Premier agreed to pay $965 million to Time Warner and its equity partner. In addition, Premier assumed $890 million in current debt, bringing the total to the $1.86 billion. As part of the deal, Time Warner licensed continued use of its Looney Tune and superhero characters to Premier.

Six Flags Theme Parks, Inc. consisted of twelve regional parks. These included eight theme parks, three water parks, and one wildlife safari park. The park chain had 22 million visitors in 1997.

Premier Parks owned more parks than Six Flags, operating 13 regional US theme parks, one more than Six Flags. These were, however, significantly smaller parks. By comparison, the total number of visitors to Premier parks in 1997 was 11 million visitors, half as many guests as the Six Flags parks. Premier was also in the process of buying six foreign parks.

After the purchase of both Six Flags and the foreign parks, Premier owned 31 parks around the world. Total combined attendance from all of these parks worldwide was 37 million in 1997.

As part of the deal, Premier Parks assumed Warner's long term agreement to purchase *Six Flags Over Texas* from the limited partnership.

After the purchase, Premier began renaming many of the parks that it already owned with the popular "Six Flags" name.

1998

Unaffected by the change in ownership of the chain, *Six Flags Over Texas* opened on February 28, 1998, with a slow day and light attendance. Ticket prices under the new management were up almost a dollar to $32.95 for adults and $26.91 for children and senior citizens.

Mr. Freeze. The *Mr. Freeze* roller coaster, which the park management and Premier Rides spent the 1997 season adjusting and refining, opened for the 1998 season. The ride cost an estimated $6.5 million dollars to construct and develop, making it the park's most expensive ride to that date. Opening of the new coaster brought the park's roller coaster count to nine.

The ride was built on the border between Good Time Square and Boomtown in the northeast section of the park. As part of the theming, the ride's queue house was built to resemble a decaying ice cream factory, with a huge ice cream man head for the entrance. The ride's tagline was "The Coolest Coaster on the Planet".

The Mr. Freeze roller coaster varies from traditional roller coasters in that it does not have a lift to pull the trains to a starting point. Instead, the

Mr. Freeze roller coaster track in 1997, during construction and testing.
Photograph by Author, 1997.

ride uses rare earth magnets mounted along the track in the station house to "launch" the train out of the station.

Mr. Freeze was built by Premier Rides and designed by Werner Stengel. Stengel is a German engineer who previously worked at Schwarzkopf Industries with Anton Schwarzkopf, the designer of the *Big Bend* and *Shockwave*. Stengel also participated in the design of the *Batman, the Ride*.

Snowy's Ice Cream Factory, home to the Mr. Freeze roller coaster.
Photograph by Author, 2014.

Using rare earth magnets and linear induction motors to propel the ride's trains out of the station house, the ride reaches a speed of 70 mph in 3.78 seconds. The ride uses 172 linear induction motors to launch the trains and another 40 linear induction motors to push the train up the last vertical track. The linear induction motors are also used as brakes to slow the trains. A total of 224 induction motors are used on the ride.

The coaster's two trains each hold twenty guests in five cars. Passengers sit in rows of two. Ride capacity is 1000 per hour. The ride operates on 1,300 feet of track and the launch tunnel is 190 feet long. During the 45 second ride, riders pull up to 4 g's.

The ride uses a substitution switch in the station house to allow running two trains. To load and unload a train, the switching table slides a small section of track holding the train to the side of the main track. As this section of track moves into the loading zone, another section of track holding a second train aligns with the ride's main track. This second train then launches and returns to the start position. When it returns to the station, the table slides the track on which it rests to the opposite side of the station. At the same time, the track holding the first train slides in position to launch while the second train loads and unloads.

Mr. Freeze trains heads to the top of the 218 foot tower.
Photograph by Author, 1998.

Running the ride requires 5,000 amp of electricity at 480 volts. The ride requires electric cabinets 150 feet long and 7 feet high.

The trains travel through a series of elements, including a 150 foot high inversion, ending in a 218 foot tall vertical section of track. Near the middle of the tower, a second set of rare earth magnets shoots the trains up again, pushing the trains nearly to the top of the track. This gives the riders the impression that the train will shot straight off the track. As the train travels up the track, it slowly loses power, until it comes to a momentary stop. During that moment, the riders experience weightlessness. The train then starts to fall back, running the same track backwards.

The theming for the ride was provided by Jack Rouse Associates. Jack Rouse designed the *Snowy's Ice Cream Factory* that houses the rides queue house, loading dock, and launch tunnel. The company also designed the features and sets inside the building and at the launch dock. In addition, they designed a Boomtown makeover, including the new railroad station and surrounding sets.

On March 25, 1998, *Mr. Freeze* finally had its promotional opening. The official initial rides were extended to members of the press, special guests, and more than two dozen men with the last names of "Freeze". One family in particular was represented by three generations of "Mr. Freeze". The ride officially opened to the general public on March 28.

In 2002, the ride's over the shoulder restraints were replaced with ratcheting lap bars.

For the 2012 season, the Mr. Freeze trains were mounted on the track backwards so that the trains left the station backwards and returned at the end of the trip with the guests facing forward.

A sister coaster was built at the same time at *Six Flags St. Louis* (Formerly *Six Flags Mid-America*). The St. Louis *Mr. Freeze* is a mirror image of the Texas coaster.

For the 1998 season, the *Mini Mine Train* was reopened, after being rebuilt to accommodate the construction and track placement of the *Mr. Freeze*.

Attendance estimates for the season were slightly below the prior season, with an estimated 2.8 million guests during the season.

Construction of new roller coasters continued during the year. Around the world, sixty-seven new coasters were opening. Thirty-three were set to open in North America for a total of 345 coasters. This compares to an estimated total of 145 coasters twenty years earlier in 1979.

In April of 1998, Disney opened *Disney's Animal Kingdom* as its fourth park at the *Walt Disney World* complex. With over 500 acres, the park is the largest park in the world.

1999

For the last season of the century, the park opened on March 6, with the start of the spring break celebration. Six Flags Theme Parks reduced children's ticket prices at all of its parks nationwide. At the Arlington park, ticket prices for children under 48 inches were dropped by nearly a third from $26.91 to $17.50. Children prices had not been this low since 1993. Adult tickets, on the other hand, rose two dollars from $32.95 to $34.99.

For 1999, the park spent $14 million dollars in what was reported to be the largest seasonal capital expenditures in the park to date. The park added Gotham City, an entirely new theme section, and opened *Batman the Ride*, its tenth roller coaster.

Gotham City is the home to Batman the crime fighter; the new section became home to the new *Batman* the roller coaster. The section was added north of Good Time Square. Predictably, the *Mr. Freeze* ride was also included in the new section.

Batman roller coaster traveling around loop. Photograph by Author, 2010.

Portions of Good Time Square, including the games area, were removed to make way for the expansion. Similar carnival games, however, are provided in both the new Gotham City area and in Boomtown.

Batman, the Ride. *Batman the Ride* opened the season following the opening of the *Mr. Freeze*. *Batman* is the park's only suspended roller coaster, with the cars riding below the track. Since they are suspended, the trains travel around the outside of the ride's loops, rather than inside. In addition to being suspended, the ride is floorless, so that the rider's legs hang below the cars.

With an initial lift height of 109 feet, the ride reaches 52 mph. Riders feel up to 4 g's. Designed capacity is 1,400 riders an hour.

Batman the Ride suspended roller coaster.
Photograph by Author, 2007.

The ride, built by Bollinger & Mabillard of Switzerland, contains 2,700 feet of track. Featured ride elements include a 77-foot tall vertical loop; a 68-foot tall vertical loop; two 40-foot tall corkscrew spirals; "s" curves; flat spins and a zero gravity heartline spin. The ride features two 32 passenger trains, with riders suspended four across.

The ride is one of seven similar *Batman* style rides installed in various Six Flags parks. All operate as *Batman the Ride*, except one, known as the *Goliath* in *Fiesta Texas*. It previously was the *Batman the Ride* at *Six Flags New Orleans*.

A media event for the new ride was held on May 26, 1999. The honorary first riders were a group of Arlington firefighters, along with the caped crusader himself. The ride opened to the public the next day.

Go-carts.   In addition to the *Batman*, an up-charge go-cart track was added between the railroad tracks and the *Shockwave*. Riders race traditional go-carts around the winding track. The track sports forty go-carts, twenty-four of which have individual seating and sixteen of which have dual seating. Only twenty carts run on the track at any one time. Track races last four to six minutes.

The track and carts cost the park $500,000. Premier Parks installed similar tracks at nine of its 25 parks. There is a $5 up-charge to race the carts.

Shows.   The 1999 season was a big year for shows in the park. Seven new shows were added at existing theaters. Corresponding with the

*Escape from Dino Island, (1999–2001)
at Adventure Theater.
Photograph by Author, 2001.*

addition of the Gotham City section, the *Batman Stunt Show* was updated to the *Gotham City Carnival of Chaos* at the *Tower Theater.* The show featured Batman trying to prevent his arch rival the Joker from interfering with the Gotham Circus.

In addition to the *Batman* show, the 3D film "*Escape From Dino Island 3-D*" replaced the *Right Stuff* at the *Adventure Theater* in the USA section. The new show was also a virtual reality presentation, with the action on the screen programmed to match the action of the seats. The show entertained guests with the story of the dangerous rescue of a dinosaur from a volcanic island. The show ran for three seasons.

A magic show, *Illusionaria*, replaced the *Hollywood Animal Action Show* at the *Good Times Square Theater.* A magician and his four assistants performed various feats of magic, including sawing two ladies in half at the same time. This show continued for three years and was followed for three years more years by another magic show, *Merlin's Magicademy.*

The *Texas Backlot Stunt Show,* featuring gunfighters and stunt performers, continued as a street show in the Texas Section.

The *Southern Palace* featured *Hooray for Hollywood,* with songs and dances from classic movie musicals. The *Crazy Horse Saloon Revue* was featured at the *Crazy Horse.* The Texas history movie, *Lone Star Legacy* was shown in the *Lone Star Theater.*

At the end of the 1999 season, the *Air Racer* was removed after sixteen seasons in the park.

Industry estimates were that attendance was down at the Arlington park 2% from 1998, with an estimated 2.75 to 2.8 million guests. One park spokesman, however, indicated that there was a 2% increase in attendance in 1999. This increase was attributed to the success of the special events held at the park during the year. As is the current practice, specific numbers were not provided.

Nationwide amusement park attendance increased 3% to 5% per year for twenty years. Every year was a new attendance record, and 1999 was no different. It was estimated that 309 million individuals visited amusement parks during the season.

Games in Gotham City Section replaced those in Good Times Square.
Photograph by Author 2007.

2000

The fortieth season saw little change in the park. The park opened on March 11, 2000. Nationwide, the average one-day ticket price for amusement parks increased $2.00 to $37.00. In Arlington, adult prices were right at the national level at $36.99 before taxes. Children's tickets were approximately half that price, at $18.50. This was up a dollar after the previous season's dramatic drop in children's ticket prices.

While the season saw some improvements to the appearance of the park, no major attraction was added.

The season brought the return of a previously removed type of ride to the park. A scrambler ride named the *Missilechaser* was installed at the former site of the *Air Racer*. Although the same type of ride, it was not the exact same unit that had previously operated in the Modern section.

At the end of the season, *Wascal's Burgers and Fries* restaurant was removed to make room for the upcoming *Wyle E. Coyote's Grand Canyon Blaster* roller coaster.

In order to take full advantage of the Six Flags brand name, Premier Parks, the company that purchased the Six Flags chain of parks in 1998, changed its corporate name to Six Flags, Inc.

Attendance for the year stayed near the number for the year before, with an estimated 2.775 million guests.

Overall, Six Flags, Inc. did not earn a profit on its revenue of more than $1 billion dollars. This was due to large capital expenditures and the large amount of money required to reduce the corporation's debt.

2001

As the new millennium began, amusement parks around the world continued their quest for the tallest, fastest, most thrilling rides. *Six Flags Over Texas* was not to be outdone in this epic battle of thrills. The 2001 season was the park's 40th anniversary and for the first time in its history, *Six Flags* added two roller coasters in the same season. *The Titan* and *Wyle E. Coyote's Grand Canyon Blaster* brought the park's coaster count to twelve. In addition, in celebration of the park's 40th Anniversary, the park introduced 17 shows and overhauled *Looney Tunes Land*.

The park opened on March 3, 2001. Ticket prices for the new season were $39.99 for adults and $19.99 for children under 48 inches. Children under 2 were free. Parking was now at $8 per car.

The Titan.   Construction of the *Titan* was one of *Six Flags Over Texas'* largest capital expenditures. The ride was built in the southwest corner of the park, west of the Texas section, in an area that had previously been outside the park. The ride is considered a "megacoaster" or "hypercoaster". These are coasters with a full circuit track and a drop height of over 200 feet. The term "hypercoaster" was first used by Arrow Dynamics for a coaster at Cedar Park. The term "megacoaster" was used by Intamin.

The media opening for the ride was April 26, 2001. The ride opened to the public on Friday, April 27th.

The ride starts with a lift hill 245-foot high. This lift leads to a 65-degree drop of 255-feet that ends in a 120-foot long underground tunnel. After topping the first hill, the ride reaches speeds of up to 85 mph. The ride track is 5,312 feet in length, making it 32 feet longer than a mile. This makes the *Titan* the longest roller coaster in the park, followed by the *Giant* at 4,920 feet and the *Shockwave* at 3,600 feet.

The three trains each hold thirty riders. Ride capacity is 1600 guests per hour. During the three and one-half minute ride, guests can experience up to 4.5 Gs.

The *Titan* is an extended version of the *Goliath* roller coaster that opened the year before at *Six Flags Magic Mountain*. When the *Titan* opened, it tied with the *Goliath* as the third tallest roller coaster in the world. The two coasters are still in the top ten of the fastest coasters and longest drops. Both rides were built by Giovanola of Switzerland.

Titan riders on first drop.
Photograph by Author, 2013.

Titan train in action, 2013.
Photograph by Author.

Although hypercoasters produced by the company are very popular, Giovanola went bankrupt in 2004.

Much of the ride extends over one of the park's parking lots. Building the ride required 2.8 million pounds of support steel and one million pounds of steel for the track. It is held together by 45,000 bolts. The ride is monitored by 175 sensors that feed ride information into a computerized control system.

At a cost of $12 million dollars to construct, the investment was not only the most expensive improvement to the Arlington Park, it was also the most expensive ride installed to that date at any Six Flags Park.

Wyle E. Coyote's Grand Canyon Blaster.   The second coaster added in 2001 was the *Wyle E. Coyote's Grand Canyon Blaster*. It was installed as part of a major revision of *Looney Tunes Land*. It was added at the previous location of *Wascals'* restaurant.

The ride is a *Big Dipper* style children's steel roller coaster. The single train has four cars, each of which can hold four riders. Chance Rides manufactured the ride. The ride travels at approximately 15 mph and has 350 feet of track. It can handle 300 riders per hour. The area around the ride is themed to resemble the canyon areas in which Wyle E. Coyote pursues the Roadrunner.

Looney Tunes USA.   In addition to the installation of a roller coaster, *Looney Tunes Land* underwent other improvements. As part of a major overhaul, the name was changed from *Looney Tunes Land* to *Looney Tunes, USA.*

In addition to the *Canyon Blaster* roller coaster, five other new small children's rides were included in the reworking of the section. A mini *Empire Tower* drop ride named *Taz's New York Adventure* was added in the same

Wyle E. Coyote's Grand Canyon Blaster roller coaster in Looney Tunes section.
Photograph by Author, 2012.

location at which the small *Porky Pig's Fewwis Wheel* had stood. For this ride, youngsters ride a bench seat that rises approximately 20-feet up the front of the "Empire State building". When it reaches the top, the seat jumps up and down as it returns to the ground level.

The second ride was the *Daffy for President Tour Bus*. Known as a *Crazy Bus* style ride, guests sit in a small bus shaped unit that rotates in a vertical circle. The ride was also referred to as the *Looney Tunes Capital Tours* bus ride in some promotional materials. It is decorated as both a Hollywood tour bus and a presidential campaign bus.

The third ride, a teacup style ride named *Yosemite Sam's Texas Tea Cups*, allows riders to ride in Texas style "oil barrel" teacups. The ride is located at the former site of the *Daffy Duck Lake* boats.

The forth ride was a miniature bumper car ride, the *Route 66 Bumper Cars*. Each car represented a different Looney Tunes' character.

These four rides were manufactured by the SBF-VISA Group.

The fifth new ride was *Sylvester & Tweety's State Fair-is Wheel*. This was the third Ferris wheel located in the section. It is a Zamperla mini-Ferris wheel. This wheel has six enclosed balloon shaped units. It is located at the site of the larger *Porky Pig's Magic Wheel*, which was removed.

In addition to adding the new rides, each of the remaining current rides in the section were renovated and rethemed. The small *Red Baron* airplane ride became the *Bugs Bunny's Spirit of St. Looie*. The miniature swing ride was moved and renamed *Michigan J. Frog's Tinseltown Parade*, also called *Michigan J. Frog's Tinseltown Revue*. The Zamperla convoy truck ride became *Speedy Gonzales' Truckin' Across America*. The miniature train ride became *Elmer Fudd's America the Beautiful Railway*.

Daffy for President Tour Bus.
The sign at the top says "Vote Daffy". The one that Daffy is holding states "Hollywood tours".
Photograph by Author, 2012.

Yosemite Sam's Texas Tea Cups.
Photograph by Author, 2012.

Taz's New York Adventure.
Photograph by Author, 2012.

Looney Tunes Tower, Looney Tunes, USA.
Photograph by Author, 2009.

A new *Looney Tunes Land Stage* was added for live outdoor shows. In order to make room for the new rides, the *Rugged Buggy* was removed from the park. The *Rugged Buggy* was the park's first off the shelf small children's ride. The *Daffy Duck Lake* small boat ride was also removed.

The Frontgate was also once again renovated. Part of the renovations included the installation of a stage around the *Silver Star Carousel* for use in outdoor shows.

Anniversary Shows. In celebration of the park's 40th anniversary, the park presented a series of new shows. The grand finale each night was *Celebrate Texas,* held on the newly installed *Carousel Stage.* The show's cast of fifty performed typical Six Flags song and dance style entertainment celebrating football, Texas, and the USA. The *Dallas Cowboy Cheerleaders* were featured performers. Each show was topped off with a fireworks display.

Replacing the *Batman* show in the *Tower Arena,* now referred to as the *Texas Arena,* was the new *Rangers & Outlaws, the Texas Rangers Wild West Adventure.* The nonstop action show was subtitled the "The Great Shafer Texas Silver Mine Incident". It recounted the adventures of Texas Ranger John Hughes and his efforts in 1892 to bring silver thieves to justice in Shafter, Texas. The show was based on actual events.

The show was produced by Robert Keith, owner of Texas Cowboys, Inc. In addition to actors, the show featured nine paint horses, a Brahman bull, a buffalo, and a Jack Russell Terrier. Keith sat upon a long horn steer while he narrated the show.

A popular feature of the show took place after each performance when audience members were allowed to talk with the characters and to view up close the animals used in the show. The live action show ran for six consecutive seasons.

American Rock was featured at the *Southern Palace*. The show presented contemporary music mixed with music of the '80s and '90s. *Big Time Review* was featured at the *Crazy Horse Saloon*. An illusionist continued to perform at *Good Times Square Theater*.

Sam Houston's Texas was featured in the *Lone Star Theater*. The show was billed as a "visual and sensory tour of the 600 year old Texas story". In the movie, Sam Houston narrated the history of the six flags that have flown over Texas. The show ran for four consecutive seasons, as well as returning for the 2007 and 2008 seasons after a two season hiatus.

The *Austin City Limits* show featured a replica of the *Austin City Limits* stage built in the Modern section. Musical numbers from the *Austin City Limits* TV show were featured.

Sylvester & Tweety's State Fair-is Wheel, the park's third children's Ferris Wheel, located in the Looney Tunes section. Photograph by Author, 2011.

Looney Tunes *Party-on America* featured a performance by five Looney Tunes characters on the *Looney Tunes Stage* in the Modern section.

The anniversary celebration also included additional street performers. Judge Roy Bean and the gunfighters performed on the streets of Texas. Wildcatter Wanda and Dry Hole Charlie did a street show with stories and songs in Boomtown. Shorty the Clown, a stilt-walker in the Modern Section, recreated the same type of performance from Six Flags in the 60s. Batman and Mr. Freeze dueled throughout Gotham City.

Western Trio, three singing young ladies, performed with the *Back Porch Beaus* on the *Backporch Stage*. *Strains of Spain* was a performance by a classical guitarist in the Spanish section.

On the 40th anniversary date, August 5th, the park held an anniversary celebration with cake and a seven-foot tall birthday card for guests to sign. On that day, anyone born during the year of 1961 was admitted for free at all Six Flags' parks.

With the introduction of the *Titan*, and the 40th anniversary celebrations, attendance for 2001 was estimated to have broken the 3 million mark. Although actual attendance figures were not released, General Manager Steve Calloway was quoted as stating that 2001 was the highest attendance year in the history of the park. Nationwide, amusement park attendance was up to an estimated 319 million guests. *Six Flags Over Texas* was estimated by Amusement

Rangers & Outlaws, "The Great Shafer Texas Silver Mine Incident"
at the Tower Arena (2001-2006). Photograph by Author, 2001.

Business to be the twentieth most visited theme park in the country for the season.

The year of Six Flags' 40th anniversary also saw the bankruptcy of Arrow Development. Beginning with *Disneyland*, Arrow was one of the first manufacturers of theme park rides. The company was a major contributor to ride development at *Six Flags Over Texas*. During 1981, Arrow merged with a German manufacturer to become Arrow-Huss. After filing bankruptcy in 2001, the company was purchased by S&S Power. At that time, Arrow became S&S Arrow, a division of S&S. S&S Power later built the *Superman Tower of Power* for Six Flags.

2002

After the major celebration of Six Flags' 40th anniversary, the 2002 season saw only minor changes in the park. The park opened on March 9th, 2002. Instead of a major new ride or special attraction, the park management hosted the *Best of Texas* festival as a new experience to attract guests to the park. In addition, a new set of shows was created for the park's theaters.

Ticket prices were up nearly three dollars to $42.89 for adults and $26.80 for children under 48 inches tall.

As an innovation, the park installed the *Q-Bot* system. Similar to reservations at a restaurant, this system was designed to lessen the time guests spent in line by providing them with a ride appointment. For $10, guests use

*Looney Tunes souvenir store at the original site of the corporate exhibits
in the new Looney Tunes, USA. section.
Photograph by Author, 2012.*

the *Q-Bot* to schedule an appointment time to ride on nine major attractions. The *Q-Bot* recorded a reservation time based on the estimated time to ride the ride based on the current line length at the time of the request. At their appointment time, the device signals the guests. They can then access the ride without waiting in line. Marketed as *Fast-lane*, the concept was developed by a company named Lo-Q, now known as "accesso".

The method has been modified since its initial installation. It was expanded to allow different levels for different prices. Higher levels allow immediate ride access and repetitive rides. In 2006, the system was renamed *Flash Pass* system. In 2011, Six Flags corporation extended their contract with Lo-Q through the 2017 season.

Best of Texas. The *Best of Texas* festival highlighted a wide assortment of Texas culture and heritage. Attractions for the event were obtained from around the state. As part of the celebration, a replica of the facade of the Alamo chapel was installed near the tower, with an Alamo museum nearby. Reminiscent of the original petting zoo, live animals representative of Texas were displayed at the *Critters of the Big Bend* exhibit.

Also on display was the embalmed body of *Old Rip*, the horny toad that, according to legend, sprang back to life after being trapped in a courthouse cornerstone for 31 years. The *World's Largest Killer Bee*, a 21 foot long bee statute, sat at the Frontgate. Fort Worth's own eight-foot tall Jackalope was also a featured attraction.

In addition to the animals on display, four armadillos participated in armadillo racing. In each race, children coaxed their favorite critter towards the

Alamo façade installed for the Best of Texas Festival.
Photograph by Author, 2002.

finish line. Each of the participating armadillos had previously been injured and rescued.

Texas food was also featured. Guests could try meals from famous Texas restaurants such as Kincaid's famous Hamburgers; steaks from Amarillo's Big Texan Steak Ranch; or Eddie Dean's East Texas Barbecue.

The event also featured Texas entertainment, with daily performances of the Light Crust Doughboys band and Tyler's Apache Belles dance team. The *Best of Texas Festival* ran from June 8 to August 11.

2002 Shows. In addition to the *Best of Texas* event, a new set of shows opened across the park. In the *Southern Palace, State of Rhythm* opened. Billed as a "musical journey through the USA", the show explored the "rhythm and beats" which form the wide varieties of American musical styles. The *Crazy Horse Saloon* featured a new musical, *Raise a Ruckus*. The revue featured favorite songs and high energy dances from *Crazy Horse* shows of previous seasons.

Merlin's Magicademy was the new show at the *Good Time Square Theater*. It featured the music, magic, and mystery of Merlin the Wizard as he trained Arthur in the art of Wizardry. Young guests in the audience could earn their "Ph.D. in Wizardry". All three of these shows began three season runs.

Space Shuttle America. Ending a three year run, the movie at the *Adventure Theater* was changed in 2002 from *Escape from Dino Island* to *Space Shuttle America*. As the name indicates, the new movie involved a simulated ride on a space shuttle.

For its second season, *The Rangers & Outlaws* show at the *Tower* amphitheater was updated with more pyrotechnical effects and more stunts. *Celebrate Texas*, featuring the Dallas Cowboys Cheerleaders, continued on the Frontgate stage. The nightly parade was *Party on America*.

At the end of 2002, the *Missilechaser* installed in 2000 was removed from the park. This particular scrambler was moved to *Six Flags Magic Mountain*.

Despite the season long festival, attendance was down for 2002, with estimated attendance at 2.65 million. It is likely that the 100 millionth guest visited the park in 2002.

2003

Superman Tower of Power (2003), with Gotham City in background. Photograph by Author, 2008.

Six Flags followed a season of new shows with a major attraction for 2003: the *Superman Tower of Power*. The park opened on March 9th with the start of a two week long *Spring Break-Out* event. Opening day was a major event, with ten different bands playing various types of music at stages all around the park. Ticket prices dropped after the rather steep increase the season before. Adult tickets for the year were $39.99. Children's tickets were $24.99.

Superman Tower of Power. Building on the popularity of the park's first two drop rides, the *Chute-Out* and the *Cliffhanger*, the park offered a new tower ride for 2003. The ride, a three leg free-fall tower, stands 325-feet tall from the ground to the top of the ten-foot tall US flag mounted on the structure. It is one of the world's tallest free falls rides. At the time that it was installed, it was the tallest structure in the park when measured to the top of the American flag.

Tower rides can be "space shot" style, in which riders are shot up the side of a structure. They can also be 'turbo drop", in which riders are raised up the structure and then shot back towards the ground.

Superman, Tower of Power (2003) ride unit.
Photograph by Author, 2005.

The *Superman Tower of Power* ride is a combination tower. Riders sit in seats mounted on the side of the rides' legs. As with a space shot ride, riders shoot up the side of the tower. They ascend 245 feet in height at speeds up to 50 mph. Then, as with a "turbo drop" ride, after being held at the top for a moment, they are shot down to the ground in an accelerated free fall also approaching 50 mph. The ride lasts 1 minute and 15 seconds.

Built by S&S Power, Inc. of Logan, Utah, each one of the three legs has three sides. Each of the three sides holds three seats, for a total of twenty-seven simultaneous riders. The ride has a capacity of 1,200 riders per hour.

The ride seats are propelled by compressed air. Riders feel 3.5 g's on the ascent and a negative .8 g's on the descent. The cost of construction was estimated at over $10 million.

The *Superman Tower of Power* was previewed with a media event on Wednesday, March 23rd, 2003. The ride officially opened to the public the following Saturday. Twelve contest winners were the initial riders for the ride's official opening. Named for Superman, the hero of comic books, TV shows, and movies, the ride followed the park's practice of naming rides after DC Comic characters.

For the 2003 season, the original *Right Stuff* movie returned to the *Adventure Theater*.

Industry estimates were that attendance for the season was flat, down to 2.6 million guests for the season. General Manager Steve Calloway, however, stated that attendance was better than that for 2002.

During the year, Six Flags took over management of *Jazzland* in New Orleans, later to be renamed as *Six Flags New Orleans*.

2004

After the installation of the *Superman Power of Tower*, the 2004 season was another year without a major new attraction. The park opened March 6, the first Saturday of the month. Spring break, however, did not start until March 13, the following week. A shorter, one week spring break season was featured rather than the two week event from the year before. A music festival was again featured in connection with the event.

Adult ticket prices rose two dollars to $41.99. Online tickets, however, were available for $29.99 for adults. These were printable at home. Children's tickets remained at $24.99.

SpongeBob Movie.   For 2004, the movie at the 100-seat *Adventure Theater* was changed once again. A younger crowd was targeted with the addition of *SpongeBob Squarepants 4D*. The show was a 4D movie based on the popular Nickelodeon character and his Bikini Bottom friends. In the story, SpongeBob chases the Krusty Krab's last hamburger pickle through various obstacles, before facing off with his nemesis, Plankton.

The show incorporated the ride's moving seats and 3D glasses with additional elements, such as bubbles and water spray. Audience contact with the bubbles and water spray constituted the "fourth dimension", making the movie "4D".

Sponge Bob, Square Pants (2004–2007), at the Adventure Theater.
Photograph by Author, 2005.

The show was produced by SimEx-Iwerks. The ride film and effects were created in conjunction with Paramount Parks, Attraction Media & Enterprises, and Blur Studios.

To complement the show, Spongebob souvenirs and memorabilia were available at the souvenir shop next to the theater.

Also for 2004, *Casa Magnetica* reopened at its original location in the Spanish section.

2004 Shows. At the *Southern Palace*, the production *It's Alright* featured the sounds of Motown legends. The show was featured along with the second season of the *State of Rhythm*. Scott Michael Foster, later known as Cappie in the TV show "Greek", was one of the featured singers in *State of Rhythm*. The show was billed as an "American melting pot of music".

The *Crazy Horse Saloon* continued its up close up entertainment with the *Rip-Roaring, Old-Timey, Saloon* musical revue.

In March of 2004, Six Flags Theme Parks introduced Mr. Six, perhaps its most recognizable spokesman ever. A product of the Doner Advertising Agency, Mr. Six is a bald, rather elderly man in a black tuxedo and large rim glasses. At relevant times, he breaks out into wild uninhabited dancing. His theme music is *"We Like to Party"* by the Vengaboys.

Used primarily in television commercials, the figure also made some personal appearances at the various parks and appeared on some souvenirs, including a series of bobbleheads. His preferred mode of a travel was on a red bus with "Six Flags" painted on the side. The tagline for the ads was "It's Playtime".

Mr. Six is considered more than a little creepy by many, including the author of an opinion piece in Time magazine. Overall, however, Mr. Six proved to be a very popular and extremely recognizable character. The ads he appeared in were very highly rated by industry surveys.

Mr. Six was dropped from TV ads in November of 2005, although his image was still used on some souvenirs and merchandise. In 2009, he made a return with his new dance companion, "Little Six", a younger version of the elder dancer.

Mr. Six was "thrown under his bus" in 2010, when over reliance on the Mr. Six advertising campaign was given by the post-bankruptcy management team as one of the reasons for low attendance at the chain's parks.

Industry estimates were that attendance at the park fell from 2003 to 2.2 million. This estimate would make the season attendance the lowest since the early 1970s. Six Flags was, however, rated by Amusement Business as the twenty-second most visited theme park that season.

During the year, Six Flags sold nine parks. Internationally, Six Flags sold its eight European parks. In the U.S., Six Flags Theme Parks sold the *Worlds of Adventure* park in Ohio to Cedar Fair.

14.

PREMIER PARKS II
2005 – 2008

2005

Six Flags opened on Saturday, March 5th, with Dallas Cowboys' owner Jerry Jones as the guest of honor. Jones was in the midst of planning and building the new Dallas Cowboy stadium less than a mile from the theme park. The stadium promised to create an even stronger entertainment district in Arlington. Six Flags is historically tied to the Cowboys football team, as Angus Wynne's brother, Bedford Wynne, was a partial owner of the team when the park opened in 1961.

A one-week long spring break event was held the week following the park's opening.

Tickets for the season stayed at $41.99 for adults. Prices rose two dollars to $26.99 for children 48 inches tall and under. Adult tickets were available online for $31.99.

2005 Shows. For the second year in a row, no major ride was added to the park. Instead, the management promoted new shows around the park as the season's fresh attractions. All of the shows were scheduled for summer runs.

The new shows included the return of the Chinese Acrobats at the *David Blackman Southern Palace*. They previously performed there in 1987. The act provided a mixture of dance, acrobatics, and martial arts.

In addition to the Acrobats of China, the *Southern Palace* featured the second season of the musical *It's Alright*.

The *Lone Star Theater* featured *Kathy Burk's World of Puppets*. Burk produced *Sarah Jane Armadillo-Superstar*, a show featuring a girl Armadillo from Amarillo. At the time, Burk had thirty years of experience producing shows for the Dallas Children's Theater. Her show featured several different types of puppets. *Kathy Burk's World of Puppets* ran for two seasons, after which time the Sam Houston movie returned to the theater.

The *Spirit of Dance* was staged at the *Good Times Square Theater.* The show featured Irish line dancers. Their performance was not, however, limited to traditional Irish dances. They also performed routines involving the tango, flamenco, and salsa styles. The show originated in Dublin, Ireland.

The *Crazy Horse Saloon* featured *Showboat's Comin'.* Featuring music of the *Showboat Neches Belle,* Captain Andy and the Neches Bell Troupers performed traditional music in the styles of Stephen Foster and Al Jolson.

Rodeo Monkey, a country rock band was featured at the *Back Porch Stage. It's Playtime* was the featured show on the *Silver Star Carousel Stage.*

Casa Magnetica also returned for the season.

Attendance for the year was estimated by industry sources to be up from 2004 to 2.31 million guests.

During the season, Six Flags moved its corporate offices from Oklahoma City, where Premier Parks was located, to New York, City. At the end of the 2005 season, *Astroworld,* the fourth park to become a part of the Six Flags system of parks, was closed and dismantled. The 161 acres on which it was built were sold. Rides and sets were sold, scrapped, or relocated to other Six Flags parks. In addition, *Six Flags New Orleans* suffered such extensive damage from hurricane Katrina that it never reopened.

Majestic Theater next to the Texas Chute-Out in the Good Time Square section. The theater was originally the Sid and Marty Krofft Puppet Theater. Photograph by Author, 2006.

2006

For its 45th Anniversary season, the park opened on March 4th, 2006, with a ceremony at the Frontgate. Park General Manager Steve Calloway presided over the proceedings. The Hardin Simmons Cowboy Band performed at the opening.

Other guests included Arlington Mayor Robert Cluck and the Dallas Cowboy cheerleaders. Morgan Matlock, the current Miss Texas, was the grand marshal for the Park's opening-day parade. Former employees from the Six Flags Association of Former Employees appeared as a group for the opening ceremony.

In honor of the 45th Anniversary, tickets for the season were "$45.00" for adults and $34.99 for children and seniors.

Park General Manager Steve Calloway addresses guests at the opening of the 45th Anniversary Season. Silver Star Coursel in the background. Photograph by Author, 2006.

Ten New Rides. In celebration of the 45th anniversary, Six Flags added nine new rides, and one non-ride attraction. This constituted the addition of more new rides in one season than any other season after the opening of the park. The new rides, added at various locations around the park, had a total hourly capacity of 5,000 riders.

Cloud Bouncer. In the Good Time Square area, two rides were added. One, the *Cloud Bouncer*, is a slow up and down ride. Eight gondolas shaped to look like baskets attached to hot air balloons move up and down a short tower. The balloons and baskets rise forty-four feet into the air, circle the central tower, and return. The ride lasts two minutes.

Each basket can hold two adults and two children. Up to 32 riders can ride at one time, for an hourly capacity of 800 riders per hour. The ride was manufactured by Zamperla and classified as a Samba Tower. It is located near the *Majestic Theater*.

Crazy Legs. Also new in Good Time Square was Crazy Legs. The ride is a centrifugal force ride with three arms that each hold seven ride gondolas. When the ride is running, the arms travel around in a circle, as well as up and down at an angle up to 40-degrees. The units reach a height of thirty feet. As the ride arms rotate, the vehicles spin around the end of each arm. Each gondola holds two guests, for a total of forty-two riders. When run with two minute rides, the hourly capacity is estimated at 900 riders.

Cloud Bouncer Ride.
Photograph by Author, 2008.

This version of the *Crazy Legs* is a *Troika* style ride manufactured by HUSS Park Attractions. The ride was previously installed as the *Warp 2000* at *Astroworld*. It was transferred to Arlington after *Astroworld* closed in 2005.

The ride is similar to the original *Crazy Legs* ride that operated from 1973 to 1982 at a location near the site of the new ride. The original ride was, however, a different type of ride.

Acme Rock-n-Rocket. In the Modern section, the *Acme Rock-n-Rocket* was built next to the *Adventure Theater*, close to where the Modern *Astrolift* station stood years before. Shaped like a cartoon firecracker rocket, the ride is similar to the *Conquistador*. Unlike the *Conquistador*, however, the *Rock-n-Rocket* turns riders completely upside-down as it swings 84-feet in the

The new Crazy Legs shown in its original blue color scheme. It was later painted red and white.
Photograph by Author, 2006.

Acme Rock-n-Rocket swings riders completely upside down.
Photograph by Author, 2008.

air and around in a full 360-degree circle. The ride lasts two minutes and thirty seconds. The rocket holds up to fifty riders, for an estimated hourly capacity of 650 riders.

Both the *Conquistador* and the *Rock-n-Rocket* were manufactured by Intamin. The *Rock-n-Rocket* is a Looping Starship style ride. Parts for the ride were relocated from *Astroworld* when the park was closed. The rocket unit in which the riders sit was manufactured for *Six Flags Over Texas*.

Bat Wing. The Gotham City section also saw the addition of two attractions. *The Bat Wing* was added near the entrance to the Mr. Freeze ride. The *Bat Wing* consists of airplane shaped units fastened by arms around a base. As the base spins, the planes travel in a circle. As it turns, riders can use a control to move the units up and down. The ride is a larger version of the popular *Red Baron* ride located in *Looney Tunes Land*.

The ride consists of fourteen planes, each modeled to resemble the Batplane. Each plane can hold up to two riders. The planes rotate at six rpm for a ride time of one minute and forty-five second. The ride was manufactured by Zamperla.

Gotham City Sprayground. Also added to Gotham City was the *Gotham City Sprayground.* This attraction, located between the *Bat Wing* and the *Mr. Freeze,* was a water spray playground. Guests could play in water shot into the air by jets located in the walkway.

Caddo Lake Barge. The *Caddo Lake Barge* was added in the Tower section. The ride consists of a boat shaped unit that spins around as it travels back and forth on a small curved base. This ride is located on the lake in front of the *Tower Theater.*

Batwing ride, similar to the smaller Red Baron children's ride.
Photograph by Author, 2010.

The ride is a Rockin' Tug style ride manufactured by Zamperla. The ride can hold up to 24 riders. Hourly capacity for the ride is 600 passengers.

Rodeo.   In the Texas section, the *Rodeo* was added near the entrance to the *Cave* ride, at the site of the original shooting gallery. Guests ride in units shaped like bulls which spin around on a carousel style base. The bulls buck up and down, and spin around, as the ride platform turns. The bulls were each custom painted to match an actual bull using photographs as guides.

Two adult guests can ride in each of the sixteen bulls. Rides last two minutes. The ride was manufactured by HUSS Park Attractions.

Boot Scootin'.   Also new to the Texas section was *Boot Scootin'*, located near the current exit for the *Texas Giant*. The location is very near to the former site of the Texas Station of the *Astrolift* ride. The ride is also a turntable style ride, with units modeled to resemble giant boots. The six boots rock up and down as the ride gently rotates at 6 revolutions per minute.

Each boot can hold two guests. The ride was also manufactured by Zamperla.

Sidewinder.   Much further away, the *Sidewinder* was added in the Texas section near the *Titan* roller coaster. The *Sidewinder* is a classic scrambler ride. The *Sidewinder* was the third scrambler style ride to operate in the park. The first two scramblers were both named the *Missilechaser*. This third scrambler, however, instead took the name of the first roller coaster in the park. This name was also appropriate for the Texas section of the park, however, since a "Sidewinder" refers to both an unsavory cowboy and a variety of rattlesnake.

*The Rodeo, a bucking bull ride, located near the entrance to Gold River Cave Ride.
"Calloways General Store", part of the ride set, is named for Steve Calloway.
Photograph by Author, 2006.*

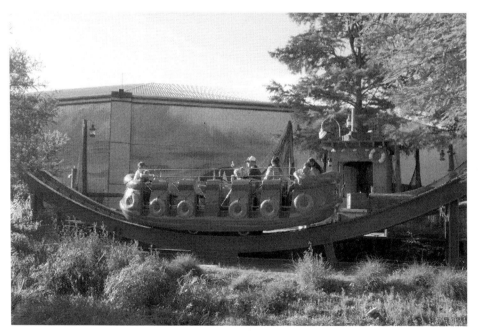

*Caddo Lake Barge. The rides spins as it slides on the track.
Tower Theater is directly behind the ride.
Photograph by Author, 2010.*

Boot Scootin' ride, another ride added in 2006.
Located across from Railroad Station in Texas, at former site of Texas Astrolift.
Photograph by Author, 2008.

Sidewinder Scrambler Ride, the third scrambler ride located in the park.
Installed in Texas section near entrances to Titan and Texas Giant.
Photograph by Author, 2013.

The *Sidewinder* has three arms, each with four ride units. With three riders per seat, the ride can hold up to 36 guests. It rides more comfortably with two guests per unit. The ride rotates at 11.4 rpm. Rides last two minutes and thirty seconds.

The ride was operated as the *Runaway Rickshaw* at *Astroworld* and was relocated when that park closed. It was manufactured by the Eli Bridge Company.

La Fiesta De Las Tazas. The Mexican section saw the addition of the *La Fiesta De Las Tazas*, which roughly translates to the "Party of the Cups". This ride is a basic teacup ride, with twelve cups decorated in traditional bright Mexican colors. The ride is located by the *La Vibora Bobsled*, where the *Sombrero* ride was previously located.

La Fiesta De Las Tazas, a teacup ride.
Photograph by Author, 2006.

Each teacup can hold up to five riders. Mounted in the center of each teacup is a wheel which riders can turn to spin the individual cup during the ride. Hourly capacity for the ride is 1,200 guests, with a ride length of one minute and thirty seconds. The ride was manufactured by Zamperla.

In order to install the *Teacups*, the *Sombrero* was moved nearer the entrance to the Mexican section, to a location that had been part of the patio to the Mexican restaurant. This was the second time the ride was moved. The move resulted in it being placed at a location nearly directly across the pathway from where the ride was originally located.

The total number of rides in the park after the expansion was forty-seven.

At the *Majestic Theater*, a musical named *Funk Nation* began a two-year run. *Rangers & Outlaws, the Texas Rangers Wild West Adventure* began its last season at the *Tower Theater*. At the *Southern Palace, The Amazing Acrobats of China* returned for a second and final season, with *Hello Texas* as the spring show. *Kathy Burk's World of Puppets* also returned for a second and final season at the *Lone Star Theater. Raise a Ruckus* returned to the *Crazy Horse Saloon* after a season off.

For the 45th anniversary, the park also doubled the number of concerts; added opportunities to dine with the Looney Tunes and Justice League characters; and added more character appearances during the day.

A 20-minute long nightly parade was held each evening just before closing. The parade featured floats representing each of the park's sections, as well as the Justice League of America and the Looney Tunes Characters.

In June of 2006, Cedar Fair Entertainment Company purchased five parks from the CBS Corporation. These included *Canada's Wonderland*; *Carowinds* in North Carolina; *California's Great America*; *Kings Dominion* in Virginia; and *Kings Island* in Ohio. The transaction was reported at $1.24 billion dollars.

Texas float from 45th Anniversary Parade.
Photograph by Author, 2006.

255

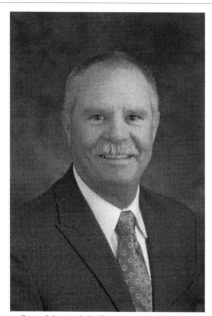

Steve Martindale, President of Six Flags Over Texas. Photograph courtesy Six Flags Over Texas, 2016.

In January of 2007, the Six Flags chain sold eight of its smaller parks for $312 million. These included Premier Park's former flagship park, *Frontier City*, together with *White Water Bay*, both in Oklahoma City; *Elitch Gardens*, in Denver, Colorado; *Darien Lake*, and *Splashtown* water park, in Darien, New York; *Waterworld*, in Concord, California; *Wild Waves*, formerly *Enchanted Village*, in Federal Way, Washington; and *Splashtown Houston*, in Houston, Texas.

At the end of the 2006 season, Steve Calloway retired as the General Manager of the park, a position that he held for 11 years. Steve Martindale was appointed as the new President of the park. Mr. Martindale began his career in 1973 as a ride operator at *Six Flags Over Texas*. He is only the third General Manager for the park since 1984.

2007

The 2007 season opened with little fanfare. The season began on March 10, with *Spring Break* kickoff. The main changes to the park at the time were upgrades in the appearance of the park, such as cleaning and painting. The major new attraction for the year, the *Coobrilia* show, did not open until June 16.

Ticket prices rose to $47.00 for adults, a two-dollar increase. Tickets for children remained at $34.99.

As part of the park makeover, additional food choices were added. Outside vendors *Panda Express* and *Cold Stone Creamery* opened locations in the park. The *Chubbie's* restaurant in Good Time Square was converted into a *Johnny Rockets* restaurant. The *Johnny Rocket* chain was owned by Redzone Capital. Redzone was owned in turn owned by Daniel Synder, at that time chairman of the board of Six Flags.

Cirque Dreams Coobrila. The big attraction for the season was the *Cirque Dreams Coobrila* show added at the *Music Mill Theater*. The theater was adapted for the show with the construction of additional runways and stages to accommodate the several different acts performed simultaneously during the show.

"Coobrila" cast members mingled with the crowd after each show.
Photograph by Author, 2007.

The name *Coobrila* is a combination of three words that described the show: The three words were **COO**ler, as the show was at night when the temperatures are lower; **BRI**ghter, referring to the elaborate lighting and colors used in the production; and **LA**ter, referring to the later times during the evening when the show was open.

The show was produced by Cirque Productions, a firm founded in 1993. Cirque Productions, which also operates as Cirque Dreams, specializes in European cirque-style shows mixed with American circus acts and specialized theatrics.

The forty-minute show featured thirty dancers, musicians, and acrobats. During the show, they appeared in one hundred and fifty elaborate costumes. The show used florescent colors with unusual sets designed to create a dreamlike image of the far side of the moon. Presenting a surreal effect with distinctive characters, costumes and sets, the show was unique to the Six Flags parks. The show was the largest ever produced at *Six Flags Over Texas*. Two and a half million dollars were spent in remodeling the *Music Mill* to host the performance.

X-Treme Country, featuring country music, was a new program at the *Southern Palace Theater*. *Showboat's Comin'* began a two-season run at the *Crazy Horse Saloon*. The show was also produced there in 2005. *Sam Houston's Texas* returned to the *Lone Star Theater* after a hiatus for the two-season run of *Kathy Burke's Puppets*.

In June of 2007, Daniel Synder's RedZone Capital bought 60% of Dick Clark Productions, while Six Flags Theme Parks, Inc. bought the other 40%. At the time, RedZone was the largest holder of Six Flags stock and

Daniel Synder was the Chairman of the Board. Both companies sold their interests in 2012.

Dick Clark was known for his American Bandstand shows. In addition, Dick Clark Productions owns "So You Think You Can Dance", "The American Music Awards", and "TV's Bloopers and Practical Jokes". The purchase led to the production of several related shows at *Six Flags Over Texas* in subsequent seasons.

In October, the *Cliffhanger* ride was imploded. Given the success of the *Superman* ride, there was much less demand for the older and smaller free-fall ride. At the time that it closed, the ride had served the park for twenty-five seasons. The *Tony Hawk's Big Spin* ride was planned for the open space created.

Also closed at the end of the 2007 season was the bumper car ride located in Good Time Square. Although the building remained, the ride itself was no longer operated. At the time it was closed, it had been in service in the park for thirty-five seasons, more seasons than any other removed ride. The *Texas Chute-out* surpassed that record in 2012, when it was removed after thirty-seven seasons in the park.

Attendance was likely around 2.7 million guests for the season.

As part of the park's facelift, Splashdown Falls was rethemed as the Aquaman Splashdown ride. The white and red pipes in the foreground are water cannons. Guests can use these cannons to spray the guests in the boats. Photograph by Author, 2008.

Tony Hawk's Big Spin roller coaster.
Photograph by Author, 2010.

2008

The park opened on March 9, 2008, with a Spring Breakout event. Ticket prices for the year dropped drastically for children, from $34.99 to $29.99. Adult tickets were $46.99. As a special promotional, both adult and children's tickets were available through the Six Flags website for the same price of $29.99. The tag line for this promotion was "Everyone pays kid's price". The new season featured a new roller coaster as the year's major attraction.

Tony Hawk's Big Spin.   The *Tony Hawk's Big Spin* ride brought the park's roller coaster count to its current high of thirteen. The ride was named for the extreme sport athlete, Tony Hawk, and his "big spin" skateboarding maneuver. The ride was the first ride in the history of the park to be named for a living person. The ride is located in the Modern USA section, on and around the former site of the *Cliffhanger.*

The ride was built at a cost of $6.5 million dollars by Gerstlauer Amusement Rides of Germany, a company founded in 1982 by a former employee of Schwarzkopf.

The ride consists of eight single car units with four seats each. The seats are inside of a round base. As the cars moves around the track, they also spin around 360 degrees on their bases in a random fashion.

Coaster cars in action on Tony Hawk's Big Spin.
Photograph by Author, 2009.

The ride lift is 53 feet high with a 27-foot initial drop. The units travel at up to 31 mph. The track is 1,351 feet long. The ride is designed for a throughput of 800 riders per hour. Each ride runs 1 minutes and 51 seconds.

The *Big Spin* is similar to other *Tony Hawk's Big Spin* rides that opened the season before at *Six Flags Fiesta Texas* and *Six Flags Saint Louis*. The first version of the ride opened under the name *Mr. Six's Pandemonium* at *Six Flags New England* in 2005. Another *Big Spin* opened at *Six Flags Discovery Kingdom* in the 2008 season. The Texas, *Fiesta Texas*, and St Louis rides are identical, while the *Discovery Kingdom* ride varies somewhat.

In 2010, the licensing agreement with Tony Hawk was terminated and the ride was renamed to *The Pandemonium*.

During the season, the park was still undergoing a million dollar makeover to revitalize its overall appearance. As part of the makeover, the food court in the Modern section was rebuilt and renamed as the *Six Flags All American Café*.

Another new show was featured at the *Adventure Theatre*. The *Sponge Bob* movie was removed and replaced with *Fly Me to the Moon*. The new movie told the story of a group of flies that find themselves on-board an Apollo rocket ship voyage to the moon. The story was adapted from a full-length feature film. The show featured the voices of Kelly Ripa and Christopher Lloyd.

Boomtown Games added to the South end of Boomtown. Mr. Freeze in the background.
Photograph by Author, 2008.

Modern Food Court after renovations. Skycoaster in the left background.
Photograph by Author, 2008.

The *Southern Palace* presented *Dick Clark's Academy of Country Music: Back Trax.* The show featured a review of the last four decades of country music. A related show, *Dick Clark's Music Awards: Rewind* featured four decades of music at the *Majestic Theatre.*

The park also featured a daily parade with the Warner characters and the Justice League superheroes.

The park announced that March 20, 2008, was an extreme high attendance day, and possibly a record setting date. Since the park no longer releases specific attendance information, however, the exact guest count is unavailable.

The *Coobrila* show was continued for another season at the *Music Mill.* As a result, summer concerts were held at the *Tower Arena Theater.*

In Myrtle Beach, South Carolina, *Hard Rock Park*, later known as *Freestyle Music Park*, opened as a "rock and roll music" themed park. One highlight of the park was a ride built by Sally Corp. and based on the Moody Blues classic song "Nights in White Satin". The park also featured a play area based on the Banana Splits. The park faced severe financial difficulties and closed after attempting to operate for two seasons.

Holiday in the Park show at the Crazy Horse Saloon.
Author shown in middle in Santa costume and stylish fanny pack.
Photograph by Julie McCown, 2001.

15.

Premier Parks III
2009 – 2012

2009

In 2009, the Arlington entertainment district expanded once again with the addition of the Dallas Cowboy Stadium to the southwest of the park. The stadium, funded in part by the city of Arlington, demonstrated in its first year the variety of events that it could host. In addition to football, the first year saw major concerts and several other sporting events.

For the third time in its history, Six Flags opened in February, opening on February 28. Adult tickets were $49.99 in the park and $31 online. Children's tickets were $31. The park continued the promotion, "Everyone Pays Kid's Price".

Glow in the Dark Parade. For the season, *Six Flags Over Texas* introduced the *Glow in the Park Parade*. The $2.5 million parade was held at several Six Flags parks. The parade opened the year before at three Six Flags parks. Designed by Gary Goddard, the parade consisted of 110 cast members and crew. Featured were sixty-five puppeteers, singers, dancers, and stilt-walkers. The costumes and floats were lit up with fiber optic lights. The parade ran from the Gotham City section to the Frontgate. It returned for a repeat performance in the summer of 2010.

Once again, the *Texas Giant* was renovated to help make the ride smoother. Approximately 1,400 feet of track was replaced to make a smoother, faster, ride.

The park opened the *Mporium*, a candy store in the Confederate section specializing in M&M candy and M&M themed items. It also sells other Mars brand candies and souvenirs.

Another *Johnny Rockets* opened at the site of the *Cactus Cantina* in the Mexican Section.

The "Glow in the Park" parade featured live and animated characters displayed in vivid optical lights. Pictured is the Gotham City float. Photograph by Author, 2009.

Country is My Rock, the story of an urban cowboy's face-off with a rural cowboy, was on stage at the *Southern Palace Theater*. The *Crazy Horse Saloon* featured the *Big Time Revue*, with music of the vaudeville halls of the 1900s. *The Best of Dick Clark's Bloopers* was featured at the *Lone Star Theater*. The *Majestic Theatre* featured *The American Music Awards: Rewind*.

November 1st of 2009 was the last opportunity to ride the original *Texas Giant* before it closed for a yearlong renovation. Estimates were that 23 million guests rode the original ride.

Attendance was down for the year. Six Flags, Inc. attributed the decrease in part to an outbreak of the swine flu.

Corporate Bankruptcy. During the season, corporate news was bigger than park news. In April 2009, the New York Stock Exchange delisted Six Flags Inc. stock due to its low price. In June of 2009, Six Flags, Inc. filed for bankruptcy to restructure $2.4 billion in debt related to the purchase of the company by Premier Parks in 1998.

Premier Park's success with previous park purchases was due in part to an ability to increase profitability of older parks through park refurbishment and added attractions. These improvements lead to increases in attendance and income. After the purchase of the Six Flags chain, the Premier management was depending on such improvements to drive increases in attendance and revenue. The corporate officers were depending on increases over the parks' presale figures of at least 3% for attendance, and 5½% for revenue, to cover the high cost of their financing. Increasing attendance was not, however, as easy to attain as hoped, since the Six Flags parks were already receiving frequent major new attractions and renovations.

The inability to keep up with the interest payments on the amounts borrowed to purchase the Six Flags chain forced the company to file bankruptcy. The filing had little noticeable effect on operations at the Texas park.

Six Flags management estimated that 24 million guests visited Six Flags parks during the season. The company reported ownership of over 800 rides and over 120 roller coasters.

2010

For the 2010 season, the *Texas Giant* was shut down so that it could be converted into a hybrid coaster with both wooden and metal components.

Adult tickets were $56.99. If purchased online, adult tickets sold at children ticket prices of $39.99.

The *Adventure Theater* movie was changed to "*Robots of Mars*", an animated feature. Guests in the motion theater joined forces with friendly robots as they protected the universe from the sinister Supervisor of Mars. The *Adventure Theater* was closed indefinitely at the end of the season.

A new Looney Tunes show, *Looney Tunes Dance Off*, was featured at the *Majestic Theatre*. The show followed the efforts of the Looney Tunes characters to win a dance contest. A trivia game show, *Dick Clark's Face the Music*, was also new for the year at the *Lone Star Theatre*. The production was an interactive game show based on music trivia. The *Crazy Horse Saloon* continued the

Titan Roller coaster track.
Ranger Stadium in background, Texas Giant in foreground.
Photograph by Author, 2008.

Big Time Revue. During the day, Mr. Six hosted the *Mr. Six Dance Party* on the *Carousel Stage.*

In addition, the *Glow in the Park* parade was held over for a second year.

Although exact figures were not released, attendance overall was reported by the management to be up at the Texas park. It is estimated that even without a major addition, the 2010 season broke the 3 million mark and was up over 2009.

In April 2010, the Six Flags corporation came out of bankruptcy. The park system showed its first annual profit since 1998. The corporate stock was relisted on the New York Stock Exchange in June of 2010. The company name became Six Flags Entertainment Corporation.

On May 12, 2010, it was announced that Mark Shapiro was no longer the CEO of Six Flags. Shapiro focused on making the system of parks more family friendly, with the addition of attractions and shows targeted to smaller children.

During the year, company documents reveal that 24.3 million visitors attended the corporation's nineteen North American park. Seventeen of these were located in the United States, one in Canada, and one in Mexico.

In August 2010, Jim Reid-Anderson was named as the new CEO of Six Flags Entertainment. After four years in New York, the corporate offices were moved from New York to Grand Prairie, Texas.

Texas Gunslinger, the former Texas Tornado, after the addition of giant revolvers in 2006.
The revolvers were moved from the Astroworld swing after the park was closed.
Photograph by Author, 2007.

During the year, Six Flags Entertainment Corporation ended all of it character licenses, except the Warner related ones. Terminated was use of the Tony Hawk name at all of the parks. Also terminated at other parks was the license for both the Wiggles and Thomas the Tank Engine.

2011

The park opened the fiftieth anniversary season with a ceremony at the Frontgate on Saturday, March 5th. Among the guests of honor where two of the sons of the park's founder, Angus Wynne III, and Shannon Wynne, as well as his daughter, Temple Wynne. (Wynne's third son is David E. Wynne.) For the opening weekend, March 5th and 6th, tickets were sold online for $19.61.

During the season, adult and children's tickets sold online for the children's park price of $34.99. At the gate, adult tickets were $55 and children's $40.

Texas Giant II.   For its 50th anniversary, Six Flags unveiled a totally remodeled *Texas Giant*. The ride was rebuilt as a hybrid metal and wood coaster. While still supported by a wood structure, the ride was rebuilt with a metal rail track system for a smoother ride. In addition, the track was completely redesigned in several sections.

New Texas Giant cars styled on a 1961 Cadillac DeVille, 2013.
Photograph by Author.

The *New Texas Giant* is ten feet taller than the predecessor, topping out at 153-feet. Top speed for the new version of the *Giant* is 65 mph, also a little higher than the original version. The initial drop is 79-degrees. At the time, this was the steepest drop in the world for a "wooden" roller coaster. It also features a wooden coaster record-breaking 95-degree bank. In fact, three turns are sharper than 90-degrees. The ride track is 4,920 feet in length.

Given the new track system, some experts do not consider the ride to be accurately classified as a wooden coaster. It is now considered for purposes of some surveys and statistics as a metal coaster.

The trains, which on the original track were standard wooden coaster trains, were replaced with ones designed to resemble a 1961 Cadillac DeVille. One of the new trains is aqua, one black metallic, and one red metallic. Each train is forty-eight feet long and holds twenty-four passengers. The lap restraints feature a saddle horn for guests to hold onto during the wild ride. Gerstlauer, manufacturer of the *Pandemonium*, manufactured the trains.

The renovations were performed by Rocky Mountain Construction of Idaho and cost $10 million. Similar renovations were made for the 2013 season by the same company to the *Rattler* at *Six Flags Fiesta Texas*. The ride was renamed as the "Iron Rattler".

The area for people who decided not to ride after waiting in line was modeled to look like a "chicken" coup, complete with the sounds of chickens.

As part of the fiftieth anniversary celebration, the park sponsored *50 Days of Fun*. These were held on the fifty days leading up to the August 5th anniversary date. On each day, a special event or promotion was held.

During the summer evenings, a special *Celebrate Texas* anniversary show was held on the *Carousel Stage* at the Frontgate. It featured the Dallas Cowboys Cheerleaders dancing in celebration of Six Flags. In addition, Mr. Six continued his *Mr. Six Dance Party* at the *Carousel Stage* during the day.

New in the *Southern Palace* was *Chart-Toppers 5.0*, a look at the last fifty years of music and dance. *Dick Clark's Face the Music* continued at the *Lone Star Theater*; *Looney Tunes Dance Off* continued at the *Majestic Theater*; and *Big Time Revue* repeated at the *Crazy Horse Saloon*.

Casa Magnetica was again opened for the anniversary season, having been closed since 2007.

The fiftieth anniversary year closed with Six Flags Entertainment Corporation sitting as the 5th largest theme park group in the world, entertaining an estimated 25.75 million guests worldwide for the season. Visits to theme parks nationwide were up nearly 4% over the year before. A total of 131.6 million guests visited the twenty largest parks in North America.

New Texas Giant heading down first drop.
Photograph by Author, 2015.

THE FUTURE

Looking back over the last fifty years, it is easy to predict that the next fifty will bring more change. As Angus Wynne predicted on opening day in 1961, "Six Flags is not complete. It will never be complete. We will continue to build to what we consider to be an institution." The park's first fifty years proved Wynne's expectations correct.

The park has grown outside the original defining railroad tracks to take in 212 acres. In 1961, when the park opened, it boosted fourteen rides and major attractions, as well as five central shows. Fifty years later, the park has three times the number of rides, in addition to an array of rides just for children. The park has seven major show venues, as well as several smaller performance areas around the park. In between, over twenty-five major rides and numerous shows and attractions have come and gone.

Six Flags Over Texas has grown from being a single park owned by a north Texas company, to the grandfather park of a nationwide chain of amusement and water parks. Over the last fifty years, ticket prices have increased an average of $1.10 per season. During that time, over one hundred and twenty million guests visited the park.

In 2013, the park opened a new swing ride, the *Texas Skyscreamer*. At 400 feet, the ride is 100 feet taller than even the *Six Flags Tower*, giving it claim to the tallest ride in the park and the tallest swing ride in the world.

Over the next fifty years, there is every reason to believe that the park will continue to change and provide innovative and unique entertainment for its guests.

ONLINE RESOURCES

Six Flags Over
Texas ~ Official Site
http://www.sixflags.com/overtexas

Parktimes ~ History of
Six Flags Over Texas
(Unofficial Site)
http://www.parktimes.com

American Coaster Enthusiasts
http://www.aceonline.org

Six Flags Association of
Former Employees
http://sfafe.net

Guide to Six Flags Over Texas
(Unofficial Site)
http://guidetosfot.com/

Six Flags Major Attractions
Years in the park as of the close of 2012 season
(Season closed is last year the attraction operated in the park.)

Attraction	First Season	Season Closed	Years in Park
Six Flags Railroad Oldest Operating Ride	1961		52
Animal Kingdom Petting Zoo	1961	1982	22
Astrolift	1961	1980	20
Missilechaser (first)	1961	1977	17
Happy Motoring	1961	1986	26
Sidewinder Roller coaster (La Cucaracha)	1961	1964	4
La Salle's River Adventure	1961	1982	22
Skull Island Play Area	1961	1982	22
Skull Island Barge	1961	1977	16
Amphitheater	1961	1967	7
Confederate Soldiers	1961	unavailable	
Lil' Dixie Carousel (Flying Jenny)	1961	1974	14
Butterfield Stagecoach	1961	1967	7
Conquistador Burro Ride	1961	1962	2
Fiesta Train	1961	1979	19
Texas Gunfighters	1961		
Crazy Horse Saloon	1961		52
Indian Village	1961	1967	7
Goat Carts	1961	1963	3
Helicopter Rides	1961	1965	5
Chaps	1962		51
Caddo War Canoes	1962	1983	22
Casa Magnetica (Not continuously operated)	1962		51
Flume	1963		50
Carousel (Silver Star) (Not continuously operated)	1963		50
Sky Crane	1963	1968	6

Speelunker Cave (Gold River transformation 1992)	1964		49
El Sombrero	1965		48
Texas Pavilion (Arena)	1965	1974	10
Runaway Mine Train	1966		47
Spindletop	1967	1989	23
Jet Set	1967	1970	4
Southern Palace	1968		45
Puppet Show (Majestic Theater)	1968		45
Cyclorama Museum	1968	1978	11
Tower (closed one season for improvements)	1969		44
Tower Slide	1969	1975	7
Mini-mine Train (closed one season for construction)	1969		44
Chevy Show (Loan Star Theater)	1969		44
Tower Theater: Dolphin Show/Aquatic Show/Stunt Show	1969	1991	22
Big Bend Rollercoaster	1971	1979	9
Rugged Buggy	1972	2001	30
Bumper Cars	1973	2007	35
Crazy Legs	1973	1982	10
Music Mill Theater	1974		39
Rotoriculious	1975	1988	14
Red Baron (Bugs Bunny's Spirit of St. Louis)	1975		38
Chute-Out	1976	2012	37
Spinnaker	1977	1995	19
Shockwave	1978		35
Sensational Sense Machine	1979	1984	6
Judge Roy Scream	1980		33
El Conquistador	1981		32
Cliffhanger	1982	2007	26
Elmer Fudd Fewwis Wheel	1982	1997	16
Roaring Rapids	1983		30

Texas Tornado	1983		30
Pac-Man Land	1983	1984	2
Great Six Flags Air Racer	1984	1999	16
Looney Tunes Land	1985		28
Avalanche	1986		27
Splashwater Falls	1987		26
Flashback	1989	2012	24
Texas Giant (Original)	1990	2009	10
Porky Pig's Magic Wheel	1991	2000	10
Convey Trucks; Sylvester Jr's Train; Martian Escape	1991		22
Batman Stunt Show	1992	2000	9
Adventure Theater	1995		18
Runaway Mountain Roller coaster	1996		17
Mr. Freeze Roller Coaster	1997		16
Barman, the Ride	1999		14
Missilechaser II	2000	2002	3
Titan Roller coaster	2001		12
Wylie E. Coyote's Grand Canyon Blaster	2001		12
Daffy Tour Bus; Taz's New York Adventure; Route 66 Bumper Cars; Sylvester & Tweety's State Fair-is Wheel	2001		12
Superman Power of Tower	2003		10
Rocket	2006		7
Cloud Bouncer	2006		7
Crazy Legs II	2006		7
Batwing	2006		7
Caddo Lake Barge	2006		7
Rodeo	2006		7
Boot Scottin'	2006		7
Teacups	2006		7
Sidewinder	2006		7
Pandemonium (Tony Hawk)	2008		5
New Texas Giant	2011		2
Sky Coaster	2013		

Six Flags System of Parks

Park	Year Opened	Year Acquired	Year Sold
Parks Built by Great Southwest Corporation			
Six Flags Over Texas - Arlington, Texas (sold to limited partnership 1969, Six Flags continues to manage)	1961	1961	
Six Flags Over Georgia - Atlanta, Georgia (sold to limited partnership 1968, Six Flags continues to manage)	1968	1968	
Six Flags Over Mid-America, St. Louis, Missouri	1970	1970	
Parks Purchased Prior to Merger with Premier Parks			
Six Flags Astroworld, Houston Texas (Closed 2005)	1968	1976	2005
Six Flags Great Adventure Jackson, New Jersey	1974	1977	
Six Flags Wild Safari Animal Park Jackson, New Jersey	1974	1977	
Six Flags Magic Mountain Valencia, California	1971	1979	
Six Flags Atlantis, Hollywood, Florida (Purchased waterpark partially complete, sold 1988)	1983	1983	1988
Six Flags WaterWorld at Astroworld (Merged into Astroworld in 2002; closed 2005)	1983	1983	2005
Six Flags Great America Chicago, Illinois	1976	1984	
Six Flags Hurricane Harbor at Magic Mountain, Valencia, California	1995	1995	
Six Flags Hurricane Harbor Arlington, Texas (1995)	1983	1995	
Six Flags Fiesta Texas, San Antonio, Texas	1992	1996	

Parks owned by Premier Parks
At Time of Acquisition of Six Flags
Theme Parks, Inc. 1998

Park	Year Opened	Year Acquired	Year Sold
Frontier City, Oklahoma City, OK (Sold by Six Flags in 2007)	1958	1982	2007
White Water Bay, (water park), Oklahoma City, OK (Sold by Six Flags 2007)	1981	1991	2007
Adventure World, Upper Marlboro, Maryland (Renamed Six Flags America)	1974	1992	
Geauga Lake, Aurora, Ohio(Six Flags Ohio) Sold to Cedar Point, 2004	1887	1995	2004
Wyandot Lake, Powell, Ohio (Sold to Powell Zoo in 2008)	1940s	1995	2008
(Six Flags) Elitch Garden, Denver, Colorado (Sold by Six Flags 2007)	1995	1996	2007
The Great Escape, Queensbury, New York; (A Six Flags Theme Park)	1954	1996	
Splashwater Kingdom, New York;	1995	1996	
Waterworld, USA, Concord, California; (Sold by Six Flags in 2007)	1995	1996	
Riverside Park, Springfield, MA (Six Flags New England)	1940	1997	
Kentucky Kingdom, Louisville, Kentucky (Managed park – Closed in 2010);	1987	1997	2010
Paradise Family Fun Park, California;			
Marine World Africa USA, California, (Operated under a management agreement).		1997	
Parks Purchased Since Merger			
Seaworld Ohio (Merged with Six Flags Ohio to become Six Flags Worlds of Adventure) Sold to Cedar Point, 2004	1970	2002	2004

ABOUT THE AUTHOR

I first started visiting *Six Flags Over Texas* in the early 60's. Although I was too young to remember the trip, I have been told that my grandmother took my brothers and myself to the park as early as 1962.

I continued to visit the park as I grew up. In the spring of 1974, it was my pleasure to be hired as a ride operator, delivering the conductor's spiel on the *Six Flags Railroad*. Over the next four seasons, I worked in the park's ride operations. Most of my career was spent on the *Railroad*, *LaSalle's River Adventure*, the *Astrolift*, the two *Log Flume Rides* and the *Tower Slide*.

I meet Lu McDaniel, my wife of over thirty-five years when we worked together at the *Log Flume Ride*. We now have two daughters, Katie and Maegan.

I graduated from the University of Texas in Arlington with a degree in Criminal Justice and then attended Law School at the University of Texas. In 1983, I graduate from U.T. Law School and began my legal career as a prosecutor with the Tarrant County District Attorney's Office. After eight years as a prosecutor, I went into private practice with my father, Frank McCown.

After law school, I started collecting Six Flags postcards. That collection transformed into a broader collection of Six Flags memorabilia and souvenirs of all sorts..

In the mid-80s, I begin to take documentary pictures of the various rides and attractions in the park. Many of the photos included in this book are from those photos. I also created **parktimes.com**, a website dedicated to preserving the history of Six Flags Over Texas.

Author, 1974, River uniform,
Photograph by Joyce McCown.

In 1999, I helped form the *Six Flags Association of Former Employees*. I have served as the association's Vice President of Administration, as well as reunion coordinator for each of the park-wide reunions.

I have practiced law in Tarrant County for over thirty years. I handle a variety of cases involving civil litigation, as well as probate and estate planning.

I can be contacted at: davis@parktimes.com

Davis McCown, Contact Information.

Index

Symbols

D

E

F

N

O

P

Q

R

S

Made in the USA
Middletown, DE
03 September 2023

37907667R00166